Lyndon B. Johnson School of Public Affairs
Policy Research Project Report
Number 63

The Effects of State Government on Economic Development in Texas Cities

A report by the
Policy Research Project on Economic Development in Texas Cities
The University of Texas at Austin
1985

ST. PHILIP'S COLLEGE LIBRARY

Library of Congress Card Number: 84-81929
ISBN: 0-89940-665-3

© Copyright 1985 by the Board of Regents
The University of Texas

Printed in the U.S.A.
All rights reserved

Cover design by Design 2

PROJECT PARTICIPANTS

Students

Carol E. Fisher

Gregory P. Garlow

Billie Gonzales

Paul D. Goren

David S. Guarino

Gretchen M. Harper

Linda Diane Jenkins

Dru Johnston

Rebecca Lancaster

Gwen W. Newman

Amy Wexlee Orum

Bill Paschall

Anthony A. Piasecki

Marc Angelo Rodriguez

Cathy Stahl

Hayden Blake Stanford

Michelle Whisenhunt

Stuart Whitlow

Participating Faculty

Glen H. Cope, Ph.D.
Assistant Professor
LBJ School of Public Affairs

Robert Wilson, Ph.D.
Associate Professor
LBJ School of Public Affairs

Table of Contents

Chapter 1: Introduction   1

Chapter 2: Regulatory - Business Environment in the State of Texas

I.	Introduction	14
II.	The Business Climate in Texas	14
III.	State Labor Laws and their Impact on Economic Development in Texas	17
IV.	Finance Related Laws and their Impact on Economic Development in Texas	21
V.	State Regulation of Public Utilities, Transportation, and Natural Resources	27
VI.	Conclusions	34

Chapter 3: State Programs and Expenditures Related to Economic Development

I.	Introduction	51
II.	Structure of Aid to Cities Affecting Economic Development	53
III.	State Activities Directly Related to Economic Development	62
IV.	Infrastructure	83
V.	Education and Training	96
VI.	Conclusions	110

Chapter 4: State Derived Powers of Local Government

I.	Municipal Government	126
II.	Infrastructure and Bonds	132
III.	Zoning, Annexation and Eminent Domain	137
IV.	Local Economic Development Incentive Tools	140
V.	Foreign Trade Zones	147
VI.	Employment and Training	151
VII.	Water Districts	152
VIII.	The Role of Texas Counties in Economic Development	156
IX.	Conclusions	163

Chapter 5: Conclusions   175

Appendix I: Urban Policy and Economic Development - Policies Used in Other States   183

Appendix II: The Role of Texas State Government in the
Administration of Federal Programs in Urban Economic
Development   204

Bibliography   210

List of Tables

Table 1.1	Population and Growth rates for SMSAs, Urban Areas and the State of Texas, 1960-80	3
Table 1.2	Share of Urban Population Among Groups of SMSAs, 1960-80	4
Table 1.3	Gross Product Location Quotient for Texas, 1959, 1969, 1978	6
Table 3.1	Share of Net Expenditures by Function Texas State Government, 1979-83	54
Table 3.2	Aid to Cities and Counties (State Sources), 1977-83	57
Table 3.3	Aid to Cities and Counties (Federal Sources), 1977-83	59
Table 3.4	Grants to Selected Cities in Texas, 1980-83	61
Table 3.5	Intergovernmental Expenditures to Municipalities by State, 1979	62
Table 3.6	Selected Park Expenditures per Capita, FY 84	81
Table 3.7	Texas Local Parks, Recreation, and Open Space Funds Expenditures, 1979-83	82
Table 3.8	Sources and Methods of Funding for Waterworks and Sewer Facilities in Texas, 1981-82	86
Table 3.9	Annual Percentage Change in Registered Vehicles, 1972-82	88
Table 3.10	Total Highway Expenditures in Nominal and Real Terms, 1972-82	91
Table 3.11	Aggregate Expenditures by Highway District for 1972-82	92

Table 3.12	Per Capita Maintenance Expenditures by Highway District for 1972-82	93
Table 3.13	Per Capita Construction Expenditures per Highway District for 1972-82	94
Table 3.14	Total per Capita Expenditures by Highway District for 1972-82	95
Table 3.15	Foundation School Program: State Aid to Independent School Districts in Texas, 1977-85	103
Table 3.16	Foundation School Program: State Aid to Independent School Districts in Texas, Percentage Change in Six-Year Period (1979-80 to 1984-85)	104

List of Figures

Figure 3.1	State Expenditures by Function, 1979-83	55
Figure 3.2	Percentage Change from Previous Year in Aid to Cities and Counties in Texas, 1978-83	58
Figure 3.3	Percentage Change from Previous Year in Aid to Cities and Counties in Texas, 1978-83	60

Foreword

The Lyndon B. Johnson School of Public Affairs has established interdisciplinary research on policy problems as the core of its educational program. A major part of this program is the nine-month policy research project, in the course of which two or three faculty members from different disciplines direct the research of ten to twenty graduate students of diverse backgrounds on a policy issue of concern to a government agency. This "client orientation" brings the students face to face with administrators, legislators, and other officials active in the policy process, and demonstrates that research in a policy environment demands special talents. It also illuminates the occasional difficulties of relating research findings to the world of political realities.

This report, which assesses the effects of state government on urban economies in Texas, is the product of a policy research project conducted at the LBJ School in 1983-84. Funding for publication was provided by the Texas Research League, the Texas Lieutenant Governor's Office, and the Lyndon B. Johnson Foundation. Clients for the project were the Texas Research League and the Lieutenant Governor's Office.

The curriculum of the LBJ School is intended not only to develop effective public servants but also to produce research that will enlighten and inform those already engaged in the policy process. The project that resulted in this report has helped to accomplish the first task; it is our hope and expectation that the report itself will contribute to the second.

Finally, it should be noted that neither the LBJ School nor the University of Texas at Austin necessarily endorses the views or findings of this study.

Max Sherman
Dean

Acknowledgments

The participants of this policy research project are indebted to many state and local government officials that contributed freely of their time to numerous inquiries and questions. We acknowledge their contribution and express our appreciation. Deserving special mention are Dr. Jared Hazleton, President of the Texas Research League and Mr. David Spurgin, Lt. Governor's Office, who represented the clients in our project. Also working closely with us were Mr. Frank Sterzl of the Texas Municipal League and Ms. Meg Wilson of the Governor's Office of Economic Development. These four individuals greatly enriched our efforts through their encouragement, guidance and criticism. Their collaboration was invaluable. We hope this report will in some way compensate those who have worked with us by contributing positively to the debate on economic development in Texas, an issue with which they were all concerned. The views expressed in this report, however, are the sole responsibility of the project paricipants and are not necessarily endorsed by others that contributed to our project.

                                             Glen Cope

                                             Robert Wilson

                                             Project Directors

CHAPTER 1: INTRODUCTION

The prospects for growth of the economy of any city or region relate to a variety of factors, including the natural resource base of the surrounding area, availability and skill levels of labor, availability of capital, economic linkages to the regional and national economy, and the size of the city or region and its economic structure. In addition, growth prospects are to some extent related to federal economic policy, the actions of state government, and the actions of local government. This project identifies and assesses the role that the state government plays in the economic development of Texas cities.

While the role of national economic policy in promoting or inhibiting growth is well recognized, the role that states can play has only recently become an area of concern. Although the State of Texas has been involved in advertising for industrial recruitment for some time, in 1983 Governor Mark White announced that his staff would henceforth emphasize development efforts and that he had reorganized his staff in order to facilitate greater state involvement. As evidence of this commitment, his office was instrumental in convincing the participating partners of a major computer research and development consortium to locate their operation in Austin.

Development efforts had already been initiated at the local level. In San Antonio, Mayor Henry Cisneros created an office whose purpose is to encourage new industries to locate in the city. A number of development strategies for different sections of the city were devised. In addition, community organizations and task forces have begun work to encourage further development. In Houston, Mayor Kathy Whitmire, elected largely in response to growing citizen dissatisfaction with the city's deteriorating infrastructure and unzoned, uncontrolled development, has worked to make the city more attractive for future growth. Several other cities also have actively pursued industry in order to increase jobs and diversify their industrial bases, especially after the economic downturn in 1983.

Such diversity in economic bases is not easy to achieve. Glickman and Wilson argue that "the essence of the problem faced by urban economic development decision makers, both in the design of targeted national policies and local government policies, is to induce existing enterprises to expand, to attract new enterprises, and to prevent firms from closing. This can be done with a variety of tools, including labor training programs, capital subsidies, land policies, facility and infrastructure provision, tax incentives and attempts to enhance the relative attractiveness of the city (or neighborhood) to firms."(1)

A variety of state policies and statutes can affect the growth prospects of urban economies. Laws governing the provision of infrastructure, the establishment of tax bases, and the delivery of specific social services are examples. Two broad categories of state activities can be defined. First, some state efforts are directly related to development, such as the activities of the Texas Economic Development Commission. Second, a state can influence economic development through efforts not primarily related to growth, but which affect the overall growth prospects of a locality. Education, derived powers of cities, state expenditure patterns, and regulatory environment are examples of the latter.

The purpose of this project is to identify the types of state programs and laws that affect the economies of cities and to answer the following questions. Are there laws which either promote or inhibit the economic development activities of the state? How does the State of Texas affect, either directly or indirectly, the economic development of local economies? Do some policies favor the growth of specific local economies at the expense of others? The answers to these questions indicate current state actions and suggest potential policies for future development in Texas.

Urban Population Growth in Texas

Since this report focuses on economic development in cities, it is useful to begin with a discussion of urban population growth in the state. Texas in 1984 is a highly urbanized state. According to the U.S. Bureau of Census definition of "urban," 75 percent of the state population lived in urban areas in 1960 and, after a substantial increase in 1970, the figure fell sightly to 79.65 percent in 1980. As Table 1.1 suggests, while the urban population grew substantially faster than total state population in the 1960s, the two growth rates were virtually the same in the 1970s.

Another definition of "urban" uses the Standard Metropolitan Statistical Area (SMSA), a category defined by the U.S. census. An SMSA, a grouping of one or more counties, must contain at least one city with fifty thousand inhabitants or more and can include one or several counties that are economically linked. The 1980 U.S. Census reported twenty-six SMSAs, consisting of fifty-five counties, in Texas. Urban population in these SMSAs, as a share of total state population, increased from 63.7 percent to 69.5 percent between 1960 and 1980, reflecting the fact that these larger cities have been growing faster than the state population as a whole. Among these twenty-six SMSAs, one finds that between 1960 and 1980 the largest ten have increased their share of urban population from 85 percent to 88 percent; the largest three--Houston, Dallas-Ft. Worth, and San Antonio--have increased their share from 57.1 percent to 62.6 percent (see Table 1.2).

In summary, Texas is a highly urbanized state in which larger cities are growing faster than smaller cities and rural areas. While the urban population in the state continues to increase at a rate higher than that of the total state population, the differences between the two rates were less in the 1970s than in the 1960s.

Table 1.1

POPULATION AND GROWTH RATES FOR SMSAs, URBAN AREAS, AND THE STATE OF TEXAS, 1960-1980

	POPULATION (in millions)			GEOMETRIC GROWTH RATES PER YEAR		SHARE OF STATE POPULATION (in percentages)		
	1960	1970	1980	1960-1970	1970-1980	1960	1970	1980
URBAN POPULATION OF 26 SMSAS	6.11	7.77	9.90	0.024	0.035	63.7	69.4	69.5
URBAN POPULATION OF TEXAS	7.19	8.93	11.33	0.022	0.024	75.0	79.8	79.5
TOTAL POPULATION OF TEXAS	9.58	11.20	14.23	0.016	0.024	100.0	100.0	100.0

Sources: The 1960 and 1970 statistics were compiled from the U.S. Census of Population and Housing data for 1960 and 1970, extracted from a computer tape of the County and City Data Book - Consolidated File - County Data 1947-1977 (Washington, D.C.: U.S. Department of Commerce, Bureau of the Census, 1979). The 1980 statistics were compiled from U.S. Census of Population and Housing 1980: Tape File 3 (Washington, D.C.: U.S. Department of Commerce, Bureau of the Census, 1982).

The State of the Texas Economy

Like its social values and politics, the Texas economy is a product of its land. The cattle kingdom created by early settlers was the basis for economic as well as social and political patterns. The discovery of oil at Spindletop in the early twentieth century led to economic power, yet also initiated a trend toward dependence upon prices for its raw material determined beyond Texas borders in national and world markets.(2)

Economic growth in Texas derived from agricultural and petroleum production can readily be explained through the economic base theory, which emphasizes the relationship between the export sector and the local sector of a specific area. The export sector consists of "firms and individuals serving markets outside the community," while the local sector consists of "firms and individuals serving markets within the community." The export sector is considered the "prime mover of the local economy."(3) Therefore, when the export sector prospers, the community as a whole prospers. If the export sector experiences hard times, the entire community's economy becomes depressed.

Table 1.2
SHARE OF URBAN POPULATION AMONG GROUPS OF SMSAs
1960-1980 BY SIZE OF SMSA

Groups of SMSAs By Population in 1980, n=number in group	Urban Population (in millions) 1960	1970	1980	Share of Total Urban Population (in percentage) 1960	1970	1980
Above 900,000 n=3	3.49	4.80	6.1	57.12	61.85	62.60
200,000 to 900,000 n=4	.98	1.18	1.54	16.07	15.20	15.53
125,000 to 200,000 n=7	.86	.95	1.17	14.10	12.26	11.82
Less than 125,000 n=12	.78	.83	.99	12.70	10.69	10.06

Source: Same as Table 1.1.

The underlying process at work is that export firms sell goods and services in markets outside the community, which brings dollars into the local economy. Wage earners spend some of these dollars on locally produced goods and services generating more employment income and production within the area.(4) The state of the local economy depends upon conditions in the export sector, expanding when the export sector expands and contracting when exports decline. The relationship between the export and local sectors and the community's entire economy can be expressed numerically in terms of a "multiplier." The multiplier indicates the degree of change in a community's total economy given a change in the export sector.

The agricultural and petroleum sectors are both export oriented, and their growth earlier in the century was the principal contributor to economic conditions in the state. Within these sectors a certain diversification occurred, such as meat processing and packing in the cattle industry and petrochemical production in the petroleum industry. In both cases local resources were being processed within the state, which brought further benefits through the multiplier effect. These industries also had a significant impact on the growth of certain cities such as Ft. Worth (agriculture) and Houston (oil). Another sector, military installations, is export in nature and it too has had a significant impact in certain parts of the state, particularly since World War II. Even though industrial diversification did occur, to a certain extent, in the export sector, the high level of export specialization still contributed to economic vulnerability and dependency on markets beyond state borders.

Much of the growth during the past twenty years has not been exclusively related to the traditional industrial sectors in Texas. Factors such as transportation facilities, access to raw materials, and a large available labor force encouraged growing industries to move to the state. The growth in "new" sectors during this twenty-year period has resulted in a shift in the structure of the economy. Table 1.3 shows a measure of industrial structure, the gross product location quotient, in Texas for 1959, 1969, and 1978. These quotients show the percentage of regional activity occurring in a sector divided by the percentage of national activity in the same sector. A quotient greater than 1.0 indicates that the particular sector in Texas is relatively more important than that sector in the national economy.(5)

There is a noticeable decline in the location quotient for both agriculture and mining, which includes the oil and gas production, over this twenty-year period. Agriculture in 1978 was relatively less important in the Texas economy than in the national economy. Although mining is of great relative importance to the state economy, its relative degree of importance has dropped significantly between 1959 and 1978. Construction, manufacturing, and the financial sectors and wholesale and retail trade have gained in relative importance during this twenty-year period. These shifts are indicative of the direction of future structural changes in the Texas economy as dependence on petroleum-related firms declines and the economy becomes more diversified.

Diversification in an export-oriented economy and resulting economic growth have been studied by Wilbur R. Thompson. In his book A Preface to Urban Economics, Thompson states:

> The very essence of long-run growth is, in fact, the transition--sometimes orderly, sometimes chaotic--of the local economy from one export-base to another as the area matures in what it can do, and as rising per capita income and technological progress change what the national economy wants done. Thus the emphasis in our growth analysis is on the process by which each round of economic development leaves an industrial legacy of skills, wage rates, business services, social overhead, entrepreneurial talent and so forth, which shapes the developmental path and constrains the policy choices of the next round.(6)

It is in these "policy choices" that the state can become involved for purposes of supporting the economic development.

Thompson discusses the effect of both the demand-side and supply-side factors on economic growth. On the demand side he relies heavily upon the export base construct. The urban area is thus perceived as primarily relying upon the major exporting industry(s) for its economic well-being.(7) There are, however, four supply-side factors of production, labor, entrepreneurship, and land, which also affect growth.(8) A city which has a comparative advantage in these four factors will be better situated for growth than other cities. A city with a highly skilled labor force, for example, may be able to attract industries searching for such

Table 1.3

GROSS PRODUCT LOCATION QUOTIENT FOR TEXAS
1959, 1969, 1978

SECTOR	1959	1969	1978
AGRICULTURE	1.28	.94	.82
MINING	5.25	4.59	4.20
CONSTRUCTION	.98	1.07	1.33
MANUFACTURING	.65	.80	.82
TRANSPORT, COMMUNICATION, AND PUBLIC UTILITIES	1.09	.98	1.01
WHOLESALE AND RETAIL TRADE	1.03	.99	1.11
FINANCE, INSURANCE, AND REAL ESTATE	.89	.94	.97
SERVICES	.88	.92	.88
GOVERNMENT	1.07	1.02	.89

Source: Extracted from computer tape "Regional Economic Information System" (Washington, D.C.: U.S. Department of Commerce, Bureau of Economic Analysis, April 1980).

a labor pool. Stages of entrepreneurial vigor may arise to help generate local industrial development and to encourage innovation through research and development.(9) Since capital is highly mobile, it is extremely important to attract individual investors who are interested in small business and local development. On the other hand, the availability of land, natural resources, and energy is essential in attracting industries dependent upon these factors.(10) A state which is involved in economic development could direct its policies and monies toward improving these factors.

A diversified economy shows more stability than a specialized economy during business cycles. In Texas, the degree of economic specialization was still evident in 1983 when growth declined considerably. A drop in world oil prices, the devaluation of the Mexican peso, severe weather conditions affecting the agricultural sector, and the national recession were primarily responsible for this slow-down. Every one-dollar drop in oil prices resulted in $40 million less in oil production tax receipts for the state and a decline in the overall state economy. The peso devaluation caused taxable retail sales to drop by 22 percent in the border region from January through July of 1983. The worst drought in the state's history caused a loss of one-half billion dollars in crops and livestock.(11) Even after accounting for these exceptional conditions, the Comptroller of the State of Texas concluded in his 1983 financial report that Texas will probably not return to the growth patterns of the previous decade, even though the state will remain an economic leader in the country.(12)

Trends in production in Texas will slowly shift from resource-based production to the manufacturing, construction, and private-service producing sectors. In 1981, 18.3 percent of the state's gross product was produced by agriculture and mining; by 2006 the percentage of production in that sector is expected to decrease to 5.7 percent. Manufacturing, which produced 18.9 percent of the state's economic output in 1981, is expected to produce 25.2 percent of this output in 2006. Texas's real gross product is predicted to increase from $105 billion in 1981 (in 1972 dollars) to $320 billion in 2006. This is an average growth rate of 4.6 percent per year. The population of the state during the same time period is expected to increase from 14.7 million to 24.6 million. The overall economic growth rate in Texas between 1981 and 2006 is expected to be 1.8 times the U.S. economic growth rate for the same period.(13)

Economic growth in Texas ultimately depends on business decisions to locate new operations or expand existing operations. These decisions are based on location factors which can be characterized as the costs and benefits of locating or expanding in a particular locale. These may vary according to the size of the firm; the good or service it produces, and whether the activity is relocating, expanding, or creating a new firm. Regardless of these variations, the location decision is always a function of combined costs and benefits of a specific locale.

Unlike the static nature of mainstream economics in which supply-demand relationships are analyzed at one place and at one particular time, much of location theory is a dynamic analysis of the fluctuating factors which promote location decisions. In this scheme, markets and firms have the ability to penetrate space and time, creating an interdependent web of economic activities. These activities produce a historical effect on the economic structure of cities: past location decisions create the economic structures which in turn influence future decisions of firms. Thus, in determining the factors which influence business location decisions, location theory also provides a historical overview of the trends affecting the economic structures of American cities.

In manufacturing, cost-oriented factors have traditionally been the major criterion of the decision process. One such factor is labor, which includes the availability of workers at the appropriate skill level and wage level prevalent in the area. Other factors include the proximity to markets, the proximity to resources, the availability and dependability of energy (utilities, electricity, natural gas, and water), financing costs, and the accessibility and costs of transportation.

As an example, water is and will be an important factor in the future development of the Texas economy. The projected water use in the year 2000 is 21.6 million acre feet, which is 2.5 million acres over that which can be dependably supplied.(14) The influence of Texas's water supply on the state's economic growth is discussed by Joseph Adair in his dissertation entitled "An Aggregate and Sectoral Analysis of Economic Growth in Texas, 1914-1972." Adair states:

> The failure to develop extensive industrial water supplies, however, has placed a severe constraint on the state's ability to base economic expansion along a proven path. This constraint insures that to maintain a long-term economic growth rate that reflects past

experience, the state must shift to a diverse array of sectors that are attracted to the region for other than raw material and heavy industrial processing activities. Texas must encourage the development of locational advantages as they pertain to a wide variety of business enterprises and exploit the benefits associated with the Sun Belt.(15)

Yet any subsequent growth in employment sectors other than those requiring raw materials and industrial processing (heavy water users) will further complicate the situation with the state's water supply because they probably will result in an increase in the population.

As traditional manufacturing operations yield to demands for high technology, shifts in the relative importance of these factors will occur. For example, the decreasing importance of the availability of skilled workers, coupled with the increasing importance of the availability of technical and professional workers, reflect the impact of automation in new manufacturing operations.(16) Similarly, in the field of technology, proximity to markets and raw materials are not of great concern. Many service sector firms, on the other hand, depend heavily on the availability of a ready market for the services they provide.

In addition to cost-oriented criteria, many subjective factors have gained increasing importance in the location decision process. Living conditions and operating environments, although not readily quantifiable, are of concern to location decisionmakers.(17)

In general, the materials-oriented appproach for explaining industrial location patterns, where transport costs were important, has been to a large extent replaced by a market-oriented approach. This change has occurred because technological advances and changes in relative prices have diminished the importance of transport considerations, thereby allowing for substantial manufacturing growth in areas that held no relative advantages in the past.

The implications of these changes for state and local activity in economic development are varied. While cities or regions which have developed a comparative advantage as transportation centers will continue to sustain growth because of agglomeration economies, other regions may become more favorable as business locations for firms which consider a more complex set of factors when choosing a site. For example, growth in the so called high-technology industries has brought to the forefront new location decision factors, often emphasizing a high quality of life for employees. In addition, as regional disparities in location advantages tend to equalize, states and localities will become more sensitive to changes in national and international economic trends. As federal policies favor some industries over others, states and cities which have developed specialized economies suffer when these policies cause resources to be moved from region to region. Economic development strategies in the future may have to encourage economic diversity to compensate for unclear directives and unstable resources from the federal level and instability in the national and even the international economy.

Although the definition of economic development has been implied throughout this discussion, it is essential here to state how the term is used in this report. The term "development" in an economic sense implies "structural change, technological advance, and resource discovery."(18) A goal of development is the rise of real per capita income and the creation of more employment possibilities. Another criterion by which development can be judged consists of the reduction of subregional disparities in per capita income. If changes (political, social, economic, and technological) in an environment result in an increase an income and available jobs, economic development has occurred.

In the context of per capita disparities in the state of Texas, a brief discussion of the role of minorities in the economy is warranted. At present, blacks constitute about 12 percent of the state's population while Hispanics make up about 20 percent. The Hispanic component has been increasing sharply due to birth rates and immigration.(19) Although blacks and Hispanics together constitute over one-third of the total Texas population, they account for nearly 60 percent of the state's poor population. Black males are less likely to be in the labor force and are more likely to remain as nonworkers through time. Hispanics are less likely to have been enrolled in school during the years they should have been finishing high school.(20)

Unsurprisingly, there is a significant gap between minorities and Anglos in terms of income levels and average occupational levels. More than one-fourth of all black and Hispanic males are employed as laborers, approximately five times the percentage of Anglo males. Similarly, the percentage of Anglo males employed in professional and technical occupations is three to four times that of blacks and Hispanics (21). In terms of income distribution, in 1973, 40 percent of all non-Anglos in Texas had incomes below the poverty line, compared to 10 percent for Anglos. In 1970, well over half (56 percent) of Hispanics and two-thirds of all black families made less than $6,000.(22)

This socioeconomic status can be attributed to longstanding sociocultural and political discrimination directed toward the minority population in the state. Some scholars argue that few successes have been made by minorities in Texas despite federal and state intervention due to significant resistance to the mobilization of minorities. According to this argument certain groups in the state economy have an interest in maintaining a large, unorganized, and politically docile labor force.(23)

Despite the few economic successes, there are indications that changes in the state's political and economic structure are forthcoming. A higher degree of politicization and participation has been evident in the last decade, especially for Hispanics.(24) It has been estimated that by 1995, Anglos will no longer be the state's racial majority group. Blacks and especially Hispanics will become a greater factor in Texas's employment and business trends. In the economic sector, Hispanics are moving out of the traditional agricultural employment and into jobs in housing construction, lumber, food-processing, and the hotel and restaurant industries.(25) For both minority groups, the greatest internal barrier to overcoming unemployment and poverty is educational. State action in developing the human resources of this growing population sector is critical to the future economic and political sophistication of the labor force.

Chapter Descriptions

The success of state government in incorporating these economic principles into its policies and actions will affect the stability and the future of the Texas economy. As suggested above, these policies can take the form of actions that explicitly affect economic development, but more often their impact is implicit or indirect. Many state actions that are not normally associated with economic development do affect the economic climate in cities. This research project examines three areas in which the state can shape the context for economic development: regulatory environment, direct state actions, and local government powers derived from the state.

The regulatory and business environment in the State of Texas has been claimed in recent years as one of the reasons behind the migration of capital and labor resources from the "Frostbelt" to the "Sunbelt." The variables used to assess the State's impact on the business climate, discussed in Chapter 2, include labor laws, banking and insurance regulations, environmental constraints, taxation levels, land policies, the availability and quality of infrastructure, and utility and transportation regulations. The purpose of this chapter is twofold:

1. To examine the state laws and programs which affect each of the specific variables used to measure the business climate in Texas; and

2. To assess how business climate in general affects economic development in Texas.

The examination in Chapter 3 of state programs and expenditures, which are referenced in this report as direct state action, covers activities most commonly perceived as characterizing a state's role in economic development. In this chapter, aid to cities and counties; the activities of the Texas Department of Community Affairs, the Texas Economic Development Commission, and the Governor's Office; and expenditures and policies related to infrastructure, education, training, and tourism are discussed. Chapter 3 assesses these actions, policies, and expenditures in terms of their impact on economic development.

As legal subdivisions, cities derive certain powers from the state. Chapter 4 examines how and if cities use these powers. In an effort to establish an inventory of the legal powers of local government that affect development, this chapter reviews legislation affecting taxation, infrastructure, bonding authority, enterprise zones, tax increment financing, and foreign trade zones, as well as legislation affecting nonmunicipal entities such as Municipal Utility Districts. Chapter 4 attempts to answer these questions:

1. What powers do governmental subdivisions have that affect economic development?

2. What are the constraints upon these powers? Under what limitations do these subdivisions operate?

3. How are these powers used by these subdivisions?

4. How do revenues and expenditures of these subdivisions reflect their relationship to economic development?

Finally, Chapter 5 presents the general and specific conclusions and recommendations that have resulted from this project.

ENDNOTES

1. Norman J. Glickman and Robert H. Wilson, "The Economic Context of Urban Policy," Working Paper no. 28 (Austin: Lyndon B. Johnson School of Public Affairs, University of Texas at Austin, 1984), p. 21.

2. Fred Gantt, Governing Texas: Documents and Readings (New York: Thomas Crowell Co., 1974), p. 5.

3. Charles M. Tiebout, "The Community Economic Base Study," Supplementary Paper no. 16 (New York: Committee for Economic Development, 1962), p. 13.

4. W. Z. Hirsch, Urban Economics Analysis (New York: McGraw-Hill, 1973), p. 187.

5. Thomas Plaut and Mildred C. Anderson, The Gross Product of Texas and Its Regions (Austin: Bureau of Business Research, University of Texas at Austin, 1983), p. 30.

6. Wilbur R. Thompson, A Preface to Urban Economics (Baltimore, Md.: Johns Hopkins University Press, 1968), p. 3.

7. Ibid., pp. 27-28.

8. Ibid., pp. 338-39.

9. Ibid., pp. 47-50.

10. Ibid., pp. 51-56.

11. State of Texas, Comptroller of Public Accounts, 1983 Annual Financial Report (Austin, November 7, 1983), p. 1.

12. Ibid., p. 8.

13. Victor Arnold, Texas - Trends and Forecasts (Austin: Bureau of Business Research, University of Texas at Austin, 1983), p. 24.

14. Ibid., p. 30.

15. Joseph Adair, "An Aggregate and Sectoral Analysis of Economic Growth in Texas, 1914-1972" (Ph.D. dissertation, University of Texas at Austin, 1978).

16. *Why Corporate America Moves Where*, A Fortune Market Research Survey of Facility Locator Decisions (New York: Time, Inc., 1982), pp. 8-16.

17. Gurney Breckenfeld, "Business Loves the Sunbelt (and Vice Versa)," *Fortune* (June 1977): 132-46.

18. Benjamin Higgins, *Economic Development, Problems, Principles, Policies* (New York: W. W. Norton, 1968), pp. 106, 378-79.

19. Beryl Pettus and Randall Bland, *Texas Government Today* (Homewood, Ill.: Dorsey Press, 1979), p. 43.

20. Ray Marshall, James L. Walker, and R. Lynn Rittenmore, *Human Resource Development in Rural Texas* (Austin: Center for Study of Human Resources, University of Texas at Austin, 1974), pp. 9-10.

21. Clifton McCleskey, Larry Dickens, and Allan Butcher, *The Government and Politics of Texas* (Boston: Little, Brown and Co., 1975), p. 15.

22. Pettus and Bland, p.48.

23. Ibid., p. 70.

24. McCleskey, Dickens, and Butcher, p. 102.

25. David Rogers, "The Latino Tide," *Wall Street Journal*, June 11, 1984, p. 1.

CHAPTER 2: REGULATORY-
BUSINESS ENVIRONMENT IN THE STATE OF TEXAS

I. INTRODUCTION

The regulatory and business environment in the State of Texas has been claimed in recent years as one of the reasons behind the migration of capital and labor resources from the "Frostbelt" to Texas. In general, the variables used to assess a state's regulatory-business environment include labor laws, banking and insurance regulations, environmental constraints, taxation levels, land policies, the availability and quality of infrastructure, and utility and transportation regulations. Taken together, these elements constitute an area's business climate, a popular measure of a state or region's capacity to attract industry. The purpose of this chapter is twofold: first, to examine the state laws and programs which affect each of the specific variables used to measure the business climate in Texas; and, second, to assess how business climate in general affects economic development in Texas.

II. THE BUSINESS CLIMATE IN TEXAS

A. Historical Basis for Business Climate

1. **Social Attitudes**. Traditions and social attitudes have played a major role in developing the business climate in Texas. The immense size of the state and the importance placed on land ownership were important factors in the formation of early social values. The early migration to Texas from the United States and Europe was motivated by the desire both to escape governmental control and to ensure individual freedom. Thus, the availability of land and the opportunities it provided helped to create a society based upon the landowner, who either conquered the soil or was humbled by it.(1)

While land was plentiful, sovereignty over it was highly contested by the groups that occupied it, including American Indians and Mexicans. As an independent country, Texas also disputed sovereignty with the U.S. government.(2) With constant threats to survival and vast distances between communities, early Texans developed a keen sense of individual responsibility. This "survival of the fittest" attitude does not imply that Texans were antisocial or antineighborly, but rather that circumstances forced each person to be responsible for his survival since the threats posed by unpredictable harvests, harsh climate, and hostile enemies were ever present.(3)

These attitudes still influence Texas's business climate. Right-to-work legislation, as well as restrictions placed on financial institutions, can be traced to the agrarian individualism which permeated early Texas society. In addition, antitrespass laws and an emphasis on private property appear linked to the importance of land ownership, while a belief in individual responsibility may perhaps contribute to Texas's rank as the state with the lowest average unemployment compensation benefits paid and the fourth lowest expenditures in welfare payments.(4) Finally, the social structure of Texas urban areas today points to the continued existence of a "frontier ethos." First populated by displaced farmers who lost everything during the Depression, Texas cities never created the "urban ethos" that characterizes such cities as Boston, Chicago, or San Francisco.(5)

2. Political Philosophies. Texas politics and government emerged from Texas society, its imperatives, and its world views. The frontier experience, the work ethic, and the attitudes of farmers and ranchers contributed significantly to several attributes of Texas politics, including supremacy of property holders rights; fiscal conservatism; aversion to regulation, taxes, and governmental power; no tolerance of criminality; and resistance to federal courts' mandating of national norms.(6) In addition, the 1876 Constitution was formulated by mostly farmers and ranchers, and their biases against corporations, big banks and strong state government were evident in such provisions as the two-thirds legislative vote required to create any private corporation and the ban against banks incorporating under any circumstances.

Great distances between communities have been noted as one factor contributing to the amorphous nature of Texas politics.(7) This relative isolation of communities made consensus building difficult. V. O. Key notes that the result was a lack of vigorous party competition, which was one factor that led to the emergence of one-party politics, in which many factions compete for recognition within the controlling Democractic Party.(8)

The tradition of agrarian protest and individualism became reflected in political expression following the agricultural distress of the late 1880s. At that time, the People's Party emerged as an action group of farmers focusing attention on what they considered the causes of their distress: banks, railroads, corporations, low prices, and tight credit. Their grass-roots effort was successful in electing several governors attentive to their concerns. (9) In 1890, James Hogg was elected governor on a platform attacking business abuses. Thomas Campbell, endorsed by Hogg, was elected in 1906 and continued Hogg's policies by strengthening antitrust legislation, increasing control over lobbies, providing for regulation of public utilities by municipalities, and encouraging measures to increase taxation in order to provide more government services.

In 1915, James Ferguson was elected and became the archetype of the Texas politician. Elected by rustics and known as the farmer's friend, Ferguson used his personality to distract voters from the issues, instead focusing on their like or dislike of "Farmer Jim."(10) Even today, Texas elections have been characterized as more dependent on personalities, mood, or local issues than on ideological, economic, or regional interests. In addition, a taxpayer's bias perpetuates the belief held by early Texans that elected spendthrifts try to persuade the people while selling out their interests.(11) Thus, the taxpayers feel they are left with politicians and businessmen they do not trust.

B. Business Climate in Texas : Recent Surveys

Despite the differing measures used by various surveys to assess business climate, Texas has consistently scored among the top five states in recent years. For example, INC. magazine's annual rating of small business climates across the United States is based on five categories: capital resources, labor, taxes, business activities, and state support. (12) Texas ranked first in this survey in 1982. Similarly, a business climate index prepared by the Federal Reserve Bank of Atlanta analyzed twenty variables grouped in three categories--government policy, labor, and quality of life. Texas was rated first in 1982 in this study.(13)

In yet another survey, Alexander Grant & Co. used twenty-two measurement factors divided into five categories.(14) These included: state and local government fiscal policies, state-regulated employment costs, labor costs, availability and productivity of labor force, and other issues including energy costs, environmental regulations, and population. Texas ranked among the top two in this 1982 survey. In general, a combination of strong capital resources, effective labor force, low tax burdens, aggressive business activity, negligent unionization, and relatively lenient regulatory policy has helped Texas achieve a top rating in these and other surveys.

C. Business Climate and Economic Development in Texas

One of the significant themes which emerges from this discussion of Texas politics, economics, and society is a dichotomy between strongly held beliefs and modern realities. Texans wholeheartedly support growth and progress yet quickly become possessive and irritated when growth results in congestion and inconvenience or requires a rethinking of old ways to handle new problems. Politically, Texans as taxpayers demand protection from the abuses of big business and government, yet as workers and business executives cling to strong laissez-faire attitudes. The state continues to develop and export its vast resources, yet resents the dependence on outside markets. These attitudes may be part of the appeal that Texas holds for newcomers since outsiders can easily assume the Texas ways without sacrificing their own beliefs.

In order to appraise the effects of the business-regulatory environment on economic development in Texas, the remainder of this chapter will examine the state laws and/or programs that affect each of the variables used to measure business climate. In addition, each factor will be analyzed for its overall effect on economic development in Texas.

III. STATE LABOR LAWS AND THEIR IMPACT ON ECONOMIC DEVELOPMENT IN TEXAS

This survey of labor laws is based on the notion that state statutes regarding labor could have a direct and/or indirect impact, through wage levels, on the decisions of firms to locate in Texas. Labor laws could have, for example, a direct bearing on the extent of union activity in the state. Because unions have often been associated with high wages and highly skilled workers, firms concerned with such factors could be attracted to or driven away from states on the basis of workers' wage and skill levels.(15)

Before discussing existing laws and their impacts on the economy, it is important to recall the earlier discussion of the culture which underlies the Texas legal system. The spirit of individualism and private enterprise runs deep in Texas, and the work ethic is firmly lodged in its dominant cultural values. In addition to these orientations, a large number of Texans embrace traditions of the Old South such as socioeconomic conservatism and elitism. These postures combine to produce an environment which is not highly conducive to the presence of labor unions or to government laws or programs designed to deal with laborers' problems. The influence of cultural values should not be forgotten when one examines the labor laws of Texas.(16)

A. Inventory of State Labor Laws

The increasingly liberal interpretation of the interstate commerce clause of the U.S. Constitution over the last fifty years has expanded the applicability of federal labor laws to include all transportation and communication enterprises, as well as most manufacturing and distribution firms. Since federal labor legislation applies to most types of employment, the jurisdiction of state labor laws is generally restricted to small retail sales establishments, services, and agriculture.(17)

An exception to the supremacy of federal labor law is found, however, in a provision of the Taft-Hartley Act (Labor-Management Relations Act) of 1947 that permitted the existence of the "union shop" agreement--an agreement between employers and employees which requires all employees (usually after a probationary period) to join the union. The Act allowed each state to determine if such pacts were to be legal within the confines of their respective borders. Firms involved in interstate commerce were not exempted from state laws regarding "union shop" contracts.(18)

In the Texas Right-to-Work Law of 1947, the legislature declared that contracts including "union shop" agreements were invalid. Some view it as ironic that the Right-to-Work Law, which provides all persons (with the exception of most state employees) the right to collectively bargain and prohibits barring or dismissal from employment because of union membership also outlaws "union shop" contracts. Although the 1947 Act did not include a specific form of enforcement, a 1951 statute defined such a contract as a conspiracy in restraint of trade and, therefore, a criminal act.(19)

Many other state labor laws regulate the internal activities of labor unions and labor strikes, child labor, and industrial accidents. Because these statutes have little relationship to economic development, they are outside the scope of this report.(20)

B. The Impact of the Right-to-Work Law and Labor Factors on Economic Development

Right-to-work (RTW) laws and their impact on wages, unionization, and economic development have received a significant amount of scholarly attention. Most studies begin with the hypothesis that RTW laws have a significant impact on the level of union activity. The large majority of these studies have concluded, however, that such laws have had little if any influence on union organizing efforts.(21) Although space does not permit an extensive review of all studies, several major analyses are summarized here. One of the frequently cited works in the area was conducted by Frederick Meyers in 1959.(22) Focusing primarily on Texas, Meyers concluded that RTW laws had no significant impact on the level of union activity within a state. He noted that many unions simply maneuvered around the law and enforced what amounted to an informal union shop agreement.

A 1961 study by Benson Soffer and Michael Korenich explored the relationship between RTW laws and economic development by evaluating such laws as a location factor.(23) The authors compared the economic growth experience of primarily agricultural RTW states with a control group of agriculturally oriented non-RTW states. They concluded that the non-RTW control group actually experienced greater economic growth than the states with RTW laws. Keith Lumsden and Craig Peterson also determined that RTW laws have little impact on unionization.(24) They tied low levels of union activity to cultural attitudes. In their words, "States with such laws have a significantly smaller percent of their work force unionized but the difference reflects tastes and preferences of the population rather than a substantive impact of the laws themselves."(25)

Both the approach and the conclusions of the Peterson and Lumsden study were challenged by Ronald S. Warren and Robert P. Strauss, who concluded in a 1978 study that there was a fairly strong reciprocal relationship between unionization and RTW laws.(26) Their findings cannot, however, refute the possibility that cultural attitudes give rise both to RTW laws and low levels of union activity.

The empirical and conceptual difficulties in testing the influence of cultural attitudes on RTW laws and unionization are substantial. It is not possible to solve the issue conclusively by statistical tests. Nevertheless, it is clear that the predominance of cultural attitudes in the passage of RTW laws also inhibits union growth. It also seems evident that RTW laws represent a significant aspect of the prevailing viewpoint toward unions and thus act as a powerful anti-union symbol. Although such laws may not convince many workers that unions are "bad," they nevertheless make clear the predominant attitude in the state with regard to union activity.(27)

The orientation of many Texans toward unions has been shaped by the history of particularly violent attempts to disrupt union activities within the state.(28) The social memory of such events influences the generations which follow. Unionization in Texas has been slowed also by the fact that certain sectors of the bulwark of the Texas economy, the oil industry, are inherently difficult to organize for the cultural reasons stated above.

Whatever the causes of the powerful anti-union sentiment in Texas, the reality remains that Texas has a very low level of union activity. As of 1978, Texas was forty-sixth among the fifty states with respect to union membership as a percentage of nonagricultural employment.(29) It should be noted, however, that Texas does have strong pockets of unionism, particularly in the Port Arthur-Beaumont area.(30)

The relationship beteween low levels of union activity and economic development is much more complex than the commonly made assertion that industries are attracted to areas with weak union support. Firms requiring high-skill labor often have little choice but to locate in areas where such labor is available and to hire union workers. Dr. Ray Marshall has noted that firms which engage in projects requiring a large input of highly skilled labor would find it almost impossible to operate without a high percentage of union labor. (31)

On the other hand, it is also true that many firms dislike the resistance encountered in union employees with regard to changes in work processes and problems related to the work environment and prefer to operate in weak union areas as a result. Thomas R. Plaut and Joseph E. Pluta (1983) note that many jobs in the contemporary economy require much less skill than those of the past, a factor which may increase the demand for low-skilled nonunion workers, who are more inclined to perform routine tasks with little resistance. (32)

The primary influence of unions on economic development revolves around their well-documented tendency to cause an increase in wages.(33) Having said this, it is important to note that the impact of unions on wages is neither as simple nor as great as is commonly assumed. Other factors play an important role in influencing the wage level of a region. The large labor supply in the South, primarily resulting from the technological displacement of farmers and farm laborers in this heavily rural region, tends to keep wages low. The history of slavery in the South, as well as the tenant farmer-sharecropper system, have also been proposed as strong factors still influencing wage levels in the South (including Texas) as compared with other parts of the nation. Thus a low level of union activity is one among a constellation of factors which leads to the relatively low-wages in Texas.(34)

As a location factor, a low wage level which is reflective of a low-skilled labor force attracts some industries and repels others. Labor-intensive firms, such as textiles and apparels, are attracted to low-wage areas. Firms which are not in a price-competitive situation and require highly skilled labor will be less attracted by low wages. Market-oriented firms are often unimpressed by low-wage areas for the obvious reason that poorly paid workers have little expendable income.(35) Capital-intensive firms, which have a relatively small percentage of their costs tied up in labor, will not rank a low wage level high on their list of priorities when selecting a location.(36)

Given that the level of unionization and the wage level (which, as we have seen, are closely related) tend to vary in importance as a location factor among industries, the ultimate impact of these factors on economic development is uncertain. This is not a question which lends itself to an easy answer. David M. Smith, after noting the contradictory findings of various studies, concluded that "the overall influence of the labor factor on plant location is thus difficult to evaluate."(37) Leonard P. Wheat indicates that the lack of interest of market-oriented firms in areas with low wage levels probably reduces the net growth resulting from low wages and light union activity to insignificance.(38) Wheat may have overstated his case, but it seems apparent that the negative features involved with low wage levels and anti-unionism reduce the impact of these factors on economic growth to the realm of minor importance.

The same conclusion cannot be drawn with regard to the influence of these factors on the composition of industry in a state. The attraction of labor-intensive industries to low-wage, nonunion areas is clearly substantiated in the literature. The assertion that highly paid, highly skilled, heavily unionized labor plays a role in attracting other types of industries is also supported by various studies. Obviously, there are other factors, such as markets and climate, which also play an important part in the location decisions of firms. But they do so in a milieu in which labor factors are crucially involved.

In conclusion, this analysis suggests that RTW laws have little substantive impact on the level of union activity, although they are important symbols within an anti-union culture. Union activity and wage levels are interrelated. They are important factors but seem to play only a minor role in the overall net growth experienced by states. Their significance lies rather in their impact on the industrial composition of states.

C. Occupational Safety and Health

Federal and state occupational safety and health regulations can influence local economic development greatly because such regulations can affect the ways in which industries operate by permitting or restricting various activities.

The federal Occupational Safety and Health Administration (OSHA) enforces national safety and health standards. Individual states may defer authority to OSHA, or they may establish their own regulations provided they are at least as stringent as the federal rules. Texas is one of twenty-six states which have ceded control to the federal agency.(39) The State has its own Occupational Safety Act, passed in 1967, but it is no longer enforced and in 1975 the state legislature eliminated funds for implementation of the statute.(40)

The state does provide a voluntary compliance effort consultation service through two divisions within the Texas Department of Health-the Occupational Safety Board and the Occupational Health Division. Under the voluntary compliance plan, an employer may request "free on-site OSHA-type consultative safety and health inspections" of their facilities.(41) State officials conduct tours similar to OSHA's, but assess no fines or penalties. The inspectors inform employers of any health and safety violations and offer advice on correcting the problems. An official in the Occupational Health Division estimates that approximately eight hundred voluntary inspections will be done in the current year.(42)

Because Texas ceded control to the federal government and enforces no regulations of its own, its safety and health standards are no more stringent than any other state and may be less restrictive to economic development than those of states with stricter regulations. These laws have no more restrictive an effect on economic development than those in other states.

IV. FINANCE-RELATED LAWS AND THEIR IMPACT ON ECONOMIC DEVELOPMENT IN TEXAS

A. State Business Taxes

State taxes are one cost of doing business and purportedly are an important business climate variable. Given that rational entrepreneurs, in their efforts to maximize profits, seek to minimize total costs, and given that significant interstate tax differentials do exist, it seems reasonable to assume that taxes play a significant role in business location decisions. The following section examines this hypothesis and assesses its implications for the state of Texas by identifying the state's major business taxes and evaluating the impact of these levies on firm location decisions.

1. History. Texas has traditionally been relatively conservative in taxation; it is one of only a handful of states which impose neither a corporate nor a personal income tax. The State Constitution does provide the legislature with the authority to levy such fees; lawmakers, however, have yet to exercise these options, relying instead on the general sales tax and selected severance taxes for the majority of the state's revenues.(43)

For many years, Texas relied on the property tax, the poll tax, and a few occupational fees for most of its funds. Despite the chronic fiscal crises which plagued the state during the first half of this century, the legislature resisted the national trend toward adopting a general sales or income tax, choosing instead to enact a series of more selective severance and sales levies. In 1961, the lawmakers finally admitted that this patchwork of relatively minor fees was simply inadequate to meet the needs of a growing state.(44)

Having at last acknowledged the problem, the legislature began serious debate on the adoption of a broad-based tax. Liberals generally supported the passage of an income tax, while conservatives rallied behind the general sales tax option. The conservative forces prevailed, and a 2 percent retail sales tax was adopted.(45)

In subsequent years, the need for additional revenues has contributed to speculation that some form of income tax would be instituted. Texas has, however, managed to avoid this alternative by periodically raising the sales tax and broadening its base.

2. Current State Business Taxes. Texas does not have a corporate income tax, but it does impose a number of levies which have a direct impact on firms operating in the state. Some of the taxes are applicable to all firms, while others are industry specific.

Sales Tax. Texas imposes a 4 percent tax on "sales, rentals, leases and use of most tangible personal property."(46) Many Texas cities impose an additional levy of 1 percent.(47) Exemptions are granted to grocery food products, prescription medicines, property which will be consumed in manufacturing or processing, property sold for resale, items taxed under other statutes, and several items used on farms and ranches in the production of food.(48) Motor vehicle sales are also exempt from the general sales tax, but are subject to a separate 4 percent levy.(49) The sales tax earned $3 billion in fiscal year 1983, which accounted for 38.9 percent of the state's total tax collections.(50)

Corporate Franchise Tax. Texas levies an annual franchise tax on all nonexempt domestic and foreign corporations doing business in the state.(51) The basic rate is $4.25 per $1,000 of the corporation's stated capital, surplus, and undivided profits. Corporations also doing business in other states are taxed according to the portion of their total gross receipts earned in Texas. In either case, there is a $55 minimum payment. Approximately 305,000 corporations pay the levy, with 66,000 paying the minimum charge.(52) Corporations with total assets everywhere of less that $1 million who have previously paid a Texas franchise tax may elect to file a "short form" and make payment according to a predetermined scale. The Texas Research League reports that nearly 39,000 firms paid fees ranging from $35 to $4,270 under this option.(53) In FY 1983, the tax provided $555 million or 6.5 percent of the state's total tax revenues.(54)

Payroll Tax. Texas's state unemployment compensation fund is supported by a payroll tax administered by the Texas Employment Commission. New businesses are charged a 2.7 percent tax on the first $7,000 paid in wages to each employee. After six calendar quarters this initial rate may be adjusted up or down, depending on the firm's employment record. All firms "which employ one or more individuals during a portion of the day in each of 20 different weeks in a calendar year or . . . pay $1,500 or more in wages in a calendar quarter are subject to the fee"(55).

Fuels Taxes. Motor fuels taxes raised $490 million or 5.8 percent of the state's FY 1983 tax revenues.(56) Gasoline, gasohol, and liquified gas are taxed at 5.0 cents per gallon, while diesel fuel is charged at 6.5 cents per gallon.

Oil and Gas Taxes. Texas imposes two severance taxes on crude oil. The Oil Production Tax, first levied in 1905, is set at 4.6 percent of the market value of all production in the state. In FY 1983, the tax earned $1.2 billion.(57) An additional $1 million was raised by the Oil and Gas Regulation Tax.(58) For this levy a fee of 3/16 of one cent is charged on each barrel of crude oil produced. Combined collections from the two levies were 14 percent of the state's overall tax receipts in FY 1983.(59)

The Natural and Casinghead Gas Tax, which is the severance tax on natural gas, raised $1.06 billion, or 12.5 percent of the state's net tax collections.(60) Firms are charged 7.5 percent of the market value of gas produced in the state.

Texas also levies a 2.42 percent fee on the gross receipts of companies providing various specified services to oil and gas producers.(61) Known as the Oil and Gas Well Servicing Act, the levy raised $9 million in FY 1983, less than 1 percent of the state's tax receipts.(62)

Public Utilities Taxes. Texas taxes the intrastate gross receipts of utility, telephone, and telegraph companies. The levies are graduated by area and population.(63) The various taxes raised $309 million in FY 1983, about 3.6 percent of the state's total tax receipts.(64)

Insurance Company Taxes. Texas taxes the gross premiums of insurance companies according to the percentage of assets the company has invested in the state.(65) These taxes earned $223.7 million, or 2.6 percent of the state's FY 1983 revenues.(66)

Hotel and Motel Tax. A state tax of 3 percent of consideration is paid by hotel and motel occupants. The legislature enacted this measure in 1959; in 1965 it granted cities the option to levy an additional charge of not more than 3 percent. State revenues from the tax were $40.4 million in FY 1983.(67)

The State of Texas imposes a relatively modest overall tax burden on firms operating within its borders. William C. Wheaton compared business tax levels among the forty-eight contiguous states and found that Texas ranks thirty-seventh. Delaware, which imposed the highest tax burden on firms, was ranked first, and Utah was last.(68)

Interstate comparisons of the various fees reveal that Texas's payroll and fuel taxes are the lowest in the nation.(69) The state's sales, motor vehicle, insurance, and oil production fees are generally average or slightly below average relative to other areas.(70) Only the corporate franchise and gas production fees are fairly high in comparison to other states.(71)

Texas has a relatively favorable business climate in terms of taxes, but does this help the state in attracting industry? The overwhelming majority of studies on facility siting indicate that taxes are not an important factor in firm location decisions. Joseph Pluta of the University of Texas Bureau of Business Research explains, "Firms locate where total costs are lowest, not where tax costs are lowest."(72)

Pluta and his colleague Thomas Plaut, both proponents of this position, assert that a number of studies have found that taxes are not a significant consideration in facility siting.(73) Pluta and Plaut conducted their own business location study in 1981, the results of which reaffirmed their earlier findings.(74)

A wealth of corroborating evidence for Pluta and Plaut's assertion is provided by Donald Liner in "The Effect of Taxes on Industrial Location."(75) Liner compiled a bibliography of eighteen business location studies; in fifteen, taxes were found to be a relatively insignificant decision variable. Most of the researchers found that labor issues, transportation, raw materials, and proximity to markets were the most influential concerns.

Robert Pollard reached similar conclusions as a result of his research.(76) TIC (the Texas Industrial Commission, now the Texas Economic Development Commission), in the course of responding to routine information inquiries, asked firms to list their criteria for a suitable location. Pollard reviewed the responses from a sample of 206 firms that made inquiries to TIC between 1974 and 1977. Only 2 percent (four firms) mentioned taxes as being a primary decision variable.

While most researchers concluded that taxes do not influence location decisions, the results were by no means unanimous. Liner cites three studies in which taxes were considered at least moderately important to decisionmakers.(77) In a Congressionally sponsored survey of 691 high-technology firms, over 67 percent of the respondents said that taxes were either a significant or very significant factor in selecting a plant site.(78)

The perception that taxes are an important decision variable appears to be very strong in Texas. The Texas Municipal League in 1979 surveyed over nine-hundred private and public sector leaders in the state and found that "tax levels were believed to be the most important ingredient of Texas' favorable business climate."(79)

Why does this dichotomy exist within the literature on location theories? John Due offers a simple yet highly plausible explanation: "The anti-tax attitude of many businessmen conditions them to stress the tax factor, as does the belief that their answers may influence the conclusions of the survey and thus ultimately bring lower taxes."(80)

The common perception that taxes are a major concern is thus perpetuated, even though there are three very convincing reasons why this is not the case:

1. The effects of state and local taxes have been cut by about half because they are deductible from federal tax liabilities(81).

2. Tax differentials, like wages or any other cost differentials between two locations, are important to businesses only to the extent that they affect profits. If a firm can offset the tax differential by increasing profits or reducing other costs, profits will not be adversely affected, and tax differentials will be largely inconsequential(82).

3. If the tax differential between areas A and B is used to finance higher quantity or quality levels of services in area A than in area B, firms may view the tax differential not as a burden, but but rather as a user charge commensurate with the

additional services provided(83).

The relative insignificance of taxes as a factor in location decisions holds important implications for Texas. The state has avoided imposing either a corporate or personal income tax largely because its severance taxes on natural resources have been so productive. As the state grows and changes, and as natural resources lose their relative prominence in the Texas economy, the state will be forced to seek new sources of revenue. These findings indicate that the state should be able to diversify its tax structure somewhat without seriously detracting from its favorable business climate. As Joseph Pluta writes:

> Texas ranks high in locational studies because it offers central location, good transportation facilities, a large work force, a growing population, good climate, a healthy economy, and a general image that favors economic growth. It does not appear likely that minor changes in the business tax base or tax rates would offset . . . these advantages.(84)

Rather than offering tax incentives to attract industry, public officials should concentrate on maintaining basic infrastructure and services. L. H. Revzan echoes this theme, which was repeated in a number of studies: "Commitment to basic infrastructure and use planning on the part of the state would be more cost effective in meeting economic development objectives than the use of tax incentives or subsidy mechanisms."(85)

B. State Banking Laws

The effect of Texas's banking laws on business activity can potentially influence economic development by regulating the flow of capital in the state. State banking regulations can encourage or impede economic development, or they can have no effect whatsoever. An inventory of state banking laws, conducted in order to determine the extent to which such statutes either facilitate or obstruct the flow of capital to various sectors of the economy, revealed that in most instances the influence of state banking laws on economic development in Texas is minimal.(86) One law which has possibly had an impact on economic growth is that which prohibits branch banking in Texas.(87) Branch banking involves an established bank's formation of an office or a branch in an area other than the primary location of the bank.

Many rural areas can only support one "full-fledged" bank, while others are unable to attract a single banking facility.(88) Support can be found for the hypothesis that prohibitions against branch banking have led to a lack of competition in such areas.(89) Several studies have concluded that in states which allow branch banking the competition from a new branch in what was formerly a one-bank town resulted in a shifting in the original bank's portfolios from low-risk securities toward commercial loans.(90) This lends support to the assertion that the lack of competition fostered by prohibitions against branch banking in Texas has led to a decrease in the availability of capital in rural areas. It must be mentioned, however, that the possible adverse impact of branch banking on economic development may have been somewhat mitigated in the last five to ten years. The recent increase in large bank holding companies has for practical purposes allowed the banking community to circumvent the "branch" prohibition. The extent to which the potential adverse impact in rural areas has been mitigated is yet to be determined.

C. State Insurance Laws and Economic Development

The relationship between the insurance industry and economic development is perhaps most clearly seen in the industry's role as a major investor and in the insistence of banks and other lenders that adequate insurance be provided before granting loans. Despite this relationship, the literature concerning the impact of insurance laws and economic development is thin. Discussions with persons involved in the regulation of insurance conpanies and a survey of the available literature reveal two areas of state insurance law which have affected economic growth in Texas: the "Robertson law" and the Catastrophe Property Insurance Pool Act of 1971.(91)

The "Robertson law" involved the taxation of "foreign" (i.e., out-of-state) life insurance companies. At the time the "Robertson law" was passed, such companies dominated the insurance industry in Texas. The statute required all incorporated stock or mutual companies offering life insurance in Texas to invest 75 percent of all reserves set aside for the future payment of policies (written for Texas citizens) in Texas securities and Texas property in accordance with the specifications of the law.(92) The "Robertson law" also provided an incentive for out-of-state life insurance companies to invest by providing reduced premium taxes to those who did so.(93)

The "Robertson law" was repealed by the legislature in 1963, and it is difficult to measure the historical impact which the law had on economic development in Texas. A 1961 study of 60 randomly selected companies of the 484 life insurance companies in Texas revealed that these 60 companies invested approximately two million dollars in the Texas economy in 1961.(94) The majority of these investments were made in the areas of first liens on real estate and insured liens on real estate, which undoubtedly had a significant impact on the promotion of home ownership through increasing the amount of money invested in Texas mortgages. Inasmuch as this was the primary intention of the originators of the legislation, one can say that the law achieved its objective.(95)

While it seems accurate to conclude that although the law had a positive and significant impact on economic development in Texas, its repeal has apparently had a minimal impact on economic growth.(96) Because Texas has now become a much more lucrative area for investments, life insurance companies no longer have to be coerced to invest in the state.(97)

Another state insurance law germane to this report is the Catastrophe Property Insurance Pool Act of 1971. In response to the three destructive hurricanes of the 1960s, this Act established a mechanism by which hail and windstorm insurance might be acquired in fourteen counties on or near the Texas coast. The first section of the Act states that the law was passed to ensure that "orderly growth and development of the State of Texas" would not be "severely impeded".(98)

The Act established the Catastrophe Property Insurance Pool Association (CPIPA). All companies writing wind and hail coverage in the state are required to be members of the association, and wind and hail insurance policies are issued through it. The CPIPA uses the premiums to cover expenses and then distributes the remainder to pool members on a formula basis. In the event of a major storm, premiums may not cover expenses and association members may be required to make additional contributions on the basis of the volume of business they do statewide and the amount of insurance they write in the designated counties. If the pool has to pay out more than $100 million in any one year, the participants can deduct their share of the losses in excess of that amount from their premium taxes. Thus the State, which oversees the program through the State Board of Insurance, covers all losses in excess of $100 million.(99) For example, Texas experienced a $27.5 million tax loss after Hurricane Alicia in 1983 because of tax deductions by participating insurance companies.(100)

Few persons doubt that the Catastrophe Property Insurance Pool Association has made a significant contribution to economic development along the Texas coast. The condominiums and subdivisions which have been erected on the shoreline in the period since the law's passage would probably not have been possible without the legislation. Bankers never would have financed such projects without the insurance provided through the CPIPA.(101)

Texas insurance laws have not had a distinctive influence on economic growth in Texas. It can be said, however, that the two statutes discussed here have made identifiable contributions to the growth of the state.

V. STATE REGULATION OF PUBLIC UTILITIES, TRANSPORTATION, AND NATURAL RESOURCES AND THE IMPACT ON ECONOMIC DEVELOPMENT

A. Public Utilities

Utilities are regulated because they are "natural monopolies." The services they render are provided most efficiently if the producer acts as a monopolist. Moreover, utilities are "affected with a public interest".(102) Government, therefore, must see to it that utilities provide the best possible services at the lowest possible cost to the public.

Utility rates, service availability, and dependability can be major factors influencing the location decisions of many firms--particularly firms that use large amounts of energy such as needed in the production of aluminum, chlorine, ferroalloys, or phosphorous.(103) According to Robert M. Ady, Senior Vice-President of the Fantus Co., an industrial location consulting firm, the relative importance of energy needs in the location decisions of all types of firms is expected to increase for the next ten years. (104)

1. Public Utility Regulation in Texas. The State of Texas regulates public utilities through two state agencies. The Public Utility Commission of Texas (PUC) sets the rates and service standards of telephone utilities; all privately owned and investor-owned electric, water, and sewer utilities operating in unincorporated areas; and all electric co-operatives. Cities, rather than the PUC, have original jurisdiction over the rates and services of electric, water, and sewer utilities operating within the boundaries of incorporated cities. Appeals concerning the rates set by the cities are received by the PUC.(105) The Gas Utilities Division of the Railroad Commission of Texas regulates gas utilities in Texas with the same type of jurisdiction as that of the PUC,(106) and both set utility rates under their jurisdictions in the same way.(107) The commissions can affect economic development in two ways: first, through the direct impact on the utilities themselves; and second, through the impact on consumers of public utility goods as determined by the rates they pay.

2. Effects on Utilities. The PUC and the Railroad Commission establish a regulatory climate for utilities, and this climate has a subsequent effect on a utility's costs of capital. Many Wall Street investment firms measure and rank the regulatory climates of the states.(108) Regulatory climate unfavorable to utilities will increase their cost of capital while reducing their availability of capital.(109) The utility, for example, will have to pay a higher interest rate on its bonds in order to attract investors. Conversely, a very favorable climate ranking decreases a utility's cost of capital. Investors see it as a sounder, safer investment and are, therefore, willing to invest at a lower rate of return.

Investment firms may give a state's regulatory climate an unfavorable rank if utilities in the state are forced to charge lower rates, even though these rates may benefit consumers in the short run. As the utility requires additional capital to finance the higher rates of interest it must pay because of the state's unfavorable climate, it may have to request higher rates from the state's PUC. In the long run, therefore, the utility rates charged consumers could actually be higher than they would have been if the state had originally received a more favorable ranking and, subsequently, lower capital costs.(110)

If they have high capital costs, utilities may delay or cancel construction and improvements needed to increase capacity and efficiency. In the long run, such utilities may require very high rates either to finance inefficient production or to initiate construction and improvements that should have been started earlier. Moreover, if construction is canceled, utilities may not be able to meet future demand.(111)

3. Effects on Rates. The average electric bills for all classes of service in Texas for 1981 were generally lower than the overall national average but were the highest in the South Central Region of the United States with two minor exceptions.(112) The average gas utility prices in Texas for 1981 by class of service were lower than the national averages but again were the highest in the South Central Region.(113)

Why were Texas's average electric bills and gas utility prices lower than the national averages? Given the enormous amounts of natural gas produced in Texas, relatively low average gas utility prices are surprising. Also, since Texas generates over 70 percent of its electricity with natural gas, a reasonably economical fuel, it is also not surprising that the state's average electric bills are lower than the national averages.(114)

Why were Texas's average electric bills and gas utility prices the highest in the South Central Region? One explanation centers on regulatory climate. For the states in this region, Texas belongs to the "very favorable" category, Arkansas and Oklahoma are in the "favorable" category, and Lousiana is in the "unfavorable" category.(115) This implies that the Texas regulatory commissioners may be relatively "pro-utility" and inclined to set higher rates. A second factor involves the method of commissioner selection employed in each state. Appointed commissioners may be more supportive of the industry and create a relatively permissive or favorable regulatory climate.(116) This may be a contributing factor to Texas's high average electric bills since the PUC commissioners are appointed. The Railroad Commission, however, is elected. This line of reasoning, therefore, does not explain Texas's high average gas utility prices.

A third explanation for the high prices lies with the determination of the rate base. All states in the region use a historical test year which tends to keep rates down, and include construction work in progress (CWIP) in their rate bases, which generally contributes to higher rates.(117) The CWIP influence on rates, however, depends upon the percentage of CWIP the commissioners allow in the rate base and the amount of construction currently in progress. The higher the percentage or the amount, the larger the rate base and, consequently, the higher the rates. The percentage of CWIP normally allowed by each state regulatory commission and the average amount of construction in progress in each state are not available. The higher Texas rates as compared to those in other South Central states may be partially explained if the Texas regulatory commissioners allow a higher percentage of CWIP in the rate base than their counterparts in the region, or if the average amount of construction in progress was higher in Texas than in the other South Central states.

Finally, the high average electric bills in Texas could be explained by the high rate of return the Texas PUC traditionally allows electric utilities, which is the highest in the South Central region.(118) Since the rate of return for Texas gas utilities was the lowest in the four-state region, rate-of-return comparison cannot explain the high Texas average gas utility prices.(119)

4. Effects on Economic Development. Because Texas's average electric bills and average gas utility prices are lower than the national averages, the state should have a competitive advantage over most of the country (except over the northwestern states regarding electricity) when recruiting firms that use large amounts of energy. Texas is, however, at a competitive disadvantage when compared with the other states in the South Central Region. In other words, in competition for attracting energy-intensive firms, Texas should do well when compared to states outside the Central South, but less well within this region.

Finally, Texas's average electric and gas utility prices carry implications for firms already established in the state. Texas firms will have an advantage over their competitors located in states with higher energy prices. A disadvantage exists for Texas firms competing with firms located in other South Central states. If all other costs are the same, when comparing a Texas firm and one of its competitors in a South Central state, the higher average electric and gas utility prices the Texas firm incurs may increase the price of its product. In this case, the Texas firm may find it difficult to market its exports. If this happens on a large scale, the rate of economic growth will be negatively affected.

B. The Regulation of Transportation

The purpose of regulating transportation is to "limit discriminatory pricing practices concerning persons, localities, routes, and traffic."(120) That is, regulation keeps rates down, particularly for small, rural shippers, and guarantees that most, if not all, areas will be serviced by at least one transportation firm. To the extent that regulation of transportation affects rates and level of service, it may also affect economic development.

As discussed in the previous chapter, transportation costs can be a major factor influencing the location decisions of firms.(121) A firm often locates either at the source of its raw materials, if its manufacturing process is weight losing, or at the market where it sells its product(s), if its manufacturing process is weight gaining.(122) If a third factor such as energy or labor costs is low enough in another area to offset the increased transportation costs of moving raw materials to and finished products from that area, the firm may locate there.(123) High transportation costs, however, may predominate over other comparative advantages of an area such as labor availability, making the area relatively unattractive for manufacturing.

In spite of the long-term trend of decreasing transportation costs, which diminishes the impact of these costs on location, the implications of the above situation can still be significant. Areas that are economically depressed because they cannot offer manufacturers either raw materials or a market but can offer cheap labor or power may remain depressed if transportation rates are high.

For many firms, these transportation costs can be a significant part of their total costs. Any firm, therefore, that must pay higher transportation costs than a competitor may be at a disadvantage. The price a firm charges for its product(s) may be higher than its competitors' prices because "transportation costs frequently play a significant role in determining the ultimate price of a product."(124)

In Texas the Transportation Division of the Railroad Commission is responsible for the regulation of all "for-hire" transportation in the state.(125) The Railroad Commission was given the responsibility to regulate the rates and operations of bus companies in 1927 and the rates and operations of trucking companies in 1929. The Transportation Division sets the rates motor carriers may charge for their services. In addition, it also sets routes, schedules, service and safety of operations.(126)

A number of studies have found that regulated intrastate trucking rates in Texas are higher than they could be, especially when compared to the rates charged by deregulated interstate trucking firms for similar distances traveled and weights trucked.(127) Furthermore, these studies concluded that the level and quality of service offered by regulated intrastate truckers was lower than that of deregulated interstate truckers.

1. Effects on the Economic Development of Texas Cities. Suppose that a Texas firm and an out-of-state firm are selling identical products in a Texas market and are therefore competitors. Further suppose that both are located at raw materials sites and generally ship equal amounts of finished products equal distances. The Texas firm uses higher-priced intrastate trucking, while the out-of-state firm uses cheaper interstate trucking. The out-of-state firm could charge a lower price for its products because of its lower overall costs, assuming that all other costs to the firms are equal or balance out and the only difference is transportation costs. The level of economic activity in the area where the Texas firm had been located will decrease.

Furthermore, a firm wishing to serve Texas markets may locate just beyond the state boundaries and use cheaper interstate trucking to move its product(s) to market. It is possible that a firm would choose an out-of-state location over a Texas location simply because of the differences in transportation costs. The Texas area that the firm in question did not choose will not develop economically because it could not compete with the out-of-state area. (This assumes again that all other factors influencing the location decision are equal.)

In conclusion, transportation regulation in Texas can have the following consequences: first, firms will tend to cluster around raw materials sources and markets (usually big cities), leaving many areas which offer other advantages such as cheap labor or energy economically undeveloped; second, Texas firms may be at a competitive disadvantage with rival firms in other states, particularly when the firms are serving Texas markets if the out-of-state firm uses interstate trucking with lower rates; and, third, Texas may experience difficulty attracting new industries, especially those that use large amounts of intrastate trucking.

C. The Regulation of Natural Resources Production

Natural resources development, which is of special importance to the economy of Texas, is regulated to some extent by the State. To the extent that this regulation controls the potential pace and costs of production, it may affect rates of economic development. The principal regulatory activity is located in the Oil and Gas Division of the Railroad Commission, which regulates the production of oil and gas, and in the Surface Mining and Reclamation Division, which regulates the production of coal and other hard minerals.(128)

The regulation of natural resources production is necessary for a number of reasons. Oil and gas producers are regulated to protect against wasteful production, storage, and transportation of oil and gas.(129) The surface minerals in the state are regulated to prevent the adverse effects to society and the environment that may occur from surface mining.(130) Activities such as these can have substantial effects on the economic development of Texas cities.

1. The Regulation of Oil and Gas Production. Authority to drill for oil and gas requires a permit from the Oil and Gas Division.(131) In order to avoid the physical waste of oil and gas, the Commission sets the "maximum permissible rate of production of both oil and gas fields in the state."(132) This ensures that all the recoverable oil and gas in a field is recovered. (If oil and gas are extracted from the ground too quickly, the drive mechanism that pushes them to the surface is destroyed and part of the oil and gas is not recovered.)

The Oil and Gas Division also determines the maximum number of wells allowable on a tract of land and whether or not a well can be drilled at all. Finally, it sets safety, storage, and transportation standards that help minimize physical waste. To protect against economic waste, the Commission prorates the production of oil and gas to market demand. That is, it sets the amount that all producers in the state can produce equal to market demand in order to keep prices stable.(133)

The Railroad Commission's effect on economic development through the regulation of oil and gas production depends upon its decisions concerning the number of wells that are approved, their locations, and the quantity of oil and gas that may be extracted from the ground. If the Commission restricts drilling in a given area, or sets the production rate at a very low level, the income lost to the area could be substantial. The area's economic development level, therefore, might remain low. On the other hand, excessively high production rates could lead to lower prices and rapid depletion of these resources, again negatively affecting growth prospects, particularly in the long run.

2. The Regulation of Surface Mining and Land Reclamation. In 1977, the federal government passed the Surface Mining Control and Reclamation Act. According to the Act, all states are required either to set standards comparable to those of the Act or to turn jurisdiction of surface mining and reclamation over to the federal government.(134) The scope and stringency of regulation are basically the same across all states. The impact of surface mining and land reclamation regulations is in the costs of reclamation. In some states the cost of reclamation per acre of land disturbed or per ton of mineral mined is higher than in others because of the characteristics of the state's terrain and the mineral deposits.(135)

A study by Walter Misiolek and Thomas C. Noser determined the costs of land reclamation to be between $6,500 and $8,000 per acre of land disturbed for large-scale mines in the United States.(136) In a separate study, Misiolek and Noser found that the reclamation costs of the Texas Gulf Mine ran between $4,009 and $5,635 per acre disturbed and between $.27 and $.35 per ton of coal mined.(137)

Regulation of surface mining and land reclamation, therefore, does increase a mining firm's total costs. The amount of the increase depends upon the characteristics of the land and the coal seam and the type and amount of equipment used in the reclamation process. These could result in slightly higher prices for coal, which could in turn result in an increase in the the cost of generating electricity. Because the cost of reclamation in Texas seems to be lower than that in most other states, due to the topography of its coal mines, the impact of regulation is less in Texas than in other states.

D. Environmental Protection Laws

Environmental protection laws are closely tied to the regulation of natural resources and may significantly affect economic development to the extent that they limit business activity. Incorporating environmental controls into an industrial facility, obtaining disposal permits, and monitoring discharges are often expensive activities. Environmental regulations can, consequently, significantly increase the costs of doing business.

The federal government has promulgated numerous national environmental regulations. Individual states often adopt similar legislation, which may be stricter than federal rules, but may not be more lenient. During the 1960s and 1970s, Texas enacted several environmental protection laws. This section reviews the three major statutes in this field and examines the impact of environmental regulations on business location decisions.

1. Air Pollution Control. The Texas Clean Air Act was adopted by the state legislature in 1967 "to safeguard the air resources of the state."(138) The statute recognizes the Texas Air Control Board (TACB) as the principal authority on all air quality issues in the state.(139) Any person building or modifying a facility which may emit air contaminants must obtain a permit to operate from the TACB. The person must demonstrate that the structure will be equipped with the best available control technology, and that the emissions from the facility will meet all federal and state standards.(140)

2. Water Pollution Control. The Texas Department of Water Resources is the state agency charged with the protection of the state's water supplies. The Department requires that businesses obtain permits for the following activities: wastewater disposal, industrial solid waste disposal, disposal of waste by underground injection, solution mining, and appropriation and use of state water.(141)

The Department of Water Resources promulgates the state's water regulations and also enforces many federal standards. The Department derives its authority for pollution control from three major state laws: the Texas Water Quality Act,(142) the Solid Waste Disposal Act,(143) and the Disposal Well Act.(144)

3. Nuclear and Radioactive Materials. The Texas Radiation Control Act recognizes the Texas Department of Health as the state Radiation Control Agency.(145) According to the provisions of the Act, radioactive materials, or devices or equipment utilizing such materials, must be licensed. The Act also stipulates that detailed records must be kept regarding the utilization, receipt, storage, transfer, disposal, and exposure of radioactive materials.(146)

4. Environmental Standards: A Comparative Overview. Federal, regional and state officials, and representatives of various environmental organizations interviewed for this report felt that Texas is generally less cautious about its environment than most other states, and not much more stringent than the federal government.(147) The Texas air quality regulations were described as more comprehensive, but not necessarily more stringent, than the federal rules, while the state's water quality regulations were generally considered slightly more strict than the national standards.

The Conservation Foundation recently released a comprehensive, rigorous review of state environmental standards.(148) The study provides the only available comparative data on environmental regulations among the fifty states. Author Christopher J. Duerksen constructed an index of twenty-three environmental and land-use indicators to measure state environmental control efforts.(149) Texas received twenty-two out of a possible sixty-three points; it was tied with Nebraska, Nevada, and North Dakota for thirty-ninth place among the fifty states, where first place represented the strictest environmental control effort.(150)

5. Environmental Regulation and Industrial Location. Environmental standards do not appear to be a significant factor in the business location decisions of most firms. Evidence does indicate, however, that pollution-intensive industries give slighlty more weight to interstate differentials in environmental regulations than do other firms.(151)

Texas could probably impose stricter environmental protection policies without harming its favorable business climate. In fact, the state may enhance its attractiveness to many firms by strengthening its pollution control efforts. As Duerksen writes, "A reputation for strong environmental protection may increase a state's attractiveness to dynamic industrial sectors that attach great importance to quality of life."(152) In other words, stricter environmental controls might actually make a state more attractive to some industries.

VI. CONCLUSIONS

This chapter has assessed the impact of Texas's business regulatory environment on economic development in the state. It is clear that historical trends continue to be reflected in the current business climate. The long-standing influence of the frontier ethos, abundant land, and the culture of individualism have led to an economic environment which tends to encourage laissez-faire attitudes. The earlier aversion to big business and financial institutions seems to have abated.

State labor laws are one example of this political and cultural environment. Texas is the only large urban state with a right-to-work (RTW) law. This analysis concludes, however, that RTW laws have little substantive impact on the level of union activity, although they are important symbols within an anti-union culture. While union activity and wage levels are interrelated and are important factors in the economy on a number of dimensions, they seem to play only a minor role in the overall net growth experienced by states. Their significance lies rather in their impact on the industrial composition of states. Thus, the existence of RTW laws has not hampered or helped economic development, although it has shaped the nature of the development by attracting labor-intensive low-wage industries to Texas. There is, however, some evidence that the research facilities of universities in Texas are attracting research-oriented firms which need highly skilled employees, such as in the microelectronic and biomedical fields.

This analysis reveals the relative insignificance of taxes as a factor in location decisions, which has important implications for Texas. The State has avoided imposing either a corporate or personal income tax largely because its severance taxes on natural resources have been so productive. As the state grows and changes, and as natural resources lose their relative prominence in the Texas economy, the State will be forced to seek new sources of revenue. These findngs indicate that the State should be able to diversify its tax structure somewhat without seriously detracting from its favorable business climate.

It is apparent that although insurance laws, especially the Robertson law, were significant in earlier years, they do not seem to have an important influence on economic growth in Texas at the present time. The only regulation which has significant economic impact now is the Catastrophe Property Insurance Pool Act (CPIPA), which has encouraged extensive development along the Texas coast. Similarly, state banking laws appear to have minimal affect on Texas's economy since state statutes neither impede nor facilitate the flow of capital to various sectors of the economy. With the exception of the prohibition of branch banking, the relative insignificance of financial regulations on economic development in Texas reflects the historical traditions of the state and the prevailing laissez-faire attitude.

The impact of the regulation of public utilities, transportation, and natural resources on economic development also reflects the state's deep-seated laissez-faire attitude, but the ramifications are somewhat more complex. Because of its vast natural resources, Texas's average gas and electric bills are lower than the national average. Thus, the state enjoys a theoretical competitive advantage over most of the country in recruiting energy-intensive firms. However, the Texas rates are higher than those of other states in the South Central Region, putting Texas at a disadvantage compared to neighboring states for utility firms that consider rates important.

Regulation of intrastate trucking in Texas has resulted in rates higher than those charged by deregulated interstate trucking firms. This is the one exception to the prevailing absence of restrictive regulations. Texas's transportation regulations may have adverse consequences for economic development, especially in areas that are more remote, where intrastate transportation is required. Texas firms may be at a competitive disadvantage with rival firms in other states, particularly when the firms are serving Texas markets, if out-of-state firms use cheaper interstate trucking. Finally, Texas may experience difficulty attracting new industries, especially those that use large amounts of intrastate trucking.

The regulation of natural resources production focuses on the oil and gas industry and surface mining. This regulation attempts to promote productivity and market stability, and clearly seeks to encourage economic development. Surface mining regulations, however, increase a mining firm's total costs, which could result in slightly higher costs for coal. This could increase the cost of electric generation and therefore might hamper economic development. However, the cost of reclamation seems to be lower in Texas than in most other states, and so the impact of this federal legislation is less significant in Texas than in many other states. Surface mining regulations are imposed by federal rather than state agencies, and therefore are not indicative of the state's attitude toward business. Texas's liberal oil and gas regulations are state imposed and actively seek to promote economic development, reflecting the prevailing laissez-faire attitude toward business.

Not surprisingly, environmental protection laws in Texas are also less stringent than in most other states. They are not more stringent than the minimum levels set by the federal government and, consquently, do not increase the cost of doing business in Texas as compared with other states. This analysis shows that environmental standards do not appear to be a significant factor in the business location decisions of most firms. Evidence does indicate, however, that pollution-intensive industries give slightly more weight to interstate differentials in environmental regulations than do other firms. In fact, Texas could probably impose stricter environmental protection policies without harming its favorable business climate.

In the case of most state regulations of the business environment, the prevailing laissez-faire ethos has created a business climate in which economic development, while not actively encouraged, is impeded as little as possible.

ENDNOTES

1. T. R. Fehrenbach, *Seven Keys to Texas* (El Paso: Texas Western Press, 1983), p. 43.

2. Ibid., p. 14.

3. Clifton McClesky, Larry Dickens, and Allan Butcher, *The Government and Politics of Texas* (Boston: Little, Brown & Co., 1972), p. 17.

4. Wilbourn E. Benton, *Texas: Its Government and Politics* (Princeton: Prentice-Hall, 1977), p. 339.

5. Fehrenbach, p. 85.

6. Ibid., p. 91.

7. V. O. Key, "Texas: A Politics of Economics," in *Texas: Readings in Politics, Government and Public Policy*, ed. Richard Kraemer and Philip Barnes (San Francisco: Chandler Publishing Co., 1971), p. 4.

8. Ibid., p. 2.

9. Fehrenbach, p. 103.

10. Key, p. 111.

11. Fehrenbach, p. 111.

12. Bruce Posner, "A Report on the States," *INC.* 4, no. 10 (October 1982): 95-102.

13. James Fisher and Dean Hanink, "Business Climate: Behind the Geographic Shift of American Manufacturing," *Economic Review* 67, no. 6 (June 1982): 20-30.

14. Alexander Grant and Co., *General Manufacturing Business Climates* (Chicago: Grant Thornton Co., 1983), pp. 10-22.

15. Interview with Ray Marshall, Professor of Labor Economics, Lyndon B. Johnson School of Public Affairs, Austin, Texas, November 22, 1983.

16. Eugene W. Jones et al., *Practicing Texas Politics* (Boston: Houghton Mifflin Co., 1977), pp. 17-19.

17. Joan M. McCrea, *Texas Labor Laws*, 3d ed. (Houston: Gulf Publishing Co., 1978), p. 1.

18. Ibid., p. 3.

19. Tex. Rev. Civ. Stat. Ann., art. 5207a.

20. For further information concerning these laws, one should see Joan McCrea's work cited above.

21. In addition to the studies described in this report, see Frederick Meyers, "Effect of Right-to Work Laws: A Study of the Texas Act," Industrial and Labor Relations Review 9 (October 1955): 77; John J. Mitchell IV, "An Analysis of the Effect of the Indiana Right-to-Work Law on Union Membership," University of Pittsburgh (unpublished); Fred Witney, "The Indiana Right-to-Work Law," Industrial and Labor Relations Review 11 (July 1958): 506; James Kuhn, "Right-to-Work Laws--Symbols or Substance?" Industrial and Labor Relations Review 14 (July 1961): 587-94; John M. Kuhlman, "Right-to-Work Laws: The Virginia Experience," Labor Law Journal 6 (July 1955): 453; John M. Glasgow, "The Right-to Work Law Controversy Again?" Labor Law Journal 18 (February 1967): 12-15; Neil A. and Caterine A. Polomba, "Right-to-Work Laws: A Suggested Economic Rationale," Journal of Law and Economics (October 1971): 475-83.

22. Frederick Meyers, Right-to-Work in Practice (New York: The Fund for the Republic, 1959), pp. 14-15.

23. Benson Soffer and Michael Korenich, "Right-to-Work Laws as a Location Factor: The Industrialization Experience of Agricultural States," Journal of Regional Science 3, no. 2 (August 1961): 54-55.

24. Craig Peterson and Keith Lumsden, "The Effect of Right-to-Work Laws on Unionization in the United States," Journal of Political Economy 83, no. 6 (December 1975): 1237-48.

25. Ibid., p. 1247.

26. Ronald S. Warren and Robert P. Strauss, "Mixed Logit Model of the Relationship between Unionization and Right-to-Work Legislation," Journal of Political Economy 87, no. 3 (June 1979): 645-55.

27. Meyers, Right-to-Work in Practice, pp. 21-22.

28. George Edwards, Pioneer-at-Law (New York: W. W. Norton & Co., 1974), pp. 157-74.

29. U.S. Dept. of Labor, Handbook of Labor Statistics, (Washington, D.C.: Government Printing Office, 1980), p. 414.

30. Interview with Ray Marshall, November 22, 1983.

31. Ibid.

32. Thomas R. Plaut and Joseph E. Pluta, "Business Climate, Taxes and Expenditures, and State Industrial Growth in the U.S.," Southern Economic Journal 50, no. 1 (July 1983): 112-13.

33. Leonard F. Wheat, Regional Growth and Industrial Location (Lexington, Mass.: D. C. Heath and Co., 1973), pp. 194-95; also see David M. Smith, Industrial Location: An Economic Geographical Analysis (New York: John Wiley and Sons, 1971), pp. 44-53.

34. Wheat, p. 26. Also see Wesley W. Mellow, "Unionism and Wages: A Longitudinal Analysis," Review of Economics and Statistics 63 (February,

1981): 43-52; and Edwin Mansfield, <u>Microeconomics: Theory and Applications</u> (New York: W. W. Norton & Co, 1982), p. 407.

35. Wheat, pp. 26-27, 192-93.

36. Interview with Ray Marshall, November 22, 1983.

37. Smith, p. 52.

38. Wheat, pp. 192-93.

39. Interview with Fred Frodyma, Office of Policy Analysis, Occupational Safety and Health Administration, Washington, D.C., February 21, 1984.

40. Interview with Walter Martin, Occupational Safety Board, Texas Department of Health, Austin, Texas, November 30, 1983.

41. "A Brief Guide to Business Regulations and Services in Texas," Comptroller of Public Accounts Publication #96-156, Austin, Texas, August 1983, p. 5 (booklet).

42. Interview with Jerry Lauderdale, Occupational Health Division, Texas Department of Health, Austin, Texas, November 10, 1983.

43. The Texas State Constitution, art. 8, sec. 1, states that "the legislature may provide for the taxation of intangibles and impose occupation taxes upon individuals and corporations doing business in the state, and the legislature may tax the incomes of both natural persons and corporations." As cited by the Commerce Clearing House, <u>State Tax Handbook</u> (Chicago, 1982), p. 617.

44. Stuart A. MacCorkle, Dick Smith, and Janice C. May, <u>Texas Government</u> (New York: McGraw-Hill, 1974), p. 233.

45. McClesky, Dickens, and Butcher, p. 304.

46. "A Brief Guide to Business," p. 22. The sales tax affects businesses as both merchants and as consumers. Businesses bear much of the sales tax burden. The Texas Research League claims that "because the tax contains generous exemptions for individual consumers and few for business, the percentage of the tax collected from the business consumer is bound to be relatively high in this state." In December 1981, the League staff suggested that 46-48 percent would be a more realistic figure, after allowing for the residential utility exemption (Texas Research League Staff, "General Business Taxes," <u>Analysis</u> 4, no. 5 (May 1983): 2-3).

47. See Chapter 5 for details on local tax options.

48. "A Brief Guide to Business," p. 22.

49. Texas levies special taxes on both the sale and rental of motor vehicles. Combined receipts from these charges accounted for 6.9 percent of the state's fiscal 1983 net tax collections. The Motor Vehicle Sales and Use Tax, set at 4 percent of the vehicle sales price, less any trade-in, raised $526 million in FY 1983. Vehicles purchased by rental companies are exempt from this tax but face a special Motor Vehicle Rental Tax, equal to 4 percent of gross rental receipts. In 1983, $18.7 million was collected. (State of Texas, Comptroller of Public Accounts, <u>1983 Annual Financial Report</u> (Austin, Tex., 1983), pp. 23 and 54). Individuals and firms purchasing vehicles elsewhere, but operating them for business purposes within the state, must also pay a levy, with credit given for taxes paid in other states. The tax raised $6.8 million in FY 1983. A fourth motor vehicle tax is placed on manufactured housing, or mobile homes. The 5 percent tax is applied to 65 percent of the vehicle's sales price. In 1983, this tax earned $32.6 million (Ibid., p. 54).

50. Ibid., p. 54.

51. As stated in "Your New Corporation and the Texas Franchise Tax," Comptroller of Public Accounts Publication #96-198, Austin, Texas, October 1982 (booklet), exemptions are granted to sole proprietorships; trusts; professional associations; partnerships; public charities; public interest, educational, and religious nonprofit corporations; national, state, and private banks; savings and loan associations; insurance companies; surety companies; and transportation companies required to pay an annual tax based on their gross receipts (p. 1).

52. Texas Research League Staff, "General Business Taxes," p. 2.

53. Ibid.

54. State of Texas, Comptroller, <u>1983 Report</u>, p. 23.

55. Interview with John C. Jennings, Chief of Tax, Texas Employment Commission, Austin, Texas, February 20, 1984.

56. State of Texas, Comptroller, <u>1983 Report</u>, p. 23.

57. Ibid., p. 53.

58. Ibid., p. 23.

59. Ibid.

60. Ibid.

61. Michael D. Jenkins and Donald L. Sexton, <u>Starting and Operating a Business in Texas</u> (Sunnyvale, Calif.: Oasis Press, 1983), pp. 11-21.

62. State of Texas, Comptroller, <u>1983 Report</u>, p. 54.

63. Utilities within the state are taxed according to the following scale:

Population of Area	Telephone	Gas, Electric, and Water
Unincorporated	1.6500%	No Tax
Inc., under 1,000	1.6500%	No Tax
1,000 to 2,499	1.6500%	0.581%
2,500 to 9,999	1.9250%	1.070%
10,000	1.9250%	1.997%
Over 10,000	2.5025%	1.997%

The State also levies two utilities taxes to defray regulatory expenses. A charge of 1/4 of 1 percent of the intrastate receipts of natural gas pipelines is imposed to cover the administrative costs the Railroad Commission incurs in regulating gas pipelines and distributing companies. The Public Utilities Commission, which monitors electric, telephone, and water utilities, is supported by a tax of 1/16 of 1 percent of gross receipts (State of Texas, Comptroller, 1983 Report, pp. 23 and 54).

64. Ibid., p. 54.

65. Insurance companies are taxed according to the following scale:

Percentage Investment in Texas	Tax Rate
75 or less	3.300%
76 to 80	3.025
81 to 85	2.750
86 to 90	2.200
Over 90	1.925

These rates apply to out-of-state insurance companies; Texas firms receive slightly more favorable rates. Seven minor specialized taxes, known as maintenance taxes, are also levied: six to support the State Board of Insurance, and one to cover the costs of administering the worker's compensation law (Texas Research League Staff, "General Business Taxes," p. 5). The maintenance taxes raised $18.4 million in FY 1983, while the occupation tax, which brought in $205.3 million in combined receipts from the levies, accounted for 2.6 percent of the state's overall tax revenues (State of Texas, Comptroller, 1983 Report, pp. 23 and 54).

66. State of Texas, Comptroller, 1983 Report, pp. 23 and 54.

67. Ibid., p. 54.

68. William C. Wheaton, "Interstate Differences in the Level of Business Taxation," National Tax Journal 36 (March 1983): 83-94.

69. John C. Jennings, Chief of Tax at the Texas Employment Commission, reported that Texas has the lowest average payroll tax rate in the nation (Interview, February 20, 1984). According to 1982 data compiled by the Legislative Budget Board, Texas also has the lowest state gasoline tax rate in the nation. The state is tied with Oklahoma for the lowest diesel fuel tax. (Wyoming is the only state which does not levy a tax on diesel fuel.) (Texas Research League Staff, "General Business Taxes," p. 5).

70. Of the forty-six states which currently have a general sales tax, twenty-four impose a higher rate than Texas while ten levy a lower fee. Eleven states charge the same 4 percent rate (as reported by the Sales

Tax Division, Comptroller's Office, Austin, Texas, November 28, 1983. The information was compiled by the Comptroller's Office from the Commerce Clearing House, State Tax Handbook, 1983).

Of the forty-five states using the motor vehicle sales tax, the Texas Research League reports that the Texas fee is lower than that found in nineteen states, higher than fourteen states, and the same as in eleven states. Comparative data were not available for the other three charges (Analysis 4, no. 6 (June 1983): 5).

Using Census Bureau Data, Texas Research League staffers found that Texas insurance taxes yield $13.29 per capita, slightly below the national average of $14.70 (Texas Research League Staff, "General Business Taxes," p. 7). The Texas Research League also found that of the nine oil-producing states, four states charge higher fees while three impose a similar charge. Two of the states charge significantly less than Texas (Texas Research League Staff, "Products of Disequalization," Analysis 5, no. 5 (May 1984): 4).

71. The Texas Research League compared the franchise tax with capital-based taxes in other states and found that Texas has a "relatively high tax rate." Pennsylvania was the only state mentioned as having a higher rate (Texas Research League Staff, "General Business Taxes," p. 2).

The Research League also compared the Texas gas production tax to the levies imposed by the other nine top producing states. After adjusting for interstate variations in tax policies, the League concluded that "Texas taxes most natural gas at rates exceeding those imposed by all other states except New Mexico" (ibid., p. 5).

72. Joseph E. Pluta, Economic and Business Issues of the 1980s (Austin: Bureau of Business Research, 1980), p. 48.

73. Thomas R. Plaut and Joseph E. Pluta, Business Climate, Taxes and State Industrial Growth in the United States: An Empirical Analysis (Austin: Bureau of Business Research, 1981), p. 9.

74. Ibid., p. 22.

75. Donald C. Liner, "The Effect of Taxes on Industrial Location," Popular Government 39 (March 1974, Supplement): 33-39.

76. Robert F. Pollard, "Industrial Location Decisions in Texas," Texas Business Review 52 (July 1978): 125-27.

77. Liner, pp. 33-39.

78. U.S. Congress, Joint Economic Committee, Subcommittee on Monetary and Fiscal Policy, Location of High Technology Firms and Regional Economic Development (Washington, D.C.: U.S. Government Printing Office, 1982), p. 23.

79. Dick Brown, "Why Firms Locate in Texas--and What That Means for City Officials," Texas Town and City 16 (July 1982): 14.

80. John F. Due, "Studies of State-Local Tax Influences on Location of Industry," *National Tax Journal* 14 (June 1961): 165.

81. Pluta, p. 48.

82. Ibid.

83. Sharon G. Levin, "Suburban-Central City Property Tax Differentials and the Location of Industry: Some Evidence," *Land Economics* 50 (November 1974): 380.

84. Brown, "Why Firms Locate in Texas," p. 13.

85. L. H. Revzan, "State and Local Tax Policies and Industrial Location Decisions," *Popular Government* 41 (Winter 1976): 14.

86. *Texas Banking Code*, art. 5 (1943, as amended to 1977).

87. Interview with Leonard Passmore, formerly General Counsel, Texas Bankers' Association, Austin, Texas, February 21, 1984.

88. Ibid.

89. Lawrence Litvak and Belden Daniels, "Innovations in Development Finance," in *Financing State and Local Economic Development*, ed. Michael Barker (Durham, N.C.: Duke University Press, 1983), pp. 79-82. One should also see R. Chandross, "The Impact of New-Bank Entry on Unit Banks in One-Bank Towns," *Journal of Bank Research* 4 (Autumn 1973); D. Fraser and P. Rose, "Bank Entry and Bank Performance," *Journal of Finance*, (March 1972); and A. McCall and M. Peterson, "The Impact of De Novo Commercial Bank Entry," *Journal of Finance* 32 (December 1977).

90. Litvak and Daniels, "Development Finance"; Chandross, "New-Bank Entry"; McCall and Peterson, "De Novo Commercial Bank Entry."

91. Interview with Evelyn Ireland, Director, Division of Research and Information Services, State Board of Insurance, Austin, Texas, December 5, 1983. Ms. Ireland is mentioned here because her comments were particularly helpful in clarifying the relationship between certain insurance laws and economic development.

92. William J. R. King, "History and Development of Insurance Law in Texas" (unpublished, n.d.).

93. Ibid.

94. Interview with Evelyn Ireland, December 5, 1983; and Charles Melvin Sackrey, "The Laws Regulating the Investment Policies of Life In-

surance Companies Operating in Texas: An Interpretation and Analysis" (M.A. Thesis, University of Texas at Austin, 1963), pp. 51-52.

95. King, p. 39.

96. Interview with William Arondahl, Director of Tax Records, State Board of Insurance, Austin, Texas, February 23, 1984. Ms. Ireland also concurred on this point. The writings of Mr. King and Mr. Sackrey also agreed on this point.

97. Interview with William Arondahl, February 23, 1984.

98. Texas Insurance Code, art. 21.49.

99. A discussion with Jim Douglas, Director of the Texas Catastrophe Property Insurance Association (Austin, Tex., February 24, 1984), was also quite helpful in gaining an understanding of some of the details of this act.

100. State of Texas, Comptroller of Public Accounts, Office of Revenue Estimating and Research, *Fiscal Notes* (Austin, Tex., January 1984), pp. 1-8.

101. Interview with Jim Douglas, February 24, 1984. Rick Gentry, researcher at the Institute for Insurance Information (Austin, Tex., February 28, 1984), agreed concerning this matter.

102. Charles F. Phillips, *The Economics of Regulation* (Homewood, Ill.: Richard D. Irvin, 1977), pp. 4-5.

103. E. Williard Miller, *Manufacturing: A Study of Industrial Location* (University Park: Pennsylvania State University Press, 1977), pp. 85-86; Robert W. Gilmer, "Regional Energy Costs and the Aluminum Industry," *Texas Business Review* 56, no. 6 (November-December 1982): 260; and Dennis J. Donovan, "Twelve Key Questions for Site Selection Decision-Makers," *Industrial Development* 151, no. 4 (July/August 1982): 12-15.

104. Robert M. Ady, "Shifting Factors in Plant Location," *Industrial Development* 150, no. 6 (June 1981): 15.

105. Public Utility Commission of Texas, "What Is the Public Utility Commission?" Austin, 1983 (pamphlet).

106. Railroad Commission of Texas, Oil and Gas Division, "A Chronological Listing of Important Historical Events, Legislative Acts, Judicial Decisions, Orders, and Other Related Data Regarding the Railroad Commission of Texas," Austin, October 1, 1980 (mimeographed appendix), pp. 5-6.

107. Whenever a utility wants to increase or decrease its rates, it files an application with the appropriate regulatory authority. The application includes a "rate filing package" containing all the data the regulatory authority will need in order to set a new rate. The rate filing package is required to include a detailed account of the utility's expenses, revenues, and operations during a twelve-month period called a "test year" (the most recent twelve months for which this information is available). The regulatory authority may then hold hearings concerning the rate change. Once all the evidence has been presented, the regulatory authority attempts to set a rate that is fair, just, and reasonable and ensures the utility a reasonable rate of return on the adjusted value of its investments. If the regulatory authority that sets the rate is an incorporated city (i.e., not the PUC nor the Railroad Commission), the rate may be appealed to the PUC or the Railroad Commission by any party to the rate proceeding. If one of the commissions sets the rate, no avenue of appeal exists. See also Tex. Rev. Civ. Stat. Ann., art. 1446c, art. 6, secs. 38 to 40; Railroad Commission of Texas, Gas Utilities Division, "Municipal Assistance Packet," Austin, 1983, pp. 4-16; Public Utility Commission of Texas, "New Rate Procedures Adopted," Annual Report (Austin 1983), p. 23; and Tex. Rev. Civ. Stat. Ann., art. 1446c, art. 4, sec. 26(a).

108. See Jeffery A. Dubin and Peter Navarro, "Regulatory Climate and the Cost of Capital," in Regulatory Reform and Public Utilities, ed. Michael A Crew (Lexington, Mass.: Lexington Books, D. C. Heath and Co., 1982), p. 143; and W. N. Davidson III and P. R. Chandy, "Regulatory Environment for Public Utilities: Indications of the Importance of the Political Process," Financial Analysts Journal 39, no. 6 (November-December 1983): 50-53.

109. Dubin and Navarro, p. 141.

110. Ibid., pp. 141-42.

111. Peter Navarro, "Public Utility Commission Regulation: Performance, Determinants, and Energy Policy Impacts," Energy Journal 3, no. 2 (April 1982): 120-21.

112. The average electric bills are from U.S. Department of Energy, Energy Information Administration, Typical Electric Bills, January 1981 (Washington, D.C., 1981), pp. 11, 233-36, and 259-61. The only two ex-

ceptions appear in the 25 kwh residential class and the 12 kw, 1500 kwh commercial class.

113. Average gas utility prices are from American Gas Association Inc., Gas Facts (Arlington, Va., 1982), p. 121.

114. Edison Electric Institute, Statistical Yearbook of the Electric Utility Industry/1979, no. 47 (Washington D.C., November 1980), pp. 22 and 49. Texas produced 6.73 trillion cubic feet of natural gas in 1981, which accounted for 34.4 percent of the total amount produced in the United States for that year (see Thomas R. Plaut, "Energy and the Texas Economy," Texas Business Review 57, no. 2 (March-April 1983): 69).

115. Dubin and Navarro, p. 144.

116. Davidson and Chandy, pp. 50-53.

117. National Association of Regulatory Utility Commissioners, Annual Report on Utility and Carrier Regulation 1981 (Washington, D.C., 1981).

118. Ibid.

119. Ibid.

120. Ann F. Friedlaender and Richard H. Spady, Freight Transportation Regulation (Cambridge, Mass.: MIT Press, 1981), p. 1.

121. Miller, p. 100.

122. Walter Isard, Introduction to Regional Science (Englewood Cliffs, N.J.: Prentice Hall, 1975), pp. 86-89.

123. Ibid., pp. 96-100.

124. Miller, p. 101.

125. Railroad Commission of Texas, Transportation Division, "How to Obtain Trucking Authority," Austin, 1983, pp. 2-4 (pamphlet).

126. Railroad Commission, "Chronological Listing," pp. 5-6; and Tex. Rev. Civ. Stat. Ann., art. 911a, sec. 4(a), and art. 911b, sec. 4(a).

The Legislature of the State of Texas originally established the Railroad Commission in 1891 to regulate the rates and operations of railroad companies in the state.

127. See Friedlaender and Spady, pp. 169-96; and Steve Fuller, Larry D. Makus, and Jack T. Lamkin, Jr., "Effects of Intrastate Motor Carrier Regulation on Rates amd Service: The Texas Experience," Transportation Journal 23, no. 1 (Fall 1983): 16-29.

128. Railroad Commission, "Chronological Listing," pp. 4, 10, 11, and 29. See also Tex. Nat. Res. Code Ann., secs. 81.051, 85.001, 85.002, 85.041 to 85.064, 85.125, 85.161 to 85.166, 85.201 to 85.207, 85.241 to 85.243, 85.352 to 85.353, 85.381 to 85.385, 86.001 to 86.004, 86.011, 86.012, 86.041 to 86.043, 86.081 to 86.097, 86.141 to 86.145, 86.181 to 86.185, 86.221 to 86.225, 111.013, and 131.

129. Railroad Commission, "Chronological Listing," p. 10; and Tex. Nat. Res. Code Ann., secs. 85.045 and 85.046.

130. Railroad Commission of Texas, Surface Mining and Reclamation Division, "Coal Mining Regulation," Austin, August 1983, pp. 46-52, and Tex. Nat. Res. Code Ann., sec. 131.

131. Railroad Commission, "Chronological Listing," p. 10; and Tex. Nat. Res. Code Ann., secs. 85.045 and 85.046.

132. David F. Prindle, Petroleum Politics and the Texas Ralroad Commission (Austin: University of Texas Press, 1981), pp. 6-7.

133. Ibid., p. 7.

134. Carol D. Rasnic, "Federally Required Restoration of Surface-Mined Property: Impasse between the Coal Industry and the Environmentally Concerned," Natural Resources Journal 23, no. 2 (April 1983): 335.

135. Walter Misiolek and Thomas C. Noser, "Coal Surface Mine Land Reclamation and Costs," Land Economics 58, no. 1 (February 1982): 67-85.

136. Ibid., p. 82.

137. Misiolek and Noser, p. 70.

138. The Texas Clean Air Act (Tex. Rev. Civ. Stat. Ann., art 4477-5) was adopted by the state legislature in 1967. Its stated purpose is "to safeguard the air resources of the state from pollution by controlling or abating air pollution and emissions of air contaminants, consistent with the protection of health, general welfare, and physical property of the people, including the esthetic enjoyment of the air resources by the people and the maintenance of adequate visibility."

139. Ibid.

140. Texas Air Control Board, Regulation 6 (31 TAC chap. 116), "Control of Air Pollution by Permits for New Construction or Modification," Austin, rev. June 10, 1983, p. 1.

141. Texas Department of Water Resources, "Basic Information Regarding Permits and Other Authorizations Issued by the Texas Department of Water Resources," Pamphlet C-11, Austin, 1979, rev. November 1982, pp. 5-16.

142. The Texas Water Quality Act (Tex. Water Code Ann., sec. 21) requires the Department to develop water quality standards for compliance with the provisions of the Federal Water Pollution Control Act. Its purpose is "to maintain the quality of the water in the state consistent with the public health and enjoyment, the propagation and protection of terrestrial and aquatic life, the operation of existing industries, and the economic development of the state; to encourage and promote the development and use of regional and area-wide waste collection, treatment, and disposal systems to serve the waste disposal needs of the citizens of the state; and to require the use of all reasonable methods to implement this policy." The Act stipulates that no form of waste may be discharged into or adjacent to any water in the state unless authorized by permit, order or regulation. The Texas Department of Water Resources enforces its water regulations through periodic inspections. The frequency of these visits is determined by the quality of the wastewater being discharged.

143. The Solid Waste Disposal Act (Tex. Rev. Civ. Stat. Ann., art. 4477-7) was passed in 1967, its purpose being "to safeguard the health, welfare, and physical property of the people through controlling the collection, handling, storage and disposal of solid waste." The State Department of Health is responsible for municipal waste, while the Department of Water Resources regulates industrial waste. The Act gives the Department the power to require and issue permits authorizing and governing the storage, processing, and disposal of solid wastes. The provisions of this Act also extend to the management of hazardous waste.

144. The Disposal Well Act (Tex. Water Code Ann., sec. 27) requires individuals and businesses to obtain a permit in order to begin drilling a disposal well or to begin converting an existing well for disposal

purposes. The Act specifies that a permit may be issued if the installation is in the public interest, no existing rights will be impaired, and both ground and surface water can adequately be protected from pollution. The Department of Water Resources can set terms in the permit "reasonably necessary" to protect fresh water supplies from contamination from the well. Inspections may be conducted to determine the local conditions and probable effects of the well.

Oil and gas disposal wells are regulated by the Texas Railroad Commission. If the well is not an oil or gas disposal well, the Department of Water Resources must send a letter to the Railroad Commission, assuring that the well will not endanger any oil or gas formation.

145. The Texas Radiation Control Act (Tex. Rev. Civ. Stat. Ann.., art. 4590f).

146. Ibid. The statute requires the agency to "institute and maintain a regulatory program for sources of radiation so as to provide for (a) compatibility with the standards and regulatory programs of the Federal Government, (b) a single, effective system of regulation within the state, and (c) a system consonant in so far as possible with other states; and to institute and maintain a program to permit development and utilization of sources of radiation for peaceful purposes consistent with the health and safety of the public." According to the provisions of the Act, radioactive materials, or devices or equipment utilizing such materials, must be licensed. The Act also stipulates that detailed records must be kept regarding the utilization, receipt, storage, transfer, disposal, and exposure of radioactive materials.

147. Interviews with Sally Davenport, Environmental Specialist Quality 4, General Land Office, Austin, Texas, February 17, 1984; John Turney, General Counsel, Texas Air Control Board, Austin, Texas, December, 1, 1983; Ken Kramer, Sierra Club, Austin, Texas, February 22, 1984; Joyce Leidy, Business Information Coordinator, Business Referral Assistance Center, Texas Economic Development Commission, February 20, 1984; Ken Kirkpatrick, Deputy Director, Water Division, Environmental Protection Agency, Dallas Regional Office, Dallas, Texas, February 20, 1984; Nancy Wentworth, Environmental Protection Agency, Washington, D.C., February 10, 1984; Jim Price, Director of Research Division, Texas Air Control Board, Austin, Texas, November 14, 1983; and Robert Silvus, Chief of Wastewater Section, Texas Department of Water Resources, Austin, Texas, November 30, 1983.

148. Christopher J. Duerksen, *Environmental Regulation of Industrial Plant Siting* (Washington, D.C.: Conservation Foundation, 1983).

149. Duerksen explains: "The indicators ranged from voting records of a state's congressional delegation on selected national environmental issues to existence of state laws that address specific environmental problems. The overall focus was on regulatory programs and expenditures for environmental quality. Each indicator was assigned a point

value based on its relative importance in assessing a state's environmental efforts, as judged by Foundation staff" (ibid., p. 218).

150. Texas lost the largest number of points in the area of expenditures for environmental quality control. The state received perfect scores in only three of the twenty-three areas reviewed: hazardous waste programs, solar energy tax breaks, and protection of wetlands and endangered species habitats. Minnesota, with forty-seven points, was ranked first; Alabama, with only ten points, was last. Environmental controls tended to be most stringent in the Northeast and along the Pacific Coast. Among the Sunbelt states, only Florida scored over thirty points; the average score within the region was twenty-two.

151. Duerksen found "a very slight tendency for states with lax environmental and land-use regulations to make relative gains in employment in pollution-intensive industries" (ibid., p. xx). John S. Hekman, in "What are Businesses Looking for? Survey of Location Decisions in the South" (Federal Reserve Atlanta 67 (June 1982): 6-19), found that business leaders ranked state and local environmental regulations and permit processing thirteenth among nineteen location decision variables. When the survey results were broken down by industry, however, chemical manufacturers were found to place a much higher emphasis than other types of firms on environmental regulations, ranking them fourth among decision factors.

In a 1974 survey of 8,846 U.S. and Canadian firms engaged in a variety of manufacturing activities, Robert Foster found that 23 percent considered zoning and environmental requirements the most important variable in facility siting; 22 percent said they were least important ("Economic and Quality of Life Factors in Industrial Location Decisions," Social Indicators Research 4 (July 1977): 247-65). While no details were given regarding the types of firms in either group, these findings nonetheless support the notion that certain types of industries are more concerned with environmental requirements than others.

152. Duerksen, p. xxi.

CHAPTER 3: STATE PROGRAMS AND EXPENDITURES RELATED TO ECONOMIC DEVELOPMENT

I. INTRODUCTION

While the State of Texas has no formal, explicit policy on economic development of cities, the state legislature formulated an official comprehensive policy, H.R. Con. Res. 61, on development of urban communities in 1971. This resolution set forth a "broad policy framework . . . to guide state agencies and officials toward coordinated action to assist urban communities." It stresses the State's role in the following:

- preserving environmental quality through urban planning, resource conservation, management and monitoring of the environment and aesthetic qualities;

- improving individual opportunities through job expansion, through democratic practices in employment, through social, educational and economic integration, and through access to housing, health care and transportation; and

- strengthening local governments.

This policy notes that since the State relies upon elected city and county officials to solve urban problems, the State must provide assistance and cooperation in various ways. In particular, the policy urges the State to (1) improve the effectiveness of law enforcement agencies, correctional facilities, and the functioning of courts; (2) alter unduly restrictive constitutional and legal provisions that adversely affect the fiscal priorities of local governments and that encourage the formation of special districts; and (3) promote citizen participation and communication with state and local officials.(1) This policy was only a resolution and its impact is therefore difficult to assess.

In addition to setting the regulatory environment, the state government in Texas and elsewhere can affect the economic development of its cities through the administration of state development programs and the expenditure of state funds related, directly or indirectly, to economic development. Texas cities benefit from state programs that retrain the unemployed, provide highways and water projects, promote industries, and educate children. The State of Texas spends large sums of money on such programs. It is therefore important to examine these expenditures and determine their relative impacts on the economic development of Texas cities.

Although this study, and this chapter in particular, will analyze a wide variety of state programs and their impact on economic development, targeted aid to depressed or distressed communities has been a policy concern for states and the federal government for some time. The most significant federal efforts have involved the Area Redevelopment Administration, the Economic Development Administration, and certain parts of the Community Development Block Grant (CDBG) program. Some states have also designed economic development programs for depressed areas.

While a recent Advisory Commission of Intergovernmental Relations (ACIR) survey of the states and their efforts to aid distressed communities indicates that many tools for effecting such aid are available in Texas, the State in the past has chosen not to adopt policies or allocate funds for depressed areas. In some instances the State has played a role in administering targeted federal programs, but in one recent case the State appeared to set a priority on targeting. The Texas Department of Community Affairs and Governor Mark White's Office of Economic Development--both discussed below in detail--have placed a high importance on economic distress in administering the Small Cities Program of the federal CDBG program. The distribution of funds is targeted to distressed communities with a population of less than fifty thousand. The relevant Department of Housing and Urban Development (HUD) guidelines require that the funds benefit low- and moderate-income persons, aid in the elimination of slums or urban blight, and meet other community development needs of particular urgency. The program also contains a discretionary fund which recently has been allocated to the Rio Grande Valley area of Texas, largely due to the efforts of Governor Mark White.

The Governor's Office of Economic Development is also trying to boost tourism in the Valley along with encouraging industry, small business revitalization, and small business start-ups. Although these efforts are not monetary, they are still significant steps.

In Texas, state activity for distressed communities is a controversial issue, and giving priority to one area over another is even more controversial. The State does play a role in shaping the conditions of cities in the state, however, as will be seen in other sections of the report.

The mechanisms Texas utilizes that directly affect the economic development of its cities can be divided into three areas. First, the State grants funds to cities, in the form of categorical or block grants, that may be used in ways that assist economic development. Second, the State administers a number of programs designed to aid the development of business and industry by improving the quality of the state's workforce. Finally, by investing in infrastructure, the State affects the economic development potential of its cities.

This chapter begins with a discussion of the structure of state aid to cities. State expenditures by function and their relation to economic development are examined. This section includes a breakdown of federal and state grants to cities and a comparison between Texas state expenditures by function and those of other states. The chapter then analyzes a number of state agencies whose programs and expenditure levels significantly affect economic development. These agencies include the Texas Department of Community Affairs, the Texas Economic Development Commission, the Governor's Office, the State Purchasing and General Services Commission, the Parks and Wildlife Department, and the Texas Tourist Development Agency. The next section of Chapter 3 addresses the link between state expenditures for infrastructure, specifically for transportation and water resources, and economic development. Chapter 3 closes with a discussion of educational expenditures and programs in the State of Texas, which accounted for over 50 percent of total state expenditures in 1983.(2) It is evident that the State recognizes education as one of its primary responsibilities. Educational expenditures affect economic development by providing business and industry with an educated, trained, and retrainable workforce.

II. STRUCTURE OF AID TO CITIES FOR ECONOMIC DEVELOPMENT

A. Total State Expenditures in 1983

State expenditures totaled $13.64 billion in fiscal 1983, about a 12 percent increase in spending over the previous year. The three most important categories of state spending are education, welfare services, and highway maintenance and construction, which accounted for 51.4 percent, 15.9 percent, and 11.2 percent respectively of total state expenditures in 1983 (see Table 3.1 and Figure 3.1). The shares of these three categories fluctuated moderately between 1979 and 1983, but no clear trends toward increases or decreases are evident.

In a ranking with other states according to per capita state expenditures, Texas ranks forty-fourth in total expenditures, thirty-first in education, thirty-fifth in highways, and forty-sixth in public welfare expenditures.(3)

B. Grants-in-Aid

Cities and other political jurisdictions depend on state aid to fund many programs. There are three principal means by which state government can provide financial assistance to localities: (1) the state can directly assume financial responsibility; (2) the state can authorize local governments to impose taxes and/or fees; and (3) the state can provide grants-in-aid to localities. In practice all three types of assistance are often pursued simultaneously. This section is concerned with only the third form of assistance, grants-in-aid to cities and political jurisdictions. State aid, for our purposes, is defined as grants to localities financed from state and/or federal revenues as designated.

State grants to localities provide partial financing for public programs of local concern and/or enhance intergovernmental financial equity within a particular state. This type of state aid represents a shared responsibility because while the state provides funds and some overall program direction, localities have some discretion.

Across the nation, the largest portion of state aid goes to school districts, the second largest to counties, and the third to cities.(4) Texas is not an exception to this trend. In fiscal year 1983, support for education, both state and local programs, comprised 51.1 percent of the total state expenditures. Texas does not follow the national trend of providing a large amount of aid to localities. Grants to counties in FY 1983 totaled only $36.6 million, while grants to cities were $34.9 million; together these comprise about 3 percent of the total state budget.(5)

1. **State Aid Expenditures in Texas.** Programs funded through state aid to cities and counties have both explicit and implicit effects on

Table 3.1

SHARE OF NET EXPENDITURES BY FUNCTION
TEXAS STATE GOVERNMENT
1979-83

	\multicolumn{5}{c}{Percent of Total}
	1979	1980	1981	1982	1983
Administrative					
Executive Departments	1.6	1.8	1.8	2.0	2.4
Business Commissions	0.6	0.6	0.6	0.6	0.7
Legislative	0.3	0.2	0.3	0.3	0.3
Judicial	0.2	0.2	0.2	0.3	0.3
Total	2.7	2.8	2.9	3.2	3.7
Services					
Welfare	17.5	15.7	16.6	14.9	15.9
Mental Health, State Homes and Corrections	5.3	5.0	5.2	6.1	5.9
Health and Sanitation	1.6	1.5	1.5	1.7	1.7
Law Enforcement	1.1	1.0	1.0	1.1	1.1
Total	25.5	23.2	24.3	23.8	24.6
Improvements					
Highways	11.9	15.5	14.5	11.2	11.2
Natural Resources	1.0	0.9	0.9	1.0	1.0
Parks and Monuments	0.6	0.6	0.7	0.6	0.6
Total	13.5	17.0	16.1	12.8	12.8
Education					
State/Local Education	46.6	45.3	45.1	47.5	46.9
Teacher Retirement Retirement	3.7	4.1	4.1	4.8	4.5
Total	50.3	49.4	49.2	52.3	51.4
Other Expenditures					
Political Subdivision	3.4	3.2	3.1	3.3	3.0
Payment of Public Debt	1.2	1.1	1.1	1.0	1.0
State Contribution to Employee Social Security	2.3	2.2	2.3	2.4	2.4
State Contribution to Employee Retirement	1.0	1.0	0.9	1.0	1.0
Miscellaneous	0.1	0.1	0.1	0.2	0.1
Total	8.0	7.6	7.5	7.9	7.5

Source: State of Texas, Comptroller of Public Accounts, 1983 Annual Financial Report (Austin, Tex., 1983), p. 37.

local economic development.(6) Programs that aid general government services, especially those that support highways and public transportation,

Figure 3.1

STATE EXPENDITURES BY FUNCTION, 1979-83
(millions of dollars)

Other Expenditures

Mental Health, State Homes, and Corrections

Highways

Welfare

Education

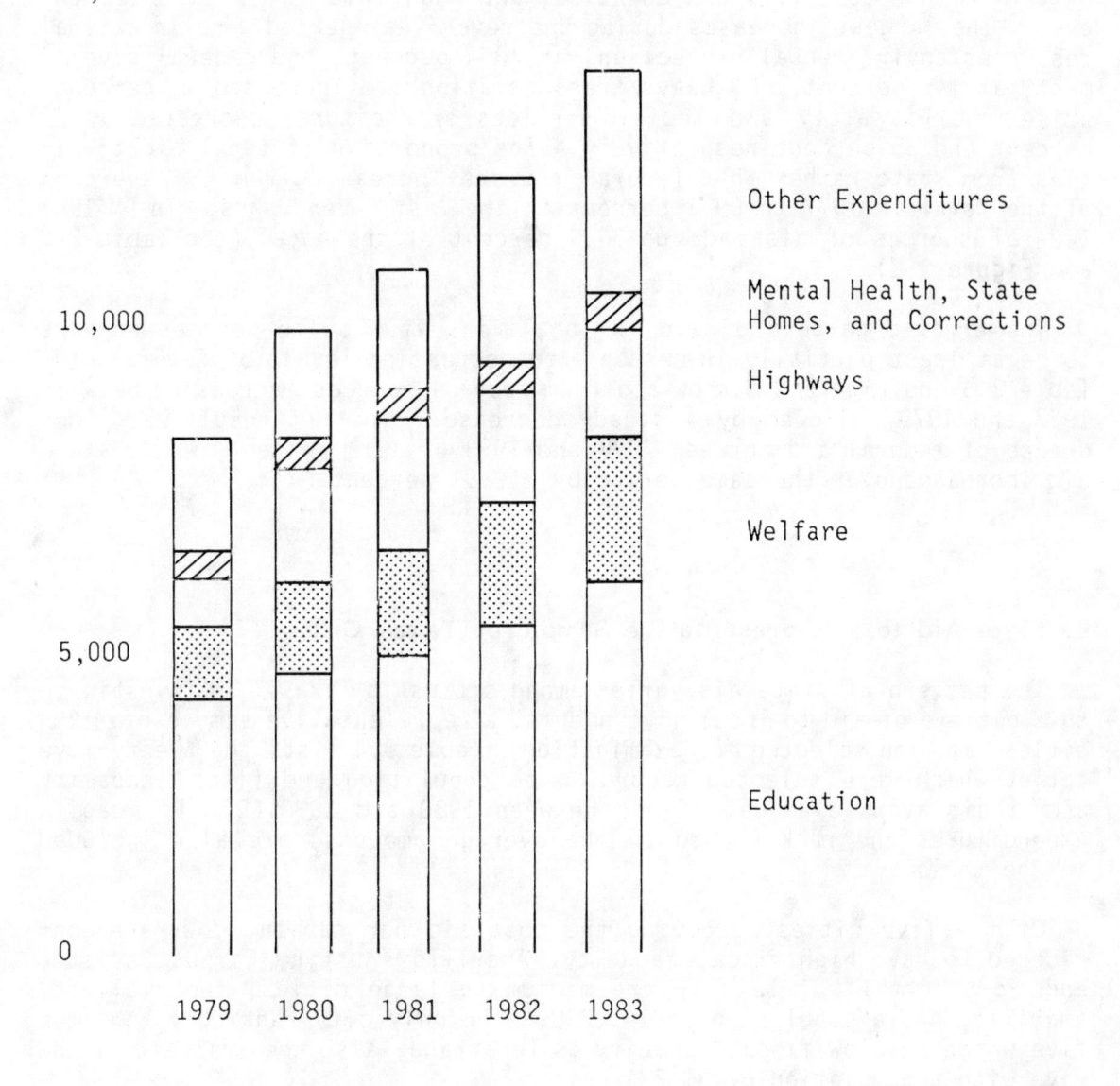

Source: State of Texas, Comptroller, 1983 Report, p.33.

directly enhance economic development, as discussed in a following section. State aid may also indirectly affect development by freeing local dollars which might be used for development-related efforts. State aid can improve equity among localities within the state by equalizing the distribution of services across regions. Intergovernmental assistance can be particularly helpful in financing costly local community and economic development efforts. Thus, it is important to examine state aid expenditures in Texas even though the amount of aid is relatively small.

The total Texas FY 1983 expenditure in the state aid category (including federal and state revenue sources) was $103.5 million, a decrease of 15.9 percent from the previous year's expenditure. Table 3.2 and Figure 3.2, which show expenditures in state aid to local governments from state revenues for fiscal years 1977 through 1983, indicate that the pattern of aid to cities and counties, and thus total aid, has been uneven. The largest increases during the seven-year period were in natural resources/environmental protection, at 1094 percent, and general government, at 145 percent. Highways/transportation aid increased 41 percent, while public safety and social services expenditures decreased by 29 percent and 35 percent respectively. The proportion of total aid to cities from state rather than federal sources increased from 48.5 percent of the total in 1977 to 69.1 percent in the last seven years. In FY 1983 federal sources of aid made up 30.9 percent of the total (see Table 3.2 and Figure 3.2).

The erratic pattern of aid to localities from state sources appears to be at least partially in response to decreasing levels of federal aid. Table 3.3 and Figure 3.3 show aid from federal sources increasing between 1977 and 1979 followed by a steady decrease. The net result was a decrease of federal aid between 1977 and 1983 of 11.2 percent, while state aid increased over the same period by 110.91 percent.(7)

B. State Aid to a Representative Sample of Texas Cities

The pattern of state aid varies among cities in Texas. To investigate this pattern of aid to local governments, a representative sample of Texas cities has been selected for examination. Table 3.4 lists the twenty-five cities which were selected according to population and fiscal capacity and their average amount of aid between 1980 and 1983.(8) Per capita expenditures and rank (based on the average amounts) are also included in the table.

Of the five cities receiving the most aid per capita, four are considered to have high fiscal capacity: Amarillo, Austin, Corpus Christi, and Fort Worth. These four are medium to large cities; the smallest, Amarillo, has a population of 149,230. The only city ranking in the top five which has low fiscal capacity is Texarkana, also the smallest of the five with a population of 31,271.

The five cities ranked lowest in average aid received are primarily very small with high fiscal capacities. Crowley and Kermit have populations under 10,000, and Sherman has a population under 35,000. All three have high fiscal capacities. The fourth city is the only one of this group with a low fiscal capacity—Mexia, which has a population of 7,094. The outlier of the group is Irving, a large city with high fiscal

Table 3.2
AID TO CITIES AND
COUNTIES IN TEXAS (State Sources)
1978-83

	1977	1978	1979	1980	1981	1982	1983
PUBLIC SAFETY							
Cities	4,246,536	0	6,457	146,252	0	0	0
Counties	294,616	0	1,094,951	946,221	104,028	3,321,455	3,378,182
Total	4,741,152	0	1,101,408	1,092,473	104,028	3,321,455	3,378,182
GENERAL GOVERNMENT							
Cities	8,099,350	10,659,938	12,389,062	14,333,396	17,815,478	23,145,041	23,548,541
Counties	10,834,762	11,316,619	11,855,741	18,246,630	20,978,171	27,818,494	23,311,521
Total	18,934,112	21,976,557	24,244,803	32,580,026	38,793,649	50,963,535	46,860,062
HIGHWAY/ TRANSPORTATION							
Cities	563,223	663,222	551,106	5,987,131	8,600,994	5,996,588	8,385,496
Counties	7,720,343	7,709,800	7,630,569	7,697,995	742,462	25,926,092	8,054,507
Total	8,283,566	8,370,022	8,181,675	13,689,626	9,343,456	31,922,680	16,440,003
SOCIAL SERVICES							
Cities	148,324	0	0	33,658	154,991	208,179	220,177
Counties	1,504,962	1,256,062	1,510,039	2,086,044	2,227,923	9,533	850,319
Total	1,653,286	1,256,062	1,510,039	2,119,702	2,382,914	217,712	1,070,496
NATURAL RESOURCES/ ENVIR. PROTECTION							
Cities	0	0	56,367	175,962	442,016	1,840,141	2,794,023
Counties	319,706	243,019	249,651	215,395	259,190	263,491	1,022,917
Total	319,706	243,019	306,018	391,357	701,206	2,103,632	3,816,940
TOTAL--CITIES	13,057,433	11,323,160	13,002,992	20,676,399	27,013,479	31,189,949	34,948,237
TOTAL--COUNTIES	20,874,389	20,525,500	22,340,951	29,191,785	24,311,774	51,339,065	36,617,446
TOTAL--ALL CATAGORIES	33,931,873	31,848,660	35,343,943	49,868,184	51,325,253	88,529,014	71,565,683

Source: State of Texas Comptroller's Annual Financial Reports, FYs 1977-83.

Figure 3.2

PERCENTAGE CHANGE FROM PREVIOUS YEAR IN AID TO CITIES AND COUNTIES IN TEXAS, 1979-83 (State Sources)

	1978	1979	1980	1981	1982	1983
CITIES	-13	15	59	31	16	12
COUNTIES	2	9	31	-17	112	-29
TOTAL	-6	11	41	3	73	-19

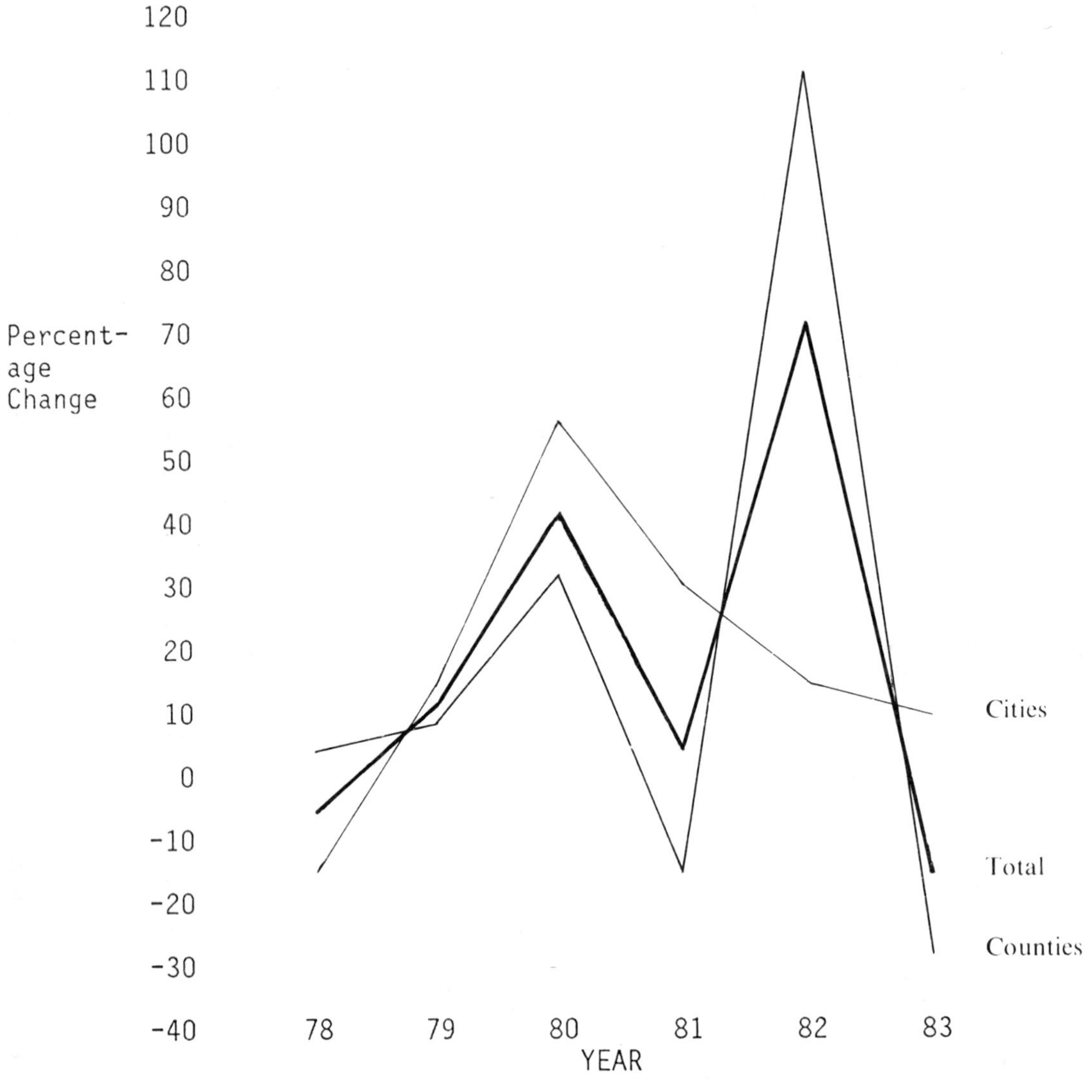

Source: State of Texas, Comptroller of Public Accounts, Annual Financial Reports 1978-83 (Austin, Tex., 1979-83).

capacity. It is a suburban community adjacent to the Dallas-Fort Worth regional airport.

Table 3.3

AID TO CITIES AND COUNTIES IN TEXAS (Federal Sources)
1978-83

	1977	1978	1979	1980	1981	1982	1983
CITY	21,599,569	25,968,632	33,909,289	29,237,888	29,870,138	23,210,530	22,044,011
COUNTY	14,385,439	16,968,917	19,201,094	18,862,200	13,671,067	11,286,919	9,907,139
TOTAL	35,985,008	42,937,549	53,110,383	48,100,088	43,541,205	34,497,449	31,951,150

Source: State of Texas, Comptroller, 1983 Report.

This survey data suggests that larger cities with high fiscal capacities tend to have higher levels of per capita aid.

Figure 3.3

PERCENTAGE CHANGE FROM PREVIOUS YEAR IN AID TO CITIES AND COUNTIES IN TEXAS, 1978-83 (Federal Sources)

	1978	1979	1980	1981	1982	1983
CITY	20.23%	30.58%	-13.78%	2.16%	-22.30%	-5.03%
COUNTY	17.96	13.15	-1.76	-27.52	-17.44	-12.22
TOTAL	19.32	23.69	-9.43	-9.48	-20.77	-7.38

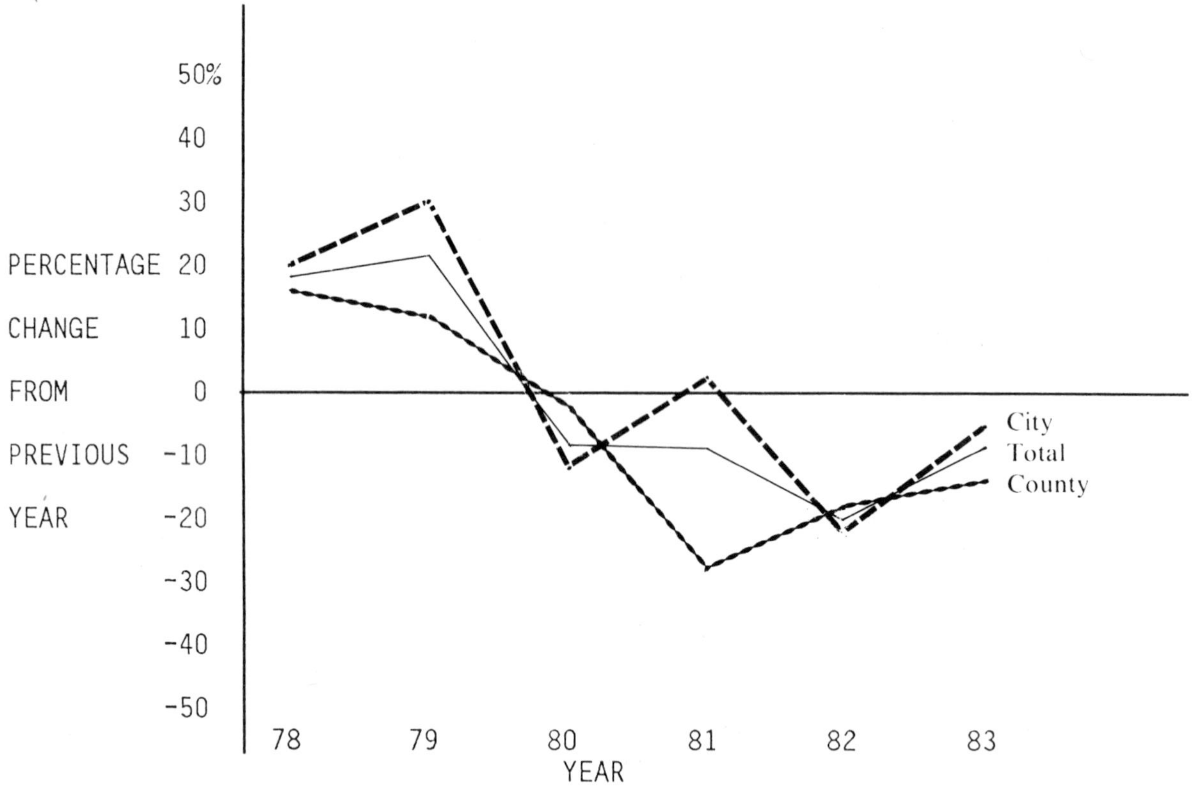

Source: State of Texas, Comptroller, 1983 Report.

Table 3.4

GRANTS TO SELECTED CITIES IN TEXAS, 1980-83

City	1980-83 Average Expenditure	Expenditure per Capita	Rank of Expenditure per Capita
Amarillo	990,924	6.64	5
Austin	2,627,593	7.60	3
Beaumont	583,990	4.94	10
Belton	36,149	3.39	15
Bryan	127,205	2.87	16
College Station	236,621	6.35	6
Corpus Christi	1,789,903	7.72	2
Crowley	7,127	1.22	24
Edinburg	54,525	2.26	20
El Paso	1,986,315	4.67	11
Elsa	12,032	2.38	19
Ft. Worth	2,991,362	7.77	1
Galveston	391,937	5.17	9
Houston	9,217,057	5.78	7
Irving	187,581	1.71	21
Kermit	936	0.12	25
Longview	174,936	2.79	17
McAllen	356,103	5.31	8
Mexia	11,063	1.56	22
Pampa	52,253	2.44	18
San Angelo	276,161	3.77	13
San Antonio	2,769,750	3.53	14
Sherman	47,239	1.55	23
Texarkana	219,629	7.02	4
Waco	398,527	3.94	12

Source: Special data compilation for the years 1980-83 by State of Texas, Comptroller of Public Accounts, in January 1984 (Austin, Tex.).

C. Comparison to Other States

In a comparison with nine other states, Texas had the lowest level of intergovernmental aid to municipalities (see Table 3.5). Intergovernmental expenditure in this comparison was defined as (1) amounts paid to other governments as fiscal aid in the form of shared revenues and grants-in-aid, (2) reimbursements for performance of general government activities, and (3) payment for specific services for the paying government in lieu of taxes. New York had the highest per capita expenditure with $320.05, and Texas had the lowest with $4.00 per capita.

Table 3.5

INTERGOVERNMENTAL EXPENDITURES TO MUNICIPALITIES BY STATE, 1979

State	Intergovernmental Expenditure	Population	Personal Income	Expenditure per Capita
Michigan	549,574,000	9,262,000	9,950	59.34
Wisconsin	633,090,000	4,706,000	9,348	134.53
Missouri	75,849,000	4,917,000	8,982	15.43
New York	5,619,399,000	17,558,000	10,260	320.05
Pennsylvania	262,903,000	11,864,000	9,434	22.16
Minnesota	402,771,000	4,076,000	9,724	98.82
Arizona	219,460,000	2,718,000	8,791	80.74
North Carolina	189,964,000	5,882,000	7,819	32.30
California	1,090,379,000	23,668,000	10,938	46.07
Texas	56,960,000	14,229,000	9,545	4.00

Source: Facts and Figures on Government Finance, 21st biennial ed. (New York: Tax Foundation Inc., 1981), p. 170.

Providing grants to localities is a mechanism that a state can use to finance development in an equitable yet discretionary manner. It appears Texas could use this mechanism more without changing its rank among the states.

III. STATE ACTIVITIES DIRECTLY RELATED TO ECONOMIC DEVELOPMENT

Over the past decade competition between regions, states, and cities for a share of the country's economic pie has increased. At stake are jobs, tax revenues, and general economic well-being. Sunbelt areas emphasize the advantages of a warmer climate, cleaner air, and low levels of unionization. Frostbelt cities cite their industrial experience and social culture. The competition is keen and becoming more acute, especially when reinvestment in industry means expanding or relocating in cities perceived as having greater potential for economic growth. Localities are taking actions to ensure that they will be successful in the competition. More and more, states are becoming officially involved in helping cities lure industry, and the State of Texas is no exception. This section of the report will discuss state programs in local jurisdictions, including programs operated by the Texas Department of Community Affairs, the Texas Economic Development Commission, the Governor's Office, the Purchasing and General Services Commission, the Tourist Development Agency, and the Parks and Wildlife Department.

A. Texas Community Development Program

One of the major federal programs providing infrastructure assistance is the Community Development Block Grant (CDBG). The State of Texas became more involved in this program in 1983 when it assumed the nonentitlement component of the program.

1. Community Development Block Grants. The CDBG program was enacted into law under the Housing and Community Development Act of 1974.(9) The primary objective of the CDBG is to develop viable urban communities by providing decent housing and a suitable living environment, and by expanding economic opportunities, principally for persons of low- and moderate-income. One restriction on the use of CDBG funds is that they must give maximum feasible priority to activities which benefit low- and moderate-income persons or aid in the prevention or elimination of slums or blight.(10)

CDBGs are the primary source of ongoing federal assistance for local community development. For the first few years of this program, emphasis was on improvement of housing and community services, primarily for low- and moderate-income persons. Legislation passed in 1977 broadened the objectives of CDBG to include economic development activities which create jobs and expand the tax base.(11) CDBGs provide cities and counties with a mechanism for financing basic infrastructure programs such as water and sewer systems and other major capital expenditure items.

There are two components to the Community Development Block Grant program: an entitlement component, which distributes funds by formula among urban jurisdictions, and a nonentitlement component, which distributes funds (also by formula) among states for competitive allocation among small cities and counties.(12) Beginning in FY 1982, states were given the opportunity to assume total administrative and program responsibility for the nonentitlement program. Texas assumed this responsibility.(13) To participate in the nonentitlement program, the State certified to HUD that it would assist small cities in planning for community development activities, provide necessary technical assistance, and obligate from the state's resources an amount equal to 10 percent of the state's federal allocation for community development activities.(14)

Thirty percent of HUD's total CDBG appropriation amount must be set aside for the nonentitlement program.(15) Local jurisdictions eligible for the nonentitlement program include general purpose units of local government (cities and counties) which are not participating or designated as eligible to participate in the entitlement portion of the federal CDBG program. Cities with a population of less than fifty thousand are eligible, unless they are participating in the entitlement program. All counties in Texas except Harris and Tarrant are eligible for funding through the nonentitlement program.(16) The nonentitlement portion of the CDBG program has been administered at the state level by the Texas Department of Community Affairs (TDCA) through its Texas Community Development Program (TCDP) since FY 1983.(17)

TDCA presently maintains community profile data for thirteen hundred eligible counties and local jurisdictions in Texas and uses these data for generating scores on selection criteria related to community distress.(18) TCDP, using the State's allocation of CDBG monies, funds eligible projects through four separate funds:(19)

- Community Development Project Fund;
- Economic Development Project Fund;
- Community Development Planning/Capacity Building Fund; and
- Emergency/Discretionary Fund.

The first three are discussed below.

The Community Development Project Fund covers housing, public facilities, and public service projects. It represents the major portion of the Texas Community Development Program. This fund is allocated among the twenty-four state planning regions by a formula designed by TDCA. The formula is based upon the number and percentage of persons living in poverty, the total population, and the number and percentage of unemployed persons.

Activities eligible for funding under the Community Development Project Fund which are likely to have impact upon economic development include acquisition of property necessary to install or improve public facilities, water and sewer facilities, street improvements, and solid waste facilities.(20)

The Community Development Project Fund grants are selected by Regional Review Committees (RRCs) and TDCA. Each of the twenty-four planning regions has an RRC consisting of twelve local elected officials who are appointed to the RRC by the Governor.(21) Grants under the Community Development Project Fund are awarded on the basis of selection criteria including measurements of community distress, benefit to low/moderate income persons, minority hiring/contracting, local tax effort, and program design.(22)

The second fund administered by TDCA through the Community Development Program, the Economic Development Project Fund, is for projects which will result in either an increase in new permanent employment within a community, retention of existing permanent employment, or an increase in the local tax base resulting in an increase in local revenues. Such projects include acquisition and preparation of property for new use through demolition, clearance and infrastructure improvement, rehabilitation of commercial areas, and technical assistance to small businesses.(23) The selection criteria for the Economic Development Project Fund include community distress, benefit to low/moderate income persons, and project design.(24)

The Community Development Planning/Capacity Building Fund is intended to provide local governments an opportunity to prepare comprehensive community plans, develop strategies, assess needs, and build or improve local capacity to undertake future community development projects. Selection of projects is on a competitive basis, with a grant maximum set at $25 thousand.(25) A number of funded planning projects in FY 1983 involved completion of Economic Development Plans; water, wastewater, and drainage studies; and data acquisition for future development activities.

2. **Analysis**. Comparisons between the HUD-administered nonentitlement program and the Texas Community Development Program revealed a greater emphasis on economic development activities in the state program. Economic development projects competed against all other eligible activities in the HUD program, and during the last two years of HUD administration, only one specific economic development project was funded in the State of Texas. By contrast, in the Texas Community Development Program, projects focusing on economic development competed within a separate funding category, to which a specific amount of funds had been earmarked. In the initial year of the TDCA-administered program, between twenty and twenty-five economic development grants were awarded.(26)

Between 1977 and 1981, HUD awarded an average of 109 grants per year with an average grant size of $365,000.(27) In the first year of state administration, TCDP awarded approximately 200 grants with an average grant size of $270,000. The TCDP award pattern was designed to give more communities an opportunity to participate in community and economic development activities.(28)

A number of interesting statistics characterized the first year of state administration.(29) Cities with a population of 1,000 to 4,999 persons received 45 percent of the TCDP grants, cities of 5,000 to 9,999 received 23 percent of the grants, and only 13 percent of the grants went to cities and counties with a population over 15,000. The average per capita income of the grantee cities and counties was approximately $5,560, ranging from a high of $8,250 in Hansford County to a low of $2,200 in Starr County. The average per capita income for the state in 1982 was $11,352.(30) The average unemployment rate of all grantees was 10.1 percent, with Bexar County the lowest at 3 percent and Starr County having the highest rate at 50.5 percent, while the state unemployment rate was at 7.4 percent.(31) The region receiving the largest number of grants was the Lower Rio Grande Region, which had an unemployment rate of 18.5 percent and a per capita income of $4,200.

A number of revisions in the Community Development Program were proposed for FY 1984 including several in the Economic Development Project Fund.(32) When ranking and selecting projects for awards, the number of new jobs created will be given more weight than the number of jobs retained, thus reflecting an emphasis on growth and development. Also, those retained jobs leveraged by private investment are to be weighted more heavily than retained jobs without that leverage. A second revision redefines permanent employment as nonpublic employment that is not dependent on TCDP funds for continuation. In order for jobs created by a project to be considered permanent, persons must remain employed in those jobs after the completion of the funded project.

3. **Economic Impact**. The Texas Community Development Program affects the economic development of small cities in three principal ways. First, through the Community Development Project Fund, TCDP finances infrastructure improvements and construction and thus makes it possible for

these local governments to use their monetary resources for other economic development activities. Expenditures for infrastructure constitute a large proportion of a municipality's budget. Federal and state aid relieves that burden and allows local governments more flexibility for planning and capacity building.(33)

Second, funds from the Community Development Program can be and often are used to leverage other sources of public and private investment. In other words, granted funds can be used as an incentive to attract private investment by local development corporations, banks and investment firms, and others with an interest in economic development. In FY 1983, 100 percent of the Economic Development Project Fund awards were used to leverage other investment.(34)

Finally, economic and community development activities are costly, particularly for small cities with a limited tax base. Without state and federal financial and technical assistance, most development activities would be beyond the financial capabilities of local communities. The Texas Community Development Program allows a greater number of cities and counties to plan for economic development, and provides those financial and technical resources necessary for an effective economic development strategy.

In light of the Reagan Administration's attitude toward domestic spending and the New Federalism approach, slow increases, if not actual reductions, in federal aid including the CDBG program are likely to place more pressure on the state and local governments as well as the private sector to assume greater responsibility for community and economic development.

B. Texas Economic Development Commission

Existing firms can contribute significantly to a state's economic stability and provide a large measure of its economic growth. It would be unwise to design policy only for attracting new firms if the existing ones are faltering. Texas, like other states, is involved in retaining industry already located within its borders.

In an effort to attract new business and industry to Texas and provide assistance to already established firms, the Texas Economic Development Commission (TEDC), formerly known as the Texas Industrial Commission, was formed. The major categories of commission activity are industrial development, business development, international development, research and data services, and financial assistance.

1. Industrial Development and Services Department. This Department coordinates three major functions for industrial development. First is attracting new business and industry to Texas, thereby creating new jobs and bringing new capital investment into the state. Tools used to promote the advantages of a Texas location include a national advertising campaign, direct mail, and telephone marketing. An industrial prospect which contacts TEDC is provided information on various cities throughout the state to aid its site location decision.(35) These activities have resulted in 335 new plant locations or expansions and the creation of 131,474 jobs from fiscal year 1979 through fiscal year 1982.(36)

Second, the department staff works directly with community leaders to prepare them for working with industrial prospects. Their programs include economic development "clinics," industrial planning seminars, and sales team training.(37)

The final step in the industrial development process is to ensure that a highly trained and motivated core labor force is available on the day that a new industry begins its operation. The Department works closely with both the Texas Education Agency and the Texas Employment Commission to meet this manpower need through a state industrial start-up training program. The program consists of (1) analysis and identification of the firm's labor force requirements, (2) design of training programs and designation of the training institution, (3) initial recruiting and screening of a work force, (4) implementation of the training program, and (5) program monitoring. These programs are jointly financed by the three agencies and the incoming industry. There have been 142 start-up training programs involving a total of 16,681 trainees during FY 1979 through FY 1982.(38)

2. The Business Development Department. This Department has the primary responsibility of working with small and minority businesses within the state. The Department must inform these businesses of opportunities for obtaining state purchasing contracts, encourage state agencies to use small and minority business in their purchasing, and maintain records on the businesses.(39) The agency also ran entrepreneurship training programs at the community college level with 4,630 participants between FY 1980 and FY 1982, but the program was discontinued.(40)

3. The Research and Data Services Department. This Department compiles and publishes social and economic information of interest to the business community, and also provides computerized information on Texas communities and industry. It is designed to serve as a support unit to the other departments.

4. The Rural Industrial Development Program. This program was created by the Rural Industrial Development Act, passed by the Sixty-second Texas Legislature in 1971. It is a loan program to encourage and facilitate industrial development, primarily manufacturing in rural areas. The program, administered by the Texas Economic Development Commission, approves and finances loans to qualified businesses at an interest rate determined by the Commission.(41)

The loans are made from a specially designated fund established by appropriations from the Texas Legislature. In 1973, $600,000 was appropriated to the fund; a grant of $300,000 from the Greater South Texas Cultural Basin Commission was added in 1978, and $1 million was appropriated in 1981 for a total of $1.9 million.(42)

Applications for loans are made by industrial development agencies. Upon approval of the application, the Commission lends the industrial development agency an amount not to exceed 40 percent of the project cost. The industrial development agency must pledge at least 10 percent of the cost of the project in funds or property and obtain financing for the remaining costs from another source.(43)

The loans are made from a revolving fund, and the Legislature may appropriate additional funds. As of October 31, 1983, the balance in the fund was $382,842.81, and the outstanding balance of the loans due to the Commission amounted to $2,027,099.99 as of August 31, 1983.(44)

The Commission made the first rural industrial loan in March 1974. From that date until August 31, 1983, thirteen cities have received a total of sixteen loans ranging in size from $25,000 to $395,000. In all cases but one, loans were made to industrial foundations in small cities, ranging in size from Trenton (1983 population of 6,911) to Corsicana (1983 population of 21,712). The one exception was a loan to the McAllen Industrial Foundation in the city of McAllen, which has a population of 66,281 (1983).(45)

Through this period the State's share in the program totaled 2.1 million dollars, which represents approximately 30 percent of the total project costs. These loans have resulted in the creation of 1,116 jobs for an average of $1,823 state investment per job. These jobs, in turn, generated an estimated $313,860 in annual state taxes.(46)

This program of assistance demonstrates one mechanism the State may utilize in its efforts to promote economic development. It also represents a form of targeting assistance, in this case to small cities.

Assessing the effectiveness of TEDC's industrial and business development programs in relation to programs in other states would prove to be unreliable primarily because of the demographic and economic resource differences that exist. However, an internal examination reveals that the old Texas Industrial Commission had realized a somewhat steady decline in most of its performance indicators during the last four years of operation. Under TEDC, almost yearly decreases have occurred in the number of new jobs created, the number of trainees in prospect simulations, and the number of start-up training programs and trainees. Some of these declines may be attributed to a slowdown in the economy and/or to the fact that many cities have developed their own programs for attracting industry. Business development programs have been hampered by the Commission's lack of enforcement authority and low budgets. Increased authority and funding, and the changes suggested by its new name (TEDC), are essential if the Commission is to have a greater role in Texas economic development. An improved status will encourage cities and entrepreneurs to seek the Commission's help more often.(47)

C. Export Promotion and TEDC

1. The International Development Division. This Division of TEDC was created in recognition of the importance of international exporting and plays an important role in promoting exports.

In 1980, U.S. exports of goods and services accounted for 12.2 percent of the gross national product, compared to 6.4 percent a decade earlier. This remarkable expansion in export activity has been traced to the growing interdependence of global economies, augmented in the early seventies by the OPEC oil embargo, dollar devaluations, and record trade deficits.(48) As a result, states have expanded their efforts in export promotion to introduce new firms to the export market and to expand the overseas sales of companies already exporting. Possible benefits from export expansion include:

1. a dynamic base for expansion of production and employment within a state;

2. a benefit from multiplier effects in producing jobs in transportation, finance, and insurance sectors, as well as increased state tax revenues;

3. a countercyclical effect that an export market can have in providing a stabilizing "cushion" when demand from abroad exceeds declining U.S. sales; and

4. an expansion and diversification of a state's economic base.(49)

For nonagricultural export promotion, the International Development Division of the Commission provides information services and assistance to small businesses new to the export market. The TEDC has cosponsored with the U.S. Department of Commerce annual trade fairs in Australia, Mexico, and Venezuela since 1977. Between 1972 and 1979, trade missions were arranged by the TEDC to South America, Africa, the Middle East, Eastern Europe, Mexico, and the People's Republic of China. In addition, the TEDC provides counseling and technical assistance to potential Texas exporters.(50) Combined trade show and mission activity in 1981 resulted in forty-nine Texas companies entering the export market and $130 million of orders written by companies.(51)

Another component of export promotion by TEDC is a branch office in Mexico City. Only two other state governments have been allowed to establish similar offices in the country (Pennsylvania and Kentucky). The main focus of the office is exporting Texas agricultural products to Mexico. In 1982, $17 million of agricultural business was processed through the office.(52) While records maintained by the TEDC staff in Mexico have indicated that a large number of business contacts are made (950 in 1979), there is still concern that Texas is not using its resources to full advantage in developing trade ties with Mexico.(53) For example, in a recent trade show in Mexico City promoting computer hardware and software, only one Texas firm attended.(54) Petroleum industry shows tend to attract more Texas participants, but a long-term export development program will need to encourage a greater diversification in products.

In Texas, a predominantly healthy economy has provided a favorable environment for exports, perhaps creating less pressure to develop specific export policies.(55) However, as regional competition for export markets continue and the likelihood of leaner state coffers persists, circumstances may motivate a more directed export promotion strategy.

In turn, a growing economy in Texas may account for the relatively small budget afforded the International Development Division of the Texas Economic Development Commission compared to other states. In 1981 the TEDC received approximately $170,000 for its export promotion activities, considerably less than Michigan ($700,000), Indiana ($600,000), or California ($300,000).(56) The FY 1984 budget for export promotion in Texas is currently set at $334,050.00. The efforts of the International Development Division of the TEDC tend to be passive or reactive in nature, functioning as a "middleman" between sellers and buyers. This may be caused in part by the antagonistic relationship that exists between private sector developers, chambers of commerce, and local governments when pursuing export markets.(57) Each of these groups wants the TEDC to meet its particular needs, creating complex and conflicting environments for the agency. Firms with export prospects want the TEDC to function as a clearinghouse, capable of making initial client assessment and eliminating unlikely prospects. Chambers of commerce, on the other hand, have traditionally viewed their economic development programs as self-sufficient and regard the TEDC as an obstacle. Local governments turn to the TEDC for protection from the overriding power of chambers of commerce and private developers and for assistance in competing on par with these other interests.

The nature of the International Development Division efforts may also be attributed to the audience which their programs attract. Export activities are usually a natural outcome of a growing, well-established firm. Most small firms view exporting as too risky given their limited resources, while most large firms maintain their own in-house export management divisions. Thus, the remaining groups include small firms on the brink of rapid growth or medium-sized firms eager to expand profits. These characteristics of firms seeking assistance may have had a role in shaping export programs. In this role, the TEDC appears to function as a "way station" for firms on their way to substantial export activities, but which need initial assistance and exposure.(58)

The most direct evidence of the impact of export activities on the state's economy appears in export-related employment figures. Growth in Texas exports of manufactured products exceeded 116 percent from 1977 to 1980. By 1983, this sector provided jobs for an estimated 285,000 Texans. (59) Analysis of export-related employment, in 1981, by major industry groups reveals that chemicals and allied products accounted for 22.5 percent of the total. Other major export sectors included nonelectrical machinery, with 21.8 percent of export-related jobs, and electronic equipment, with 19 percent of the export workforce.(60)

As discussed in Chapter 1, basic, export-related employment can be expected to generate additional supporting or nonbasic employment, due to the multiplier effect of export-related jobs in either an industrial sector or region. In 1980 supporting employment provided 80 percent as many jobs as direct export employment in one sector, for example.(61) Thus, local economies are affected more by support industries which follow major exporting sectors than by the exporters themselves.

From a state viewpoint, Texas's historical strong business climate may have reduced the need for governmental attention that should be given to export promotion. State exporting strength, as a result, is not necessarily proportional to a state's commitment to export promotion programs. The relatively positive performance of Texas as an exporter can be traced to the elements which have traditionally determined its business climate, rather than to any specific export promotion efforts carried out by the State.

C. Governor's Office

In most states, the primary responsibility for economic development rests with a cabinet-level agency or an autonomous board or commission, such as the Texas Economic Development Commission. In a recent expenditure and salary survey conducted by the National Association of State Development Agencies, only nine of the forty responding states indicated that the governor's office was the primary agency responsible.(62) The governor, nevertheless, can perform very important functions with regard to economic development, such as creating an image of a probusiness state government. Particularly in this period of the "New Federalism," with its emphasis on state initiatives, the governor must take the lead to promote cooperation between business and government.

In Texas, Governor Mark White assumed such a role in the nationwide competition for the site selection of the newly formed Microelectronics and Computer Technology Corporation (MCC). A statewide task force of prominent leaders, headed by Governor White, invested unprecedented amounts of time, energy, and resources to bring MCC to Austin, Texas. As reported in the August 1983 issue of Austin, these leaders "see their efforts as a high-risk, long-term investment in the economic and political future of Austin and the state."(63)

Another example of Governor White's initiative in attracting industry to Texas involves the 3M Company's decision to locate close to Lake Travis near Austin. The company plans to employ 1,500 or more workers by 1990. According to newspaper reports, "White's office was heavily involved in recruiting the company, which has been in contact with the state for about a year." Lewis Lehr, 3M Chairman, "had a private dinner with White last October and discussed state support for the business community."(64)

Until recently, however, explicit economic development policy, as distinct from a probusiness attitude, has not been given a high priority by Texas governors. While Governor William Clements encouraged long-range planning through the Texas 2000 Commission, his otherwise apparent lack of interest reflected a general complacency about the Texas economy, which was perceived as strong and healthy by previous governors, the comptroller, and the legislature; there appeared to be no need to concentrate on policy or programs for economic development.(65)

Several occurrences have contributed to the recent emphasis upon economic development, but the primary stimulus has been the weakening of world oil prices, with its subsequent effect on oil exploration and production in Texas. Another major event contributing to the economic crisis in Texas was the repeated devaluation of the Mexican peso in 1982, causing collapse of trade along the Texas-Mexico border. To add to the state's financial woes, in 1983 the worst drought in a century hit West Texas and an early freeze wiped out citrus crops in the Rio Grande Valley.

Realizing that gas and oil resources would eventually be depleted, the two most recent governors, former Governor William P. Clements and present Governor Mark White, have stressed diversification in the state economy to reduce dependency on oil and gas. Clements and White both made efforts to examine current economic development issues through long-range planning and task force studies, as described in the following paragraphs.

1. The Texas 2000 Commission. This Commission was created by Governor Clements in April 1981 in an effort to emphasize economic development through long-range planning. This Commission predicted that 3.2 million people would enter the Texas labor force during the 1980s and 1990s, thus creating the need for 164,000 new jobs per year. In its final report, the Commission noted the need for diversification of the state's economy, especially into high technology and information systems.(66)

The final report also contained forty-two recommendations relating to the following seven areas of concern: water, energy, agriculture, transportation, research and development, government finance, and relations with Mexico.(67) According to the final report, how Texas deals with, or fails to deal with, these critical issues will determine the future of the Texas economy and quality of life in Texas. The Commission also encouraged the State to continue long-range planning and to adjust state actions and policies as circumstances change and knowledge increases.(68)

2. Task Force on Small Business. Governor Clements also established a Task Force on Small Business in October 1981 for the purpose of designing a coordinated state strategy to encourage and promote the growth of small businesses. One of the subcommittees created within the task force examined financing alternatives open to the State for promoting small businesses. It proposed an innovative franchise tax credit program, but the tax was not well received because of a number of apparent weaknesses in the program.(69)

3. Task Force on Emergency Jobs and the Unemployment Trust Fund. In January 1983, Governor Mark White created the Task Force on Emergency Jobs and the Unemployment Trust Fund, whose charge was to make recommendations regarding the lagging economy and the solvency of the Unemployment Compensation Trust Fund. The Job Training and Educational Committee of the task force investigated mechanisms to create "high-tech" jobs in Texas, such as (1) supporting the establishment of new-technology firms and targeting existing firms for development; (2) exploring the use of state and local retirement funds as possible sources of capital; and (3) encouraging banks to develop capitalization programs for emerging technologies.(70)

4. Governor's Office of Economic Development. In addition to task forces, Governor White also established an Office of Economic Development in September 1983. With an initial budget of approximately $700,000 and a staff of eight professionals, this office works with the Texas Economic Development Commission to enhance economic development in the state. The office has primarily a coordinating function, attempting to link educational institutions, job training programs, labor leaders, private employers, state agencies, and cities and counties with financial and marketing institutions in order to create a working partnership. Staff assignments are divided by economic development issues, including science and technology development, industrial development, trade expansion, tourism enhancement, and finance strategies.(71)

Of the many projects coordinated or monitored by the Governor's Office of Economic Development, the following four represent major programs which offer significant potential for job expansion:

1. Small Business Revitalization Program. The Governor's Office of Economic Development markets this federal program to bankers, mayors, chambers of commerce, and other promoters of business. The program began in February 1984, and it is expected to generate $200 to $300 million in capital investment and create twenty to thirty thousand jobs over the next four years.(72)

2. Small Business Innovative Research Program (SBIR). This program was created in the late 1970s through the U.S. Department of Defense, but was expanded in early 1982 to provide federal dollars to small businesses engaging in innovative research in fields other than defense as well. The Governor's Office markets the program to prospective businesses.(73)

3. Science and Technology Council. This Council will be established to advise the Governor on major science policy issues.(74)

4. Interagency Council on Economic Development. Governor White created this Council on January 24, 1984, to formulate policies for coordinating economic development programs administered by Texas state agencies.(75)

5. Export Promotion Activities. Strong leadership is important for effective state export promotion strategies. The current administration has been active in supporting and participating in trade missions. In addition, the Governor's Office of Economic Development has announced a new program entitled Texas Trade Expansion Strategy, emphasizing development of new-to-market, new-to-export business. However, the need for coordination of information between localities, TEDC, and the U.S. Department of Commerce district offices has not been addressed and will likely remain one of the most needed changes of policymaking structures.(76)

Recently, Governor White has proposed two economic development programs which include export promotion tools. These include:

- Advantage Texas Corporation, which provides technical assistance and information by computer network links between regional councils of government and the TEDC office.

- Future Texas Corporation (FTC), which brings "movers and shakers" together and charges them with being ambassadors for foreign trade promotion. Established by an executive order, FTC will not face constitutional or legislative financial restrictions because it will not utilize public funds for its projects.(77)

Despite the lack of a comprehensive and concentrated attempt by state government to develop an export policy, Texas is currently ranked as second among the states in value of exports, only topped by California.(78)

6. Film Productions. The Texas Film Commission (TFC), created in 1971 as a division of the Governor's Office, is responsible for attracting film and television production to Texas and building a climate in Texas in which the industry can thrive. The Commission develops programs to familiarize those outside the industry with its financial potential and to encourage local talent.(79) They produce a source book for the industry, "The Texas Production Manual," and the newsletter "Film Services." The sources of capital to finance movie production, encourage new film talent, and distribute films, however, exist largely outside Texas.(80)

TFC Assistant Director Dana Shelton describes the state agency's role as a preproduction service. They "deal specifically in script breakdowns, location needs, liaison, and all the initial contacts necessary to establish a production."(81) However, with its small staff of six and budget of $265 thousand, the agency must limit its services to the productions that need the most attention.(82)

From 1980 to 1983, the Film Commission worked with production companies filming eighty-three major projects in Texas, as well as hundreds of TV commercials, documentaries, educational films, and corporate communications features. The industry has spent $500 million in Texas from 1980 to 1983.(83) Thirty major film and television shows were produced in Texas (in part or in entirety) in 1983.

Texas provides several ways for producers to lower their budgets, including relatively lower costs of living and of labor as compared to California and New York. The State of Texas also does not require producers to obtain a permit or to pay a location fee in order to shoot in Texas, and film casts and crews are not subject to the hotel/motel occupancy tax if they become "permanent residents" by occupying a hotel room for at least thirty consecutive days.(84) However, the primary reason that producers come to Texas, according to TFC Director Joel Smith, is the "great availability of crew people who can do quality work." The full range of support services available enables producers to shoot on location without having to bring the necessities of modern filmmaking across the country.(85)

When production companies film on location, they spend an estimated 25 to 50 percent of their budget in the location community.(86) The Texas Film Commission has estimated that 40 to 45 percent of a film's budget would be spent in Texas.(87) When budgets range from one to million dollars, the state and the community will receive a significant economic boost. It is also estimated that for every dollar spent directly by the production company, another four or five dollars more is spent by the cast and crew.(88) Estimates on long-term multipliers for the film industry range from 3.0 to 6.9.(89)

From the above discussion, it is clear that film and television production has a significant economic impact on the state of Texas. The state's natural and professional resources, as well as the TFC's promotion and technical assistance, attract substantial dollars from other states.

With the demand for film/tape productions increasing, it appears that this industry will continue to show growth in Texas.

D. State Purchasing and General Services Commission

The state procurement dollar is a significant force in the Texas economy and an important source of revenue for many businesses throughout the state. In fiscal year 1982-83, procurement expenditures on behalf of state agencies amounted to $662 million, and the agencies themselves spent an additional $1.5 billion. It is estimated that almost one-third of these state agency dollars went to Texas small and minority businesses.(90)

In the broadest sense, the term "procurement" describes the whole process whereby classes of resources (supplies, materials, services, equipment) required by the State of Texas are obtained. Some of the control and coordination of this activity is handled by the Central Purchasing Division of the State Purchasing and General Services Commission (SPGSC).(91) State statute authorizes three types of purchases for the Commission to use. Invitations for bid are issued with all three types:

1. Open-Market Purchases. This type of purchase is initiated by submission of an individual requisition to the Commission from a state agency. Based upon this requisition, the Commission issues an invitation for bid, soliciting firm prices on fixed quantities for a specified delivery. The Commission issues the successful bidder an open-market purchase order.

2. Term Contract Purchases. This type of purchase is initiated by the Commission through the issuance of invitations for bid for common-use supply items based upon estimated quantities, for a fixed price, for a specified term. The successful bidder is awarded a contract against which individual agencies may issue contract orders through the Commission for specified quantities.

3. Multiple-Award Contract Purchases. This type of purchase is employed by the Commission as a variation of term contract purchases where there is a demonstrated need for multiple levels of performance capabilities and/or quality in a particular commodity used by state agencies. In such instances, which are relatively rare, competitive bids will be solicited and a single award made for each level so identified.

There are 180 classes of commodities from which purchases are made by state agencies or by the Commission. In addition, contractual awards for engineering, construction, consulting, and various other services are integral parts of state procurement. Fifty-two percent of all state purchasing for FY 83 was for construction contracts, and the individual agencies have virtually complete autonomy over this process.

In 1975 the Sixty-fourth Legislature passed the Small Business Assistance Act (SBAA), which stresses the importance of small businesses to the American economy and identifies the types of assistance to be given to small business, primarily in the form of procurement and technical assistance. Under this Act the State Purchasing and General Services Commission and each state agency are encouraged to establish annually small business procurement and assistance goals, including the goal of awarding 10 percent of all purchases to small businesses.(92) Agencies are urged to inform small businesses of state procurement opportunities, include small businesses on master bid lists, inform entrepreneurs of the rules and procedures relating to bidding on and procuring contracts, waive bond requirements where feasible, and monitor the effectiveness of the Act itself.

The SBAA does not restrict its mandate to the promotion of Texas small businesses. However, the State Purchasing and General Services Act, which establishes the State's purchasing system, requires that purchase preference be given to Texas products.(93) It reads: "The commission and all state agencies making purchases of supplies, materials, or equipment shall give preference to those produced in Texas or offered by Texas citizens, the cost to the state and quality being substantially equal." Records maintained by the Commission on its purchases indicate that Texas small businesses have received, in recent years, an average of 20 percent of procurement dollars spent. During FY 1983, state agencies contributed a total of about 39 percent of their purchasing funds to the coffers of Texas small businesses.

By action of a rider in a 1983 appropriations bill, minority businesses in Texas are also designated to receive encouragement and assistance in bidding for state procurement contracts.(94) The State Purchasing and General Services Commission is required to maintain records concerning (1) the number and identification of all minority-owned firms doing business with the State through the Commission and (2) the number and dollar volume of purchases from those businesses; all other state agencies are required to maintain similar records for delegated purchases. This information is to be made available in an annual report to the Legislative Budget Board and the Governor's Office of Management and Budget.

Minority businesses received 1.58 percent of the Commission dollar volume during FY 1983, and SPGSC files show that most of those dollars were received by minority businesses located in Texas. Until 1983, the various state agencies were not required to maintain records of their business dealings with minority businesses. The data made available for FY 1983 show that 2.12 percent of their expenditures went to minority business.

Advancing the cause of economic development for Texas businesses through state procurement policies is being approached from several fronts: the Governor's Office, the state legislature, and two agencies, the State Purchasing and the Economic Development Commissions. The emphasis is on small and minority businesses. Texas businesses that do not fall within the small or minority definitions can only rely on the preferential treatment mandate for Texas products provided in the State Purchasing and General Services Act and, of course, on their presumed ability to compete more effectively for state contracts.

Other legislative mandates have given some boost to the less resourceful small and minority businesses, although the laws only speak in terms of suggested and self-imposed goals. The purchasing and economic development agencies, lacking regulatory authority, are powerless to ensure that goals are being set and met. These agencies are relegated to the tasks of encouraging adherence, providing information, and compiling statistics.

Recent action by Governor Mark White, however, may provide a significant impetus for encouraging individual state agencies to justify their actions or inactions. By executive order on May 19, 1983, the Governor directed each state agency engaged in procurement of goods and services to "annually establish small and minority participation goals of ten (10%) percent, thirty (30%) percent thereof representing purchase and service contracts solely for minority business enterprise." By examining state agencies as a group, it is evident that the goal for small business is being fulfilled, but the goal for minority business has not yet been realized. The next step is to institute a means for addressing noncompliance.

If the perennial goal of the State is to guarantee that Texas businesses receive a minimum number or dollar amount of state purchasing contracts, thereby promoting their continued economic viability and development, then the most reliable means is through explicit legislation and enforcement. Change in current legislation will depend on how well voluntary compliance works and the degree to which legislators feel that state government should become involved in this strategy.

E. Tourism and Travel

Tourism, the so-called industry without a smokestack, is very important to the Texas economy. In 1982, 35.4 million people traveled to Texas and spent $13.7 billion. As a result Texas ranked third nationally in tourism, behind California and Florida. Three Texas counties (Harris, Dallas, and Tarrant) experienced visitor expenditures of over $1 billion each, and seventeen more counties realized over $100 million.(95)

While tourists spend money for pleasure, their dollars purchase goods and services and generate employment. In 1983, the travel industry generated 283,917 jobs, equivalent to a payroll of $2.9 billion. In addition, state and local governments received $317 and $162 million, respectively, in taxes from travelers.(96)

Tourism is clearly a major industry, and although the reasons for travel are many, state and local governments can and do affect this industry. Two state agencies were specifically created to promote travel. These agencies are the Texas Tourist Development Agency and the Travel and Information Division of the State Department of Highways and Public Transportation.

Created in 1963 by the state legislature to stimulate travel to and within the state, the Texas Tourist Development Agency (TTDA) had a budget of $1.7 million and a staff of twelve in 1983. During the year, 70 percent of the budget ($1.2 million) was invested in national and international print media advertising, including magazine advertisements, newspaper advertisements, and direct mail promotions.(97)

TTDA recognizes the importance of local organizations' publicity efforts and offers organizations such as local chambers of commerce, local development agencies, and municipalities technical assistance and advisory services. Services include "selling" the community on the positive effects of tourism, evaluating the best way to capitalize on natural advantages, and aiding in the preparation of promotional literature. (98) TTDA also promotes travel by providing various services to travel agents and travel writers, and by promoting the state at trade shows.(99)

The other major state agency involved with tourism and travel is the Travel and Information Division of the State Department of Highways and Public Transportation (SDHPT). With a budget of approximately $2.5 million and a staff of seventy-six, this agency provides general tourist-related information services. About one-half of its budget ($1.3 million) is used to operate the twelve travel centers located around the state. Ten centers are located on interstate and other major highways on the state's borders; the other two centers are the Judge Roy Bean Visitor Center in Langtry, Texas, and the tourist information center located in the state capitol.(100) The travel centers distribute state maps and twenty-one different pieces of Texas travel literature; the cost of printing the promotional literature accounts for the other half of this agency's budget.

The Travel and Information Division also publishes a monthly magazine, Texas Highways, which is a travel stimulant. The various travel opportunities, calendar of events, and vacation spots in Texas described in the magazine encourage its 320 thousand subscribers to stay in Texas to vacation--or, in the case of out-of-state subscribers, to travel to Texas. The State does not expend any tax revenues on the publication of this magazine, because its $3.2 million subscription income supports the magazine.(101)

Between the budgets of both of these agencies, the State spends about $4.3 million on direct promotion of travel and tourism. This represents a small investment, considering the millions collected from tourists through state and local taxes, including hotel/motel occupancy taxes.

In a survey conducted by the National Association of State Development Agencies in 1982, state development agencies were asked to provide budget information on activities conducted by the agency, including state tourism expenditures. Thirty-one states reported tourism budgets ranging from $11,254,100 in Alaska to $181,000 in Nevada; the average budget expenditure was $ 2,100,422. On a per capita basis, the range was extremely broad, with Alaska spending $28.00 per capita and California spending $0.02 per capita; average expenditure was $0.43 per capita. The Texas tourism budget was reported as $1,719,700, which included only the Texas Tourist Development Agency. Texas apparently did not report the budget of the Texas Travel and Information Division. Using the TTDA budget figure, however, Texas ranked twelfth in total budget dollars and twenty-ninth on a per capita basis (with $0.12), among the thirty-one states. Only New York and California spend less per capita on tourism than Texas.(102)

One of the major reasons that tourism ranks as a major industry in Texas is the number of conventions held in Texas cities. More conventions are held in Texas than in any other state except California. Leading the state is Dallas, which is ranked third in the nation in the total number of meetings and total attendance. Its 1,808 meetings in 1983 generated $536 million.(103)

The state legislature also assisted tourism and travel by passing a "liquor by the drink" law and a hotel/motel occupancy tax law in 1971. Not only were more hotels and motels built as a result of the laws, but TTDA and SDHPT receive 3 percent of the room tax for travel promotion. A recent amendment to the law allows cities to raise their portion of the tax from 4 percent to 7 percent and spend it on new convention centers, historic preservation, and enhancing arts, which in turn will draw more visitors.(104) See Chapter 4 for more discussion on the local governments' share of the room tax.

1. Other Tourist-Related Activities. In order to encourage visitors to stay longer, cities have to offer a variety of entertainment alternatives. For example, John Mosty, San Antonio's Convention Bureau Chief, indicated that "the leisure tourist is more interested in the city's overall attractions like the climate, general beauty, the zoo and the historic things that set us apart." This concept is echoed by Fort Worth Convention Bureau Executive Director Jeff Russell: "The more things we have to offer, the longer visitors will stay. The key is to sell everything we have--our art museums, the new Omni Theater, the zoo, the Japanese Gardens and parks."(105) Texas is helping to bolster the arts and historical resources through the Texas Commission on the Arts and the Texas Historical Commission.

The Texas Commission on the Arts, created in 1965, provides state support for the development of the arts. For FY 83, the agency was appropriated approximately $2 million ($1.5 million in state funds and $0.5 million in federal funds) and funded approximately three hundred arts organizations.(106)

The Texas Historical Commission was created in 1953 to provide leadership and coordination in the field of historic preservation and to protect the historical and archeological resources of the state. The Commission identifies and marks sites and structures of historical interest to the state, reviews and recommends properties eligible for the National Register of Historic Places, and provides consultative services to individuals, groups, or museums engaged in historical preservation in the state. The state legislature appropriated $1.1 million to the Commission in FY 1982, while the federal government granted it $517 thousand.(107)

In addition, the Historical Commission, through its Main Street Program, provides consultative services to small cities of Texas in the revitalization and economic development of the downtown business districts, including preservation of architecturally important buildings. In 1981, the Main Street Program received a total of $98,256: 49 percent ($48,566) in state appropriations, 39 percent ($38,000) in federal grants, and 12 percent ($11,690) from corporate and foundation funds. As a result of this activity, $2,884,276 was invested in building purchases and rehabilitation of historic buildings in the five participating cities. In 1982, the program was funded by a grant from the Governor's Office in the amount of $154,000.(108)

2. Texas Parks and Wildlife Department. Tourism is also promoted and enhanced by the Texas Parks and Wildlife Department, which provides parks, recreation areas, historical parks, natural areas, and fishing piers.(109) Between 1958 and 1983, the number of Texas parks doubled from 58 to 116, and now occupy nearly 200 thousand acres. This expansion was justified by the needs of the increasing state population and the demands of increased park visitation. From 1973 to 1983, park visitation increased from 13 to 18 million people, an increase of 30.2 percent.(110)

Although it is difficult to quantify the total dollar amounts spent on outdoor recreation in Texas, the following 1981 statistics are representative indicators:

- According to the TTDA, an estimated $7.3 billion dollars were spent on recreational travel in Texas.

- An estimated $1.1 billion in gross retail sales of recreation equipment were reported to the Comptroller of Public Accounts, excluding sales of sporting goods sold in department stores and sales of recreational vehicles.

- According to the Texas Employment Commission, there are fifty-four thousand people employed full-time in manufacturing, selling, and serving recreation consumers.(111)

In addition to these indicators, Texas has approximately 4 million anglers and 1.5 million hunters, according to the 1980 National Survey of Fishing, Hunting, and Wildlife Associated Recreation. These individuals are spending $2.5 billion annually, primarily on equipment, supplies, and travel. The survey also estimates that Texas has approximately 8.5 million users of outdoor resources, including boaters, campers, and swimmers.(112)

From 1972 to 1983, expenditures by the State for park development and major repair projects totaled almost $100 million.(113) The Department's FY 84 budget allocates approximately $22.2 million for acquistion, development, and repair of state parks. These expenditures are listed by region in Table 3.6.

Responsibility for allocating these funds rests with the Comprehensive Planning Branch of the Texas Parks and Wildlife Department. Although the state planners are guided by the Texas Outdoor Recreation Plan (TORP), the above data indicate that these funds are distributed on an uneven per capita basis among park regions, which is not surprising given that parks and natural resources are also unevenly distributed across the state.

An uneven per capita distribution of state funds also exists in the Texas Local Parks, Recreation and Open Space Funds (see Table 3.7). In this program, the State awards grant money to eligible political entities, such as city parks departments, to fund acquisition or development of a park or recreational area. The local government must be willing and able to provide 50 percent of the cost of the project, either in cash or in kind (e.g., volunteer workers that are willing to donate time and/or labor), which may account for some of the disparity in distribution patterns.

Table 3.6

SELECTED PARK EXPENDITURES PER CAPITA, FY 84

Region	Expenditure(a)	# Counties	Population(b)	$ per Capita
1	$ 925,139.76	73	1,285,021	$ 0.72
2	7,692,200.50	29	1,232,191	6.24
3	5,065,737.40 (c)	30	929,279	5.45
4	865,940.49	22	3,030,800	.29
5	1,337,536.97	20	483,804	2.77
6	2,054,463.11	17	1,194,375	1.72
7	1,255,983.75	17	1,047,604	1.20
8	2,564,133.56	21	3,783,236	.68
9	485,524.79	26	1,223,463	.40
Totals	$22,246,660.33	255	14,209,773	AVG. $ 2.16

Sources:
a. Expenditures were derived from unpublished computer printouts of FY 84 Budget Reports, Parks and Wildlife Department of Texas; figures include only state funds budgeted for acquisition, development, and repair of state parks.

b. Population figures are based on 1980 federal census data, as reported in the 1984-85 Texas Almanac, ed. Michael T. Kingston (Dallas, Tex.: A. H. Belo Corp., 1983), pp. 353-66.

c. Expenditure includes $4,106,309.23 for acquisition of Franklin Mountains State Park.

From the beginning of the program in late 1979 until October 31, 1983, approximately $21.3 million of state funds have been committed to local units of government for development of ninety-eight park projects. While initially only urban areas (Standard Metropolitan Statistical Areas as determined by the last federal census) were eligible for these funds, in 1983 rural park projects also became eligible.(114)

Although the State's activities are supplemented to a large degree by local chambers of commerce, convention bureaus, and city officials, the State is clearly involved in promoting and developing tourism in the state. These activities are accomplished through direct advertising; promotion of legislation for the motel/hotel occupancy tax; assistance and consultative services to local governments/organizations; developing, promoting, and protecting recreational and historical resources; and direct grants to local entities for parks and the arts.

F. State Facility Location

Table 3.7

TEXAS LOCAL PARKS, RECREATION AND OPEN SPACE FUNDS EXPENDITURES, 1979-83

County(a)	Expenditures(b)	Population(c)	$ per Capita
Harris	$ 6,785.686	2,409,547	$2.82
Tarrant	2,352,318	860,880	2.73
Dallas	2,022,738	1,556,390	1.30
Travis	1,986,552	419,573	4.73
Nueces	1,774,339	268,215	6.62
Collin	1,685,142	144,576	11.65
Brazos	699,593	93,588	7.47
Brazoria	604,346	169,587	3.56
Galveston	423,602	195,940	2.16
Lubbock	393,584	211,651	1.86
Cameron	382,535	209,727	1.82
Hidalgo	359,000	283,323	1.27
Williamson	218,793	76,507	2.86
Bexar	213,756	988,798	.22
Kaufman	206,615	39,029	5.29
Jefferson	150,000	250,938	.60
Denton	141,875	143,126	.99
El Paso	125,993	479,899	.26
Comal	120,000	36,446	3.29
Montgomery	90,875	128,487	.71
Gregg	87,972	99,495	.88
Bowie	80,842	75,301	1.07
Potter	59,274	98,637	.60
Grayson	42,264	89,796	.47
Tom Green	29,000	84,784	.34
Totals	$21,036,694	9,414,240	AVG. $2.62

Sources:

a. Counties are ranked by total state expenditures received from the inception of the program in 1979 through October 31, 1983. Note: Until August 31, 1983, only Standard Statistical Metropolitan Areas were eligible to receive state funds under this program.

b. Figures are truncated to nearest dollar; amounts derived from data provided by the Texas Parks and Wildlife Department, Grants-in-Aid Branch.

c. Population figures are based on 1980 federal census data, as reported in the 1984-85 Texas Almanac, ed. Michael T. Kingston (Dallas, Tex.: A. H. Belco Corp., 1983), pp. 353-66.

The creation of permanent, well-paying jobs is vital to the maintenance and development of the economic base of a city. When a new business or industry locates in an area, the benefits accrue to many parts of the community. Wages for the new workers, more tax revenues for the city, and a decreased burden on social services are some of the results. A similar boost occurs in a local economy when a major state facility locates in the area, even though the locality is deprived of revenue due to tax exemption of state property.

Under authority of the State Purchasing and General Services Act, the site selection process for most of the smaller state agencies is handled by the Facilities Planning Department of the State Purchasing and General Services Commission.(115) Their planning is generally for small administrative offices, which create very few new jobs where they locate. Examples are the Department of Public Safety, the Department of Human Resources, and the Texas Department of Health Administration.

The largest state agencies, which build the largest facilities and provide the greatest number of new jobs, are likely to have their own real estate and facilities planning divisions and thus make their own site selection decisions. These agencies include the Parks and Wildlife Department, the Texas Department of Mental Health and Mental Retardation, the State Department of Highways and Public Transportation, and the various state colleges and universities.

There is no indication that the siting of state facilities is being used as an economic development tool. Although it cannot be denied that legislators may pursue certain state facilities for their districts knowing that some economic benefits will be realized, the fact is that the primary criteria for locating a facility are the service population and service needs, the distance between similar facilities, and community receptiveness. Siting of facilities will, consequently, probably not become an important component of the State's economic development strategy.

IV. INFRASTRUCTURE

A. Water Resources Development

Water has always been and will continue to be a most precious natural resource for urban as well as rural areas of the state of Texas. Because of the state's vast size, variety of climates, and topographical and geographical characteristics, water needs vary substantially around the state. For example, at any one given time in the state, a local district in East Texas may be battered from a recent hurricane while an area in West Texas is suffering from a severe drought. A district in West Texas may not have the amount of water necessary to run a petrochemical plant but may have enough water available to run a food-processing plant. As a result, water resources of the state cannot be evaluated through statewide aggregates--that is, it would be misleading to analyze the average acre/feet of water in the state and then label it as a water-rich or water-poor state.

This section of the report begins with a discussion of the effect of water resource development on economic development. This is followed by an analysis of the direct state action through the Texas Department of Water Resources (TDWR). Finally, recommendations on actions that should be taken by the State that would affect water resource development in the state are presented.

For purposes of this section of the report, direct state action is defined as the role TDWR plays in using the information it generates (water availability studies, projected water demands, etc.) in water resources planning and the financial resources it administers for specific water resource development.

1. Water Resources and Economic Development. Water resource development is important to economic development. The traditional market failure perspective of analyzing water resources states that externalities (that is, effects on third parties) dominate water resource allocation, thereby necessitating legal restrictions on water transfers.(116) Resource economics, a relatively new school of thought, approaches water resources through a market perspective which maintains that water crises can be solved through market solutions. The literature on this issue is very new.(117)

In both perspectives, there are three major costs: the cost of defining and enforcing property rights, the cost of defining the water needs of different regions, and the cost resulting from the possible contamination of available drinking water supplies.(118) These three costs are all a function of the quantity of water necessary for the level of economic activity found in an area.

In the opinion of some, government intervention is necessary for water resource allocation. Government intervention can control third-party effects of water resource allocation and monopolistic characteristics of some water resource providers. Proponents of this intervention also believe that it would promote conservation and scientific management of water resources.(119)

2. Water Usage and the Texas Department of Water Resources. In Texas, five industrial groups account for more than 90 percent of the state's water usage. The industries are petrochemical production and refining, which use water for cooling purposes; paper production, using water as input for pulp; primary metals, using water for reaction and cooling; food processing, using water as input of the product; and agriculture, using water for irrigation.(120) The first three industries are concentrated in the eastern area of the state while the last two are scattered around the state.

TDWR establishes the principles by which water resource development in the state will take place. TDWR projects state population, water availability, water usage, and needed future capital investment in its planning division, which uses computer and advanced analytical techniques. Local governments and private interests use this information to solve their respective water resource problems.

In Texas, surface water, of which river basins are the largest components, is owned by the State and managed by TDWR. Texas has fifteen major river basins and eight coastal basins. These basins have approximately 3,700 designated streams and tributaries, and more than 80,000 miles of streambed. TDWR has established water quality standards for 16,000 miles of these streambeds.(121) There are 179 major reservoirs (27 federal and 152 nonfederal) with 5,000 acre/feet or greater total capacity in Texas.(122) In addition, there are ten reservoirs presently under construction (seven federal and three nonfederal).(123)

The aquifers in the state are the major components of its ground water. More than 50 percent of Texas is underlaid by seven major aquifers and sixteen minor aquifers.(124) These aquifers receive annual recharge of about 5.3 million acre/feet and contain about 431 million acre/feet of water in storage that is recoverable using conventional technology.(125) The State does not control the ground water nor its usage, but does work to prevent pollution or waste in ground water supplies. Texas follows the "English" or "common-law" rule that a landowner has an absolute right to take for sale or use all ground water which he/she can produce from his/her land.(126)

The Texas Water Development Board administers the Water Development Fund, which is a loan program for water resource development in the state.(127) This Fund is relatively small in that only 4.46 percent of all expenditures (local, state, and federal) on water resource development in the state originated in this Fund in 1983 and was only 3.43 percent in 1982 (see Table 3.8). The Fund provides capital to small municipalities with low bond ratings or poor tax bases that cannot secure funding from other sources. Loans are often made to municipalities with out-of-date sewage systems in order to install new systems of a size adequate only to accommodate present needs and not future growth. For these reasons, it can be concluded that the program essentially promotes economic stabilization, but does not promote economic development.

In 1982 almost 75 percent of all water resource development was financed through the sale of tax-exempt bonds including general obligation bonds, revenue bonds, and water district bonds. Revenue bond financing accounted for over 50 percent of the public market financing. Federal funds from the Environmental Protection Agency (EPA) and the Corps of Engineers accounted for 22 percent of development financing in 1982. These federal funds are channeled through the Water Quality Grants Division of TDWR.

Several other agencies also affect water resource development in the state. The Texas Department of Health administers legislation that regulates the disposal of municipal and mixed municipal-industrial wastes. It also establishes drinking water standards for public water supplies, reviews the plans for construction of drinking water projects and sewer projects, administers the provisions of the federal Safe Drinking Water Act, and maintains surveillance of all drinking water supplies. The Railroad Commission of Texas regulates water pollution resulting from the exploration, development, and production of petroleum, natural gas, surface mining, and geothermal resources. It also has responsibility for and jurisdiction over transportation enterprises operating within Texas. Other state agencies that affect water resource development in some capacity are the General Land Office, the Parks and Wildlife Department, the Texas Department of Agriculture, and the State Soil and Water Conservation Board.

Table 3.8

SOURCES AND METHODS OF FUNDING FOR WATERWORKS AND SEWER
FACILITIES IN TEXAS, 1981-82
(thousands of dollars)

	1981 Dollars	1981 Percent	1982 Dollars	1982 Percent
Federal Funds	181,912	30.74	187,615	21.98
Public Market Financing	383,436	64.80	636,750	74.59
Texas Water Development Board	26,412	4.46	29,290	3.43

Source: Interoffice Memo, November 10, 1983, Texas Department of Water Resources, Planning Division, Austin, Tex.

TDWR generates a great deal of information for its permit process, various review activities, and for water resource planning in the state. The ability to actually influence development, however, is limited by its budget allocation, and local governments carry the principal responsibility for financing and constructing water resource development.

3. Recommendations. The issue of water resource development by the State of Texas is very complex because of the vast size of the state, differences between surface water ownership and ground water ownership, and the different types of economic development activity taking place throughout the state. After some basic analysis, however, some recommendations can be made.

- A comprehensive study is needed on the effect of water resource development on economic development. TDWR has the expertise and technology available to produce such a study.

- A second study is urgently needed on financing methods for future water resource development. Population growth coupled with federal legislation will require Texans to improve sewage treatment plants at a cost of more than three billion dollars by the year 2000.(128) The capability of some municipalities to continue debt financing for water systems is questionable.

- The State should increase financial resources allocated to water resource development. Determination of the type of water resource development needed in an area should continue to be handled by the local political subdivisions. Increased resources are crucial in light of recent trends in the decline of federal funds.(129)

B. Transportation

1. The Role of Transportation in Regional Economic Development. The development of any region is partially dependent upon access to resources and to outside markets, or more generally to its physical position relative to other regions. Transportation systems are designed to overcome the "frictions" (distances, natural obstacles, etc.) imposed by geography. As such, transportation systems shape the distribution of activities and influence the share each region contributes to the national product.(130)

By linking consumption and production centers within and outside a region, transportation facilities play a distinct role in conditioning the pattern of growth. Good interregional connections facilitate the movement of factors of production to centers of production.(131) Transportation linkages, in essence, serve to integrate the economy of an area with the larger economy to which it belongs. Transportation systems may also perpetuate growth shifts, encouraging growth to "spill over" from developing areas to underdeveloped areas.

This section will focus primarily on the impact of highway systems, which are a major responsibility of state government. Highways can and do play a positive role in regional economic development. Curtis Harris points out in his study on the economic effects of highway systems that a major system may affect an area's economy in three ways:

- If construction expenditures are large and they are spent in the region, they will generate employment and income in other sectors of the economy with through multiplier effects.

- New or improved highways reduce the interregional transportation costs and thus have an effect on the location of industries.

- New highway systems reduce the amount of traffic congestion within a region, making it more attractive as a location for industry and people.(132)

The absence of an adequate transportation system, on the other hand, may adversely affect the development of a region. Growing regions with limited transportation infrastructure will almost certainly require additional facilities to support further growth. Failure to provide additional facilities will create bottlenecks in movements of goods and may also cause traffic congestion in the area, which may in turn force industry to locate in less congested areas. In addition, bottlenecks and congestion will slow the movement of goods, thereby causing transportation costs to rise.

2. The Role of the State Department of Highways and Public Transportation. The highway system in Texas is especially important because of the vast geographic size of the state. As of 1984, Texas had 71,103 state highway miles. Since nearly 43 percent of all Texas towns rely soley upon trucks for freight service and all agricultural produce, livestock, and dairy products, the highway system is particularly important to the livelihood of all Texans.(133) In addition, the number of registered vehicles has been growing at a rapid rate (see Table 3.9).

Table 3.9

ANNUAL PERCENTAGE CHANGE IN REGISTERED VEHICLES,
1972-82

Year	Registered Vehicles	Annual % Change
1972	8,512,782	
1973	9,026,670	.06
1974	9,549,670	.05
1975	9,714,831	.02
1976	10,169,920	.04
1977	11,152,302	.09
1978	11,297,938	.01
1979	10,085,254	-.01
1980	11,989,419	.16
1981	12,418,020	.03
1982	12,722,555	.02
Total	116,641,121	

Source: State Department of Highways and Public Transportation, Biennial Report, 1983 (Austin, Tex., 1983).

The agency responsible for transportation and related activities in Texas is the State Department of Highways and Public Transportation (SDHPT). The primary responsibilities of the Department are to provide and maintain a comprehensive system of highways and to assist in the development of public transportation. Other secondary responsibilities will not be considered here.

Implementing highway programs is the delegated responsibility of the twenty-four districts which cover the entire state. Districts are responsible for the design, location, construction, beautification, and maintenance of highways within their domain. They are also responsible for multimodal public transportation planning and the administration of public transportation programs in conjunction with the various headquarter divisions in Austin. Each district is composed of several counties, except the Houston Urban Project Office, which is primarily responsible for creating a system of expressways within the central areas of Houston.

Most Texas highways have been designed to last twenty years, and many existing miles of highways have exceeded this "design life." A recent

Table 3.10

TOTAL HIGHWAY EXPENDITURES IN NOMINAL AND REAL TERMS, 1972-82

	Nominal	Real (1972 dollars)	% of Total
Maintenance	$2,024,734,928	$1,271,194,732	20
Construction	7,860,071,295	4,948,500,111	80
Total	$9,884,806,223	$6,219,694,843	100

Source: State Department of Highways and Public Transportation, *Annual Financial Reports, 1972-82* (Austin, Tex.).

nance expenditures, the top districts were the rural, sparsely populated ones, with the more heavily populated districts spending much less. The difference in maintenance expenditures per capita between the top district and bottom district amounted to $376 per person (see Table 3.12).

Construction expenditures per capita portray a slightly different story. Once again the small rural districts spent the highest amount per person on construction projects with the exception of District 21 (Pharr headquarter). At the lower end were the Pharr, El Paso, and Austin districts. The Houston, Dallas, San Antonio, and Fort Worth districts all ranked higher than in maintenance expenditures, but still were in the bottom half (see Table 3.13).

Rankings of total expenditures per capita reveal no new patterns. Small rural districts again spent the most total dollars per capita. With the exception of the Pharr district, the districts that spent the least per capita were those that are heavily populated, incorporating major metropolitan areas (see Table 3.14).

Rankings by expenditures indicate that the smaller, rural districts were the most successful in obtaining funding for highway projects. Heavily populated districts have, on the other hand, done less well, at least on a per capita basis. This study, however, has not attempted to do any needs assessment, and therefore a strong conclusion on the relative success of districts cannot be made. It does seem, however, that maintenance requirements would be greater in districts with more heavily traveled roadways. Yet heavily populated districts were at the bottom of the rankings in maintenance expenditures per capita.

One possible explanation of these findings may be that a large, heavily populated area achieves economies of scale in its transportation networks, and therefore requires less funding to construct and maintain roads. A second possible explanation is that the highways in the heavily

Table 3.11

AGGREGATE EXPENDITURES BY HIGHWAY DISTRICT, 1972-82
IN 1972 DOLLARS

Rank	District	Headquarter	Amount Spent
1	12	Houston	$964,331,982
2	18	Dallas	654,694,949
3	15	San Antonio	527,331,486
4	2	Fort Worth	462,139,634
5	5	Lubbock	245,735,722
6	13	Yoakum	243,595,966
7	20	Beaumont	236,067,629
8	14	Austin	227,162,783
9	4	Amarillo	219,705,826
10	21	Pharr	210,322,078
11	6	Odessa	210,076,039
12	16	Corpus Christi	209,653,316
13	9	Waco	205,943,190
14	7	San Angelo	186,834,966
15	19	Atlanta	175,534,992
16	10	Tyler	173,907,630
17	1	Paris	161,166,327
18	24	El Paso	161,057,240
19	17	Bryan	155,909,387
20	8	Abilene	149,669,111
21	3	Wichita Falls	134,359,107
22	11	Lufkin	133,868,017
23	25	Childress	87,188,744
24	23	Brownwood	83,438,724

Source: State Department of Highways and Public
Transportation, Annual Financial Reports, 1972-1982
(Austin, Tex.).

populated areas were built more recently than those in rural areas, therefore requiring less work and upkeep. This may explain the difference in maintenance expenditures, but still does not account for the gap between construction expenditures per capita. A final explanation for the expenditures gap may be that the rural highway district engineers have applied more political power when lobbying the Highway Commission for construction and maintenance funds. Further study is needed to determine which of these or some other plausible explanation accounts for the urban-rural expenditure gap.

Correlation analysis was used to investigate the relation between per capita expenditures and changes in population and employment for the twenty-four districts. It was found that per capita expenditures were negatively correlated with the rate of urban population growth and em-

Table 3.12

PER CAPITA MAINTENANCE EXPENDITURES BY HIGHWAY DISTRICT, 1972-82 IN 1972 DOLLARS

Rank	District	Headquarter	Amount Spent
1	25	Childress	$ 415
2	7	San Angelo	251
3	23	Brownwood	242
4	13	Yoakum	225
5	8	Abilene	203
6	1	Paris	200
7	17	Bryan	194
8	11	Lufkin	181
9	3	Wichita Falls	168
10	4	Amarillo	167
11	19	Atlanta	163
12	5	Lubbock	141
13	6	Odessa	118
14	10	Tyler	111
15	9	Waco	105
16	20	Beaumont	99
17	16	Corpus Christi	94
18	14	Austin	79
19	15	San Antonio	73
20	21	Pharr	70
21	2	Fort Worth	64
22	24	El Paso	49
23	18	Dallas	46
24	12	Houston	39

Source: State Department of Highways and Public Transportation, <u>Annual Financial Reports, 1972-1982</u> (Austin, Tex.).

ployment growth (Pearsons correlation coefficients of -.46 and -.60, and Spearman rank correlation coefficients of -.51 and -.65 respectively), indicating that districts with relatively high rates of growth in population and employment had relatively low per capita expenditures for highways. While the available data do not provide the basis for determining why this relationship exists, two plausible hypothesis can be advanced.

One explanation of negative correlations between rates of employment and population growth and expenditures per capita during the observation period is that while expenditures, for the most part, grew during the observation period, they may not have kept pace with the rapid growth in population and employment in many Texas areas. This argument seems rea-

Table 3.13

PER CAPITA CONSTRUCTION EXPENDITURES PER HIGHWAY DISTRICT, 1972-82 IN 1972 DOLLARS

Rank	District	Headquarter	Amount Spent
1	25	Childress	$1208
2	7	San Angelo	831
3	6	Odessa	628
4	13	Yoakum	615
5	4	Amarillo	529
6	19	Atlanta	506
7	23	Brownwood	471
8	5	Lubbock	442
9	11	Lufkin	429
10	3	Wichita Falls	428
11	8	Abilene	422
12	17	Bryan	415
13	1	Paris	397
14	20	Beaumont	371
15	2	Fort Worth	365
16	16	Corpus Christi	347
17	15	San Antonio	338
18	9	Waco	332
19	18	Dallas	281
20	10	Tyler	280
21	12	Houston	276
22	14	Austin	272
23	24	El Paso	272
24	21	Pharr	243

Source: State Department of Highways and Public Transportation, *Annual Financial Reports, 1972-1982* (Austin, Tex.).

sonable given Texas's growth rates during the 1970s and 1980s. Census figures show that since the mid-1970s Texas has been one of the fastest growing states in the nation.(141) Thus, a valid argument can be made that employment and population outgrew highway expenditures in many districts, thereby causing negative correlations.

Another explanation is that if areas of rapid population and employment growth were highly urbanized, the low level of expenditures might reflect economies of scale found in large cities rather than the inability to meet needs. In other words, fewer miles of highways were needed to service the growth in the economy and population of a large city. To test this explanation we used regression analysis to analyze the relationship between growth rates and per capita expenditures, holding constant the effect of the size of the urban population in the highway district. This analysis confirmed that even when urban population size is taken into

Table 3.14

TOTAL PER CAPITA EXPENDITURES BY HIGHWAY DISTRICT, 1972-82
IN 1972 DOLLARS

Rank	District	Headquarter	Amount Spent
1	25	Childress	$1623
2	7	San Angelo	1083
3	13	Yoakum	840
4	6	Odessa	746
5	23	Brownwood	713
6	4	Amarillo	697
7	19	Atlanta	669
8	8	Abilene	626
9	11	Lufkin	610
10	17	Bryan	609
11	1	Paris	598
12	3	Wichita Falls	597
13	5	Lubbock	584
14	20	Beaumont	470
15	16	Corpus Christi	442
16	9	Waco	437
17	2	Fort Worth	429
18	15	San Antonio	411
19	10	Tyler	391
20	14	Austin	351
21	18	Dallas	328
22	24	El Paso	321
23	12	Houston	315
24	21	Pharr	313

Source: State Department of Highways and Public Transportation, _Annual Financial Reports, 1972-1982_ (Austin, Tex.)

account, growth rates in population and employment were negatively related to per capita expenditures. While these results do not necessarily refute the economy of scale explanation, it would be prudent to expect that significant maintenance expenditures will be needed in the future for these heavily used highway networks.

4. Conclusions. Analysis of historical highway expenditure data has given insights into three areas: changes in levels of total expenditures, regions that were the major recipients, and the effect on economic growth. Three conclusions can be drawn from the study:

- a large sum of money was expended on highway projects in Texas in the 1970s and early 1980s, but relative to other state programs highway spending declined;

- on a per capita basis, small rural highway districts were the recipients of the most highway disbursements; and

- a clear relationship between highway expenditures and economic growth cannot be shown for the ten-year observation period, which may be explained by an inability to meet the needs of rapid growth or economies of scale in large cities.

V. EDUCATION AND TRAINING

The following discussion examines the role of education and training in economic development. It will outline several state-supported programs that have an effect on local economic development. The state role in the Job Training Partnership Act as well as the Foundation School Program, the junior colleges, and several vocational education programs is to provide basic skills to members of the workforce. Expenditures in Texas education and training programs will be compared with other states. This analysis will also include data on attendance, completion, the types of training being offered, and the quality of students in Texas.

A. The Job Training Partnership Act in Texas

The Job Training Partnership Act (JTPA), passed by Congress in October 1982, replaced the Comprehensive Employment and Training Act (CETA). The purpose of JTPA is to establish job training programs which will increase the productivity of the nation's workers by preparing youth and adults for entry into the labor force and by enhancing the skills of the unemployed and underemployed.(142) JTPA shifts the major responsibility for employment and training programs from the federal government to a statewide partnership composed of the governor, local elected officials, and the private sector, represented by individuals appointed to Private Industry Councils (PICs) at the state level. JTPA equalizes authority between the private and public sectors with respect to local policymaking, planning, administration, and program operation. JTPA provides states, in cooperation with the private sector, with a mechanism for designing and operating an employment and training program specifically suited to meet state and local labor market needs.

Funds through the JTPA program are allotted to the states by a formula weighting equally three factors, providing one-third on the basis of each area: substantial unemployment (areas above 6.5 percent), excess unemployment (above 4.5 percent), and the number of economically disadvantaged persons in the state.(143) Allocation of funds to the local service delivery areas within the state are made on the same basis.

The goals for implementing JTPA in Texas were developed by the Governor and the State Job Training Coordinating Council (SJTCC).(144) The three goals established for the JTPA program in Texas include: increasing the long-term employment stability of participants, improving their earned incomes, and promoting the creation of high-quality jobs in Texas through the attraction of new firms and industries.(145)

The Job Training Partnership Act has five titles, four of which are particularly important to the discussion of the Texas job training and employment program.(146) Title I covers the state and local service delivery system and administration. Title II establishes training services for disadvantaged youth and adults. Title III deals with employment and training assistance for dislocated workers, and Title V makes possible the coordination of JTPA and the United States Employment Service.

1. Title I - Service Delivery Areas and Administration. JTPA funds are allocated directly to the State of Texas, where the Governor and the administering agency, in coordination with the SJTCC and the local Private Industry Councils, direct JTPA funds to areas of greatest need.(147) JTPA gives the Governor maximum discretion in the development and targeting of programs.

The purpose of the State Job Training Coordinating Council is to provide recommendations and advice to the Governor on policies, goals, and standards for the development and implementation of effective job training and employment programs; and to plan, coordinate, and monitor the provision of those programs and services in the state(148). The Governor, aided by the SJTCC, designated thirty-four service delivery areas (SDAs) in the state. Each SDA encompasses one or more complete labor market areas within which integrated planning and delivery of services can be achieved.(149) Each SDA is controlled by a local partnership formed by a Private Industry Council and local government officials of the area.

Governor Mark White designated the Texas Department of Community Affairs (TDCA) to administer JTPA. The Employment and Training Division of TDCA provides local SDAs with technical assistance and program direction. The Job Training Partnership Act funding level for Texas for FY 1984 was $119.7 million. These funds were allocated by formula among the Title II programs and the Title III program.(150)

2. Title II - Training Services for Disadvantaged Youth and Adults. JTPA Title II is divided into two sections, A and B. The Title IIA funds are used for general employment and training services in the thirty-four SDAs, and Title IIB funds are used exclusively for the Summer Youth Employment and Training Programs.(151)

Seventy-eight percent of the funds under Title IIA are allocated to the local SDAs by the same formula used for the state allocation. At the SDA level the PIC and the local elected officials determine the specific participant and activity/service mix for the SDA.(152)

Services made available to youth and adults with Title II funds include job search assistance and counseling, remedial education and basic skills training, on-the-job training, outreach to make individuals aware of and encourage the use of employment and training services, and upgrading and retraining.(153)

Sixteen percent of the Title IIA funds are allocated for education coordination, the Older Workers Program, and state administration costs.(154) The remaining 6 percent is allocated for the Performance Incentive/Technical Assistance Fund.(155)

Title IIB provides for the Summer Youth Employment and Training Programs.(156) These programs are to be conducted during the summer months for economically disadvantaged youth. They are similar to those programs offered by SDAs to youth and adults with Title IIA funds.

The basic measure of performance for adult training programs under Title II is the increase in employment and earnings and the reduction of welfare dependency resulting from participation in the program.(157) In addition to this measure, a number of other factors are used to evaluate performance of youth programs, including the attainment of recognized employment competencies established by the PIC in each SDA; elementary, secondary, and postsecondary completion, or the equivalent; and enrollment in other training programs or apprenticeships, or enlistment in the Armed Forces.(158)

3. Title III - Worker Adjustment Program. Title III, the Worker Adustment (Dislocated Worker) Program, addresses the needs of eligible individuals who have been terminated or laid off and are unlikely to return to their previous industry or occupation; have been terminated as a result of any permanent plant or facility closure; or are long-term unemployed with limited opportunity for reemployment.(159) These needs are to be met by an appropriate mix of activities including job search assistance, training, job development, or relocation. Title III also encourages programs conducted in cooperation with employers or labor organizations that provide early intervention in the event of closures of plants or facilities.

Title III funding is available in two parts, with 75 percent allocated to the states by formula and 25 percent reserved by the U.S. Secretary of Labor for discretionary purposes. These reserves are made available to states for the purpose of providing training, retraining, placement, relocation assistance, and other aid to individuals who are affected by mass layoffs, natural disasters, and federal government actions, or who reside in areas of high unemployment.(160) Texas was allocated $5.6 million by formula for FY 1984, on a one-for-one match basis.(161)

The Worker Adjustment Program in Texas uses demonstration projects to treat a targeted problem area through retraining or relocating area workers. When a project is completed in one area, efforts are redirected to another targeted area. TDCA's Employment and Training Division has targeted three areas of high unemployment in the state for services provided through this program. These areas are Brownsville, Houston, and the Beaumont-Port Arthur area. The areas next in line for targeted demonstration projects are the Gulf Coast area around Houston, North East and East Texas, and the El Paso area. Programs are operated for two years.(162)

4. Title V - Coordination of JTPA and the Employment Service . Title V of JTPA coordinates the state Employment Service with the JTPA system. Title V amends the Wagner-Peyser Act, which established a national system of public employment offices created to provide job matching services for employers and workers. The state employment service has been administered by the Texas Employment Commission (TEC) since 1936 and is funded by a formula based on the state civilian labor force and unemployment rate.(163) TEC and TDCA/JTPA have developed a Local Employment Service Plan, which provides for a basic labor exchange service, a labor market information service, and coordination with state and SDA efforts in job training.(164)

Coordination with other state and federal economic development efforts would enhance those programs operated under JTPA. A portion of the JTPA Title IIA Performance Incentive/Technical Assistance Fund has been set aside to augment the Small Business Revitalization program initiated by the Governor's Office of Economic Development.(165) JTPA funds will be utilized in conjunction with various federal business incentives, such as urban development action grants and Small Business Administration programs, to leverage private sector investment for job creation.

The staff of TDCA expressed the need for a statewide employment development fund held in reserve by the State to be used for economic emergencies and unique economic development opportunities.(166) As required by statute, SDAs obligate their allocation of JTPA monies at the beginning of each program period for specific employment and training activities. Funds are not set aside at this level for unforeseen development opportunities. The reserve fund would be designed for those SDAs in need of supplemental funding selected on the basis of unemployment rates, existence of other resources, and local economic trends.(167)

The administrators have promoted the idea of JTPA as a resource available to all groups involved in economic development activities. Increasing the awareness of the Texas Economic Development Commission, the local chambers of commerce, and other relevant agencies and organizations has been of primary importance during the initial period of implementation.(168)

5. JTPA Role in Economic Development. State government and the private sector view JTPA as an opportunity to coordinate state employment and training efforts with labor market needs. CETA gave the private sector limited opportunities for input, and left state government with a limited role in the overall administration of the program. The vast majority of CETA funds were allocated directly to local government sponsors who had total discretion, subject to Department of Labor review, over the use of the funds. Provision was not made for coordination of job training programs with statewide employment goals. The key to JTPA's success will be the partnership between state and local government officials and private industry.(169)

JTPA's success will be measured by an increase in employment stability and earned incomes of the participants in the training and retraining programs. Effects, whether positive or negative, will be of a long-term nature, and future analysis of JTPA programs should emphasize success or failure in meeting the labor market needs of the state.

B. Education

The provision of educational and vocational training serves two purposes in economic development. Education affects the level of training in the workforce and contributes to a region's "quality of life." Many types of economic activity, and the expansion of these activities, require the availability of a well-trained and educated workforce. A state plays an essential role in the development of such a workforce by contributing funds to educational programs. The role education plays in developing a properly trained workforce is stated in a recent report studying the feasibility of a state occupational education program for Texas.

> Human capital is the bedrock of economic development and education is a vital link between the present and future economies of the state. The press for continued economic growth and development obliges public and private sectors to cooperate in developing a highly qualified workforce for the achievement of industrial productivity goals.(170)

The premise in economic development theory that a well-educated workforce is essential is evident in the state of Massachusetts. A recent article in the Dallas Morning News attributes Boston's rapid shift from "old-tech" to "new-tech" to the region's excellent public schools (and not to the universities of the area). The public schools in New England have traditionally been well supported and have produced a "workforce that is literate, trainable and retrainable".(171)

The training and development of human capital is essential to meet the needs of a diversified economy. In Texas, as there is a gradual shift from natural resource production to computer- and "high-tech"-based industry, the State will play an important role in providing training programs to develop a diversified pool of labor. Public policy toward education must recognize this need.

Education plays another role in economic development as a component in the "quality of life" in a region. This factor may not be as tangible as the development of a workforce, but it is just as important. Many types of businesses and industries place a high priority on the "quality of life" factor and will consider the quality of life in certain areas before moving their operations and employees to new regions. A well-supported, quality educational system may be an incentive in a firm's relocation decisions.

Of concern, however, is the quality of the state's technical and scientific education programs--both at the postsecondary and public school levels. Whereas Texas's economy has been traditionally linked to its natural resources--oil, gas, food, and fiber--economic prosperity in the high-tech fields, especially, will be linked to the state's human resources. Adapting to this changing economic base is at the heart of all economic development activities. Does Texas have the human resources and/or the appropriate educational system available to meet the challenge? Can Texas provide new and changing industries with a well-trained and well-educated workforce? Some evidence suggests that improvement may be necessary. Only 16 percent of the adults in Texas are college graduates, and only 61.4 percent of the adults have high school diplomas. Texas is slightly below the national average in both instances. In contrast, 73 percent of the adult population in California and Massachusetts have high school diplomas. More astounding is the fact that only 68 percent of the ninth graders in Texas complete high school--a 32 percent dropout rate. Texas ranks thirty-ninth in this category. While its spending for public education has improved, the State's per pupil expenditure is still 15 percent below the national average.(172)

Texas must have an adequately trained and technologically literate labor force to compete and grow economically. To do this, the State will likely need to increase expenditures on public schools. Several studies have shown that states with above average per pupil expenditures produce above average achievement in student test scores.(173) Educational funding can therefore be considered an investment in the future productivity of the state and its people.

1. The Foundation School Program. The establishment of Foundation Programs for elementary and secondary schools occurred throughout the nation in the early 1900s. At that time schools adopted the now common nine-month, twelve-grade schedule. States mandated certain educational objectives that were to be met by all districts. Many of the rural communities could not impose tax rates that were high enough to meet the requirements set by the states. A mechanism of state-local financing was set up whereby the state would provide a minimum level of support, that is, a foundation, for all school districts. The intent of such programs was to minimize inequalities that existed among school districts.(174)

Although this process improves equity in the funding among school districts, several potential problems do exist. The districts with a strong tax base can still levy taxes to supplement funds received through the Foundation Programs. The "rich" districts can thus afford to pay teachers higher salaries and to include expensive supplements to the curriculum. The "poor" districts are subject to the levels established by the state and can suffer hardships if prices of essential goods change after appropriations are distributed. Nevertheless, the Foundation School Programs guarantee that a minimum level of funding for educational programs is distributed throughout a state.(175)

The Foundation School Program of Texas identifies the State of Texas as being responsible for a substantial portion of the finances supporting public education. The intent of the legislature is that "each student enrolled in the public school system shall have access to programs and services that are appropriate to his or her educational needs and that are substantially equal to those available to any similar student, notwithstanding varying local economic factors."(176) Chapter sixteen of the Texas Education Code delineates the responsibility of the State and documents the formulas used to compensate school districts under the Foundation School Program.

Actual funding for the Foundation School Program is documented in Tables 3.15 and 3.16. The tables indicate the amount of Foundation funds used solely for vocational education purposes and the total funding levels appropriated by the state legislature for 1977 through 1985. Vocational education is important relative to economic development, yet only 6 percent of the total state aid to school districts is earmarked for that purpose. As economic development becomes more important in the state policy arena, it will be interesting to note if this figure increases. Table 3.16 does show that the level of vocational funding appropriations has increased by 58 percent from FY 1979 to FY 1984. This is contrasted with a 47 percent increase in the total funding provided to local school districts by the State. These figures represent a nominal increase of approximately 10 percent annually over a five-year period.

The minimum support levels provided by Foundation School Programs have been criticized in the past because many were set too low to provide services that could meet reasonable standards.(177) The Foundation School Program must be formally evaluated to ensure that it provides an adequate minimum level of funding for each school district and that is the most effective and equitable way to fund local school districts.

2. The Junior College System. The State of Texas supports 47 public community college/junior college districts, which offer more than 140 different technical and vocational programs.(178) The legislature created junior colleges to provide two-year technical programs leading to certificates or associate degrees and vocational programs designed to meet employment standards in semiskilled and skilled occupations. The educational program also includes courses in the arts and sciences designed for those students at the freshman and sophomore levels who will transfer to four-year colleges or universities. Continuing education programs for adults are also offered for "occupational or cultural upgrading".(179) The legislative design for the program includes an admissions policy that is favorable to disadvantaged students. The junior colleges have an open door admissions policy, and each junior college district is encouraged to meet the needs of the local community.(180)

The junior college districts provide more than 90 percent of the postsecondary technical and vocational training in the state.(181) The legislature appropriated $491.9 million for junior colleges during the 1980-81 biennium. In the 1982-83 biennium this was increased by over 42 percent to $700.2 million.(182) It is important to note that the appropriation for junior colleges during the 1982-83 biennium accounted for only 5.6 percent of the total state expenditures for education.

A junior college system which provides vocational training to adults can aid an economic development strategy by retraining individuals whose skills are obsolete and by improving the skills of other workers, while allowing them to maintain full-time work schedules.(183) Furthermore, businesses and companies moving into Texas cannot always be depended upon to provide training programs for their own employees. These businesses may be attracted to a state which has adequate community colleges and vocational programs. These programs must be flexible to meet the needs of new businesses coming into the state. A cooperative working relationship between Texas government, business, and industry and educational institutions to research labor and market trends should be encouraged.

3. Texas State Technical Institute. While the public community and junior college system offers both general academic programs and occupational training, one state-supported institution, the Texas State Technical Institute (TSTI), offers occupational education programs exclusively. TSTI is one of 162 institutions nationwide of this type, and the only Texas institution which provides job-ready graduates for business and industry.(184)

TSTI maintains a highly cooperative relationship with the state's businesses and industries. Through the 2,800 industrial advisory commit-

Table 3.15

FOUNDATION SCHOOL PROGRAM:
STATE AID TO INDEPENDENT SCHOOL DISTRICTS IN TEXAS,
1977-85

Year	Total Funding	Funding for Voc. Ed.(1)	Percentage of Foundation Funds for Voc. Ed.
1977-78	$1,703,209,000	NA	---
1978-79	1,724,216,000	NA	---
1979-80	2,490,942,740	$155,470,441	6.2
1980-81	2,693,173,129	171,887,800	6.4
1981-82	3,218,300,869	183,559,000	5.7
1982-83	3,493,378,950	215,785,103	6.2
1983-84	3,669,665,447	234,343,000	6.4
1984-85	3,781,277,018	246,193,000	6.5

Source: Texas Education Agency (TEA), Foundation School Program files, provided by Omar Garcia, Supervisor, Appliction Review Section, TEA Division of State Funding, Austin, Texas.

1. Vocation education costs include salaries, operating costs, transportation, and contracts. Data in this form were not available for 1977-79.

tees (representing over 1,800 businesses and industries), TSTI responds to the needs of Texas businesses for economic growth by updating its training programs and by adapting special training services for employers.(185)

TSTI's four campuses (Amarillo, Harlingen, Waco, and Sweetwater) offer over 113 training programs to over 10,000 students. Thirty-one of the programs have been identified as priority occupations in Texas in a study on vocational education in Texas conducted by the Research Triangle Institute.(186) The primary goal of TSTI is to teach necessary skills which are immediately usable in the workplace, and which may be applicable to future job restructuring as the economy changes.

Beyond program offerings, the effectiveness of TSTI can be measured in terms of student enrollment and state financial support. TSTI's projected 1984-85 student enrollment of 11,903 represents a 57 percent increase over the 1980-81 levels. Enrollment for 1986 is expected to surpass 14,000 students. Annual gains for the past ten years have averaged 9 percent, with a 21 percent increase in 1983.(187) Total state financial support for postsecondary vocational education at TSTI increased by 82 percent in the 1982-83 biennium to a total of over $90 million.(188)

4. Vocational Rehabilitation Programs. Texas's population in 1983 of approximately 15.3 million included an estimated 15 percent potentially

Table 3.16

FOUNDATION SCHOOL PROGRAM:
STATE AID TO INDEPENDENT SCHOOL DISTRICTS IN TEXAS,
PERCENTAGE CHANGE IN SIX-YEAR PERIOD (1979-80 - 1984-85)

Foundation Funds	1979-80	1984-85	Percentage Increase
Vocational Education	$ 155,470,441	$ 246,193,000	58
Total Funding	2,490,942,740	3,781,277,018	47

Source: Texas Education Agency (TEA), Foundation School Program files, provided by Omar Garcia, Supervisor, Application Review Section, TEA Division of State Funding, Austin, Texas.

classified as handicapped.(189) Of this number, 20 percent or about 300 thousand persons are eligible for some form of rehabilitation program. The Texas Rehabilitation Commission and the Texas Commission for the Blind (TCB) are the principal agencies providing training assistance to disabled persons in Texas.(190)

For FY 1982, the vocational rehabilitation program served 67,474 disabled Texans (14 percent more than the prior year). The average cost per client for a successful rehabilitation resulting in employment was $4,134 in 1982.(191)

The Commission conducted a cost-benefit study on successful completers in 1982, finding that prior to rehabilitation, 24 percent of the clients (11,415) were employed and earned a total of $1.75 million per month. Upon successful rehabilitation the employed clients earned a total of $9.6 million per month. In annual income this amounted to approximately $20.9 million before rehabilitation services and $91.1 million after rehabilitation services had been received.(192) The study also found that former clients of the agency will contribute approximately $20.4 million more in state, local, and federal taxes than if they had not received the vocational rehabilitation services--a 1000 percent return on the investment.(193)

The Texas Commission for the Blind is the other primary state agency with the mandate to provide vocational rehabilitation services. These services are provided on an individualized and contractual basis much like the Texas Rehabilitation Commission.

5. State Programs for the Economically Disadvantaged. The Texas Department of Human Resources (DHR) administers the welfare programs in Texas. Of specific interest to this report is DHR's assistance to eligible recipients through the Aid to Families with Dependent Children Program (AFDC). DHR disburses AFDC payments and coordinates with other state agencies in the provision of support and referral services for job training programs specifically for the AFDC client.

One such effort is the Work Incentive Program (WIN). WIN is a joint effort with the Department of Human Resources and the Texas Employment Commission (TEC) to assist AFDC recipients to become self-sufficient through suitable and gainful employment. The TEC provides employment services while DHR provides approved social services for the same AFDC clients so they may engage in employment, training, or other manpower programs. These services include the provision of child day care, family planning, and health-related services.

There are eleven WIN project areas in the state including the fourteen cities and thirteen counties within which over 60 percent of the AFDC population is found.(194) Funding for the WIN program is a state/federal match (10:90). For the fiscal year 1982, 17,853 recipients registered for the WIN program (up from 12,000 the previous year).(195)

Texas was the first state in the nation to create an employment program for low-income older persons with the creation of the Senior Texans Employment Program (STEP). It provides part-time jobs to approximately 1,100 low-income older persons (55 and older) in over 400 employment/training projects in 105 counties.(196) The State has appropriated approximately $1 million for each of the past two biennia. Federal funds (Title V of the Older Americans Act) have averaged about $3.8 million per year.(197)

In summary, while vocational rehabilitation services provided to Texas's eligible citizens effectively place individuals in employment and WIN provides employment services to welfare recipients, these training services are provided largely with federal funds. Texas's priority for job training efforts (and financial support) is with the public schools and postsecondary institutions. The State provides little direct financial assistance otherwise. If this trend is to continue, the State should at least provide a coordinated information and referral system to the various users.

6. Expenditure Comparisons. Education is the single largest component of state expenditures. Since 1960 state expenditures for public schools and higher education as a percentage of total state expenditures have grown from 36.07 percent to 47.51 percent in 1982.(198) The annual growth rate for educational expenditures has continually outdistanced the growth rate of total state expenditures. There are several reasons for this increase: the State has continued to assume a larger portion of public school financing, new institutions have been created, and vocational education programs have been strengthened.

In terms of 1982-83 state expenditures for public elementary and secondary education, Texas ranks second nationally with $8.3 million; California is first with $9.5 million. While the state provides one-half the cost of education, it has continued to increase its share of funding support under the Foundation School Program.(199)

Current expenditures per pupil provide a different view of state educational expenditures. In 1972, Texas spent approximately $650 per pupil, which placed the state forty-sixth among all states; and $2,012 per pupil in 1982, which placed the state thirty-eighth. The average per pupil expenditure for the country as a whole, according to the U.S. Department of Education, is $2,473.(200)

A Carnegie Foundation report states that total public elementary and secondary school expenditures as a percentage of personal income for Texas have slipped from 5.4 percent to 4.5 percent. This represents a drop in the fifty-state ranking from twenty-fifth to thiry-sixth in the last ten years.(201) In contrast, per capita income for Texans has increased 170 percent from 1970 to 1984, compared to a 141 percent increase for the United States. Texas ranks eighteenth among the fifty states with a per capita income of $11,419.(202)

Enrollments in both public and elementary and secondary schools in Texas averaged a 5.3 percent growth in the last ten years--compared to a -14.0 percent rate for the nation. When separated into elementary and secondary figures, elementary enrollments increased 23.3 percent (-11.1 percent nationwide), and secondary enrollments decreased by -16.4 percent (-17.9 percent nationwide).(203)

The ethnic distribution of the state's enrollment in public schools is an important factor. The minority enrollment of 45.9 percent in Texas is comprised of 30.4 percent Hispanic and 14.4 percent Black.(204) The large student population necessitates additional educational program costs such as bilingual instruction and programs for the limited-English-proficient students. Texas increased the State's financial support in 1982-83 for bilingual education by over 97 percent from the 1981-82 funding levels.(205)

The educational "infrastructure" of Texas and the country is important to economic development. The educational system must adequately and appropriately train Texas's citizens to meet changing economic needs. Texas's personal income per capita has increased from 90 percent of the national average in 1972 to 100.5 percent in 1982.(206) But as previously noted, Texas's national ranking for total public elementary and secondary school expenditures as a percent of personal income has declined in the last ten years. If state expenditures for public education affect the quality of education and subsequently the economic development of the state, a constant positive relationship between citizens' incomes and spending on education should be maintained.

7. The Quality of Education Programs in Texas. The greater demand being placed on the educational programs of the state will cause increased concern about the quality of instructional programs in Texas. Some measures of the quality of educational programs that begin to answer these questions are attendance rates, pupil/teacher ratios, and test scores.

The average daily attendance (ADA) in schools across the country decreased from 41.3 million to 36.9 million between 1975-76 and 1981-82.(207) This 10 percent decrease in ADA nationwide is contrasted with a 5 percent increase in ADA in Texas during the same period. The ADA in Texas increased from 2.55 million in 1975-76 to 2.69 million in 1981-82.(208)

As the state has grown, the percentage of those enrolled who are in attendance (and counted as part of the ADA) has grown. In 1974-75, 91 percent of the students enrolled were in average daily attendance in Texas public schools. This figure increased to 94 percent during the 1982-83 school year.(209) Large school systems traditionally have difficulties keeping students in class. This increase in attendance is a positive sign that educators hope will continue as programs expand. Another positive sign is the pupil/teacher ratio for the state. In 1975-76 there were 17.8 pupils per classroom teacher. This figure dropped to 16.3 pupils per teacher in the 1982-83 school year.(210)

It is an extremely difficult task to assess accurately the skills of students who utilize the educational programs of the state. If one goal of economic development is a diversified labor force equipped with skills, discipline and the ability to be trained and retrained, it is important to assess whether or not schools can train individuals in this way. Completion rates and test scores are two means, though somewhat flawed, for assessing the success of programs and schools.

The completion rate for individuals in occupational programs at the high school level during the 1980-81 school year was 53.6 percent of those who initially enrolled.(211) In contrast, the completion rate for students in occupational programs at the postsecondary level was 22.5 percent in 1980-81.(212) Since more than 90 percent of the students in postsecondary vocational programs are students in the junior colleges, one must question the effectiveness of these programs. Either the individuals are finding jobs prior to the completion of their programs or they are quitting without job placement. It is interesting to note that the highest completion rate during the 1980-81 school year at the postsecondary level was in the trade and industrial occupation programs with 30 percent of those enrolled completing their programs.(213)

Although test scores may have questionable validity because of socioeconomic or cultural biases, they do provide information on the number of high school graduates in the state who are pursuing higher education. Advocates of liberal arts training as the appropriate method to build a diversified labor pool will look to higher education as an essential part of the training process. In this light, it is important to note that 32 percent of the high school seniors in the state took the SAT in 1982.(214) This figure, which indicates the intent to enroll in a college or university, ranks twenty-second among all states and the District of Columbia.

Although test scores are subject to criticism as inaccurate tools for measurement, educators in the state should still be concerned by the recent results published by the Carnegie Foundation for the Advancement of Teaching. Even if one accepts that the scores may decrease as more people take the tests, it should still be alarming that Texas ranked forty-fourth on verbal scores and forty-sixth on the mathematical scores in 1982.(215) This represents a drop from fortieth on verbal and forty-second on mathematics in 1972.(216)

The State of Texas should be concerned about the quality of its educational programs. The students who are enrolled in the elementary and secondary programs today will make up the workforce for the state in the next twenty-five years. If the state wishes to sustain today's level of economic activity, these youngsters must be provided with equitable opportunities for quality training. A state whose per pupil expenditures rank thirty-eighth and whose test scores are as low as forty-sixth nationwide does not offer an entrepreneur an optimistic view of the future. Vocational programs with completion rates of only 22.5 percent among postsecondary students do not offer encouragement that a well-trained workforce will exist in this state. Although the University of Texas and Texas A&M University are well funded, many other educational programs in the state are in need of support. These programs will continue to face challenges as school enrollment grows. Texas's educational programs must also be able to meet the demand placed upon them by the increased economic activity in the state, which results in a dependence on the training of a qualified, capable workforce.

The State is attempting to address some of these problems. The Sixty-seventh Legislature (1981) passed several major educational reform bills which will greatly affect both the training and preparation of Texas teachers and students.

- H.B. 246, the public school curriculum reform school bill, designated twelve subject areas as the essential elements of a well-balanced curriculum. The new curriculum will be implemented by the 1985-86 school year.(217)

- High school graduation standards will be raised from the present eighteen to twenty-two credits for students in the advanced area, and twenty-one for students in the general/vocational course of study.

- Mandated competency testing for students entering a teacher education program and an exit exam as a prerequisite to teacher certification have been required beginning in 1984.(218)

Numerous national and state task forces and interim committees have been established to find ways to meet the changing demands being placed on the nation's educational systems. Texas is no different. The Sixty-eighth Legislature (1983) created the Select Committee on Public Education to study and make recommendations to improve the state's educational system.(219) Business and industry involvement with the public schools should not stop with vocational educational programs. Greater cooperation between private industry and schools--not only with financial support, but also in curriculum--is needed. One such partnership, the Adopt-a-School concept, has generated interest across the nation for the past decade. The Adopt-a-School idea encompasses several methods whereby local businesses and industry provide personnel and resources to a particular school. An example in Texas is found in the Houston Independent School District (HISD). The HISD Business/School Partnership program (involving 116 schools) uses business people extensively as tutors, teacher assistants, and special lecturers.

A central issue of concern to the Select Committee is the role of vocational education in public schools. Some reports suggest that vocational education should be eliminated since it is not an effective way to train people for the workforce. Others suggest leaving the program within the school system but outside the core curriculum requirements.(220) As already noted, Texas's State Board of Education is proposing dual graduation requirements for the general and vocational programs. There appears to be little consensus as to the proper role of the public schools with regard to vocational training. Three different types of roles have been proposed for high school vocational programs: (1) skill training, with occupation specialization; (2) career exploration and counseling guidance services, leaving specific skills training to industry or to postsecondary programs; and (3) linking vocational and academic training with on-the-job experience.

The Texas Select Committee on Public Education recommended that the emphasis on vocational education should follow the second view--career exploration. A recommendation of the Governor's Task Force on Emergency Jobs and the Unemployment Trust Fund echoes this thought with its suggestion that on-the-job training should be given a high priority as an effective educational method with an emphasis on industry-specific training.(221)

Alongside the vocational education question is the issue of increased and upgraded graduation requirements for all high school students. U.S. Department of Labor sources say that the lack of math and science skills of today's youth will severely hamper our high-tech society--particularly in the military.(222) Heavy industries are rapidly implementing technologies which will require a technically trained workforce.

With increased graduation requirements and the impetus to strengthen (toughen) existing courses comes the fear that the changes will force an increase in the already high dropout rate. Some view vocational education as the key to keeping students in school and believe that students will be benefited by merely receiving a high school diploma. The evidence supporting these claims, however, is questionable. A longitudinal study in 1980 of high school sophomores and seniors found a higher dropout rate for sophomores in vocational programs than in the general program.(223)

If it is assumed that the proper place for vocational education is outside the public schools, the State should increase its financial commitment to institutions such as the Texas State Technical Institute. TSTI has maintained a good record of employability of its students available for employment: for 1982, 70.8 percent of the students obtained employment in a field related to training, 22.7 percent of the students were employed in a field unrelated to training, and 6.5 percent were unemployed.(224)

There are other methods by which the State could encourage the effective vocational training of students. One is to encourage businesses and industry to participate in Adopt-a-School programs and create close business/school cooperatives. On-the-job-training should be given a priority emphasis as an effective educational method. The American Society for Training and Development found that employee training is the nation's largest category of job-training spending, with expenditures on the order of $20-30 billion per year. This is equal to approximately half the cost of all of higher education.(225)

Training and educational efforts of any type should be based on sound labor market information. An information system should be designed to effectively and efficiently respond to economic demands and predict required education and training programs. Such a system should provide a coordinated system for information flow both for prospective employees and employers. Texas's current lack of a coordinated effort is a serious handicap. Texas has approximately sixteen state agencies and five commissions which either have vocational education/training responsibilities or regulate them. The Research Triangle Institute report recognized this drawback and recommended a central coordinating body--the State Board of Education.

It is evident that the quality of educational offerings and their results are an essential factor in economic development. The top priority of the State should be to provide an educational program on an equitable basis to its citizens so they will be prepared to work and support its economy in the future. Businesses already moving into the state may be able to encourage this process to occur. Texas has been slowly shifting from an agrarian and natural-resource-based economy to one that is dependent on the growth of businesses within urban centers. As this has occurred, the population has moved from the agricultural communities to urban areas, as represented by the growth of Houston, Dallas, Ft. Worth, Austin, and San Antonio. The economic slowdown throughout the country has also caused a large in-migration of workers from all parts of the nation. A more urban population will demand more from the educational establishment. In turn, the services delivered will be subject to more scrutiny and criticism from the public.

The legislature must be concerned with establishing and maintaining quality programs that will aid economic development in Texas. Solutions will most likely require increased funding for educational programs. Several approaches, however, can be taken along with increasing financial support to improve educational services. First, funding mechanisms such as the Foundation School Program must be formally evaluated to ensure that they are the most equitable and efficient way to finance the schools. The quality of the educational programs should also be evaluated. Standards of accountability must be set for administrators, instructors, and students to ensure that students are receiving the best educational opportunities possible. The economic development of Texas depends on how well Texas can compete with other states and countries in attracting business. The educational programs of the state must be designed to meet the same competitive challenges which the state must face.

VI. CONCLUSION

The State of Texas promotes economic development in its cities through many state programs. By granting funds directly to cities, the State directly or indirectly encourages growth. The State also enhances development by providing education, highways and roads, water resource programs, and job training programs. These constitute a foundation upon which cities can build a solid economy capable of future growth. Through its procurement policies, the State supports many businesses, thereby creating jobs and income in numerous areas. Finally, the State increases the amount of money flowing into Texas and enlarges local economic bases by maintaining state parks, promoting Texas products, and encouraging business and industry to move to Texas.

Each of these programs affects economic development in different ways and to a varying extent. Through education and training programs, the State influences development in two ways. First, the State can maintain a workforce able to meet the future needs of business and industry by providing quality education and training programs. Second, the existence of a well-educated, well-trained, and retrainable workforce may attract new businesses to the state. Texas must maintain, if not improve, the quality of its education and training programs in the future in order to affect economic development positively.

Infrastructure also plays an important role in economic development. At present, a political consensus has yet to be reached in Texas about planning for future water needs and providing adequate sources of funding for future water projects. The State should work toward such a consensus if it wants to avoid disrupting development. While the State does invest heavily in highways and roads, which in turn has an effect on the economy of the state, the empirical analysis in this chapter could not confirm that faster-growing districts were receiving a relatively larger share of the investment. This suggests that planning efforts may need to become more sensitive to future economic growth prospects in various parts of the state. Another conclusion was that the maintenance of the existing highway system will undoubtedly become a critical issue in the near future.

Direct state expenditures on numerous other programs also influence economic development. State grants to cities for development is one such program. As indicated above, Texas is below the per capita national state average for spending of this type. One avenue of greater state support of local economic development would be through increasing the size and/or number of its grants. In addition, since procurement policies as well as expenditures on tourism and parks also support economic development, the State could use these activities in promoting economic growth.

This chapter has demonstrated that state programs affect urban economic development even though many of the programs were not designed specifically for that purpose. While a precise evaluation of each program could not be made for this report, it is clear that if the State chooses to pursue a serious policy of support for economic development, it will be necessary to coordinate these efforts, both within state government and with local governments. Local activities related to economic development are discussed in Chapter 4.

ENDNOTES

1. "Official Comprehensive Policy on Development of Urban Communities," H.R. Con. Res. 61, 62d Leg., 1971 Tex. Gen. Laws 1: 4002-4.

2. Texas Comptroller of Public Accounts, 1983 Annual Financial Report (Austin, Tex., 1983), p. 37.

3. Facts and Figures on Government Finance, 21st biennial ed. (New York: Tax Foundation Inc., 1981), p. 170.

4. Advisory Commission on Intergovernmental Relations, The States and Intergovernmental Aids, The Intergovernmental Grant System: An Assessment and Proposed Policies, vol. A-59 (Washington, D.C., February 1977).

5. Texas Comptroller, 1983 Report, pp. 48-49.

6. "State Aid to Cities and Counties" is a category in the State of Texas Comptroller of Public Accounts' Annual Financial Report under "Grants to Political Subdivisions." Aid to cities and counties includes the program categories of Public Safety/Law Enforcement, General Government, Highways/Transportation, Social Services, and Natural Resources/Environmental Protection.

7. Texas Comptroller, 1983 Report, pp. 48-49.

8. Population figures were taken from U.S. Department of Commerce, Bureau of the Census, 20th Census of the United States, 1980: Population, vol. 1, pt. 45, Texas (August 1983), pp. 8-17. Fiscal capacity was determined by a combination of average per capita income and per capita tax revenue.

9. Housing and Community Development Act, 1 U.S.C. 101, PL 93-383 (1974), 1: 713-15.

10. U.S., Executive Office of the President, Office of Management and Budget, Catalog of Federal Domestic Assistance (Washington, D.C. : GPO, 1983), p. 360 (hereafter cited as CFDA).

11. Advisory Commission on Intergovernmental Relations, Block Grants: A Comparative Analysis (Washington, D.C., October 1977), p. 6.

12. U.S. President, CFDA, p. 360. Appendix II provides a detailed discussion of the CDBG/entitlement program.

13. Texas Department of Community Affairs (TDCA), 1983 Texas Community Development Program: Applications and Procedures Manual (Austin, Tex., July 1983), p. 4 (hereafter cited as TCDP Manual).

14. National Council for Urban Economic Development, CUED's Guide to Federal Economic Development Programs (Washington, D.C., 1981), p. 70-H.

15. Ibid.

16. Texas Department of Community Affairs (TDCA), "CDBG Entitlement Counties and Participating Cities," Austin, Tex., 1983 (informational tract provided by TDCA).

17. TDCA, TCDP Manual, p. 1.

18. Ibid. The goals and objectives of TCDP are:

- To improve community facilities to meet the needs of low- and moderate-income residents;

- To improve housing conditions for persons of low and moderate income;

- To expand economic opportunities that create or retain jobs for low- and moderate-income persons; and

- To provide assistance and public facilities to eliminate conditions hazardous to the public health and of an emergency nature.

19. Ibid., p. 7.

20. Ibid., p. 8.

21. Ibid., p. 4.

22. Texas Department of Community Affairs (TDCA), "Texas Community Development Program: 1984 Proposed Procedural Changes," Austin, Tex., 1984 (informational tract provided by TDCA), pp. 4-5 (hereafter cited as "TCDP Proposed Changes").

23. Ibid., p. 2.

24. Texas Department of Community Affairs (TDCA), Community Development Program: Final Statement, as submitted to U.S. Department of Housing and Urban Development, Community Planning and Development Division (Austin, Texas, June 13, 1983), p. 11.

25. Ibid., p. 22.

26. Interview with Joseph Kayne, Director, Community Development Programs, Texas Department of Community Affairs, Austin, Texas, February 22, 1984.

27. Texas Advisory Commission on Intergovernmental Relations, Background on the HUD CDBG Non-entitlement Program (Austin, Tex., 1983).

28. Interview with Joseph Kayne, February 22, 1984.

29. All percentages based on data provided by TDCA (unpublished computer printout), Austin, Tex.

30. The Texas Almanac (Dallas, Tex.: A. H. Belo Corp., 1983), p. 405.

31. Ibid., p. 409.

32. TDCA, "TCDP Proposed Changes," p. 7.

33. U.S. Department of Housing and Urban Development (HUD), Developmental Needs of Small Cities (Washington, D.C., 1979), p. 5.

34. Interview with Joseph Kayne, February 22, 1984.

35. Plant location requirements are obtained on a report form in order to assist the firm in identifying the most suitable areas in the state. A number of criteria are listed such as site, utilities, transportation, financing, and environmental needs.

36. Texas Sunset Advisory Commission, "Final Report on Business and Professional Agencies to the Governor of Texas and Members of the Sixty-eighth Legislature" (Austin, Tex., January 1983), vol. 1, pp. 173-174.

37. Ibid., p. 180. The agency also conducts capital formation clinics to ensure that community leaders are aware of all potential sources of financing, especially for land and buildings.

38. Ibid., p. 181. The benefit of start-up training is that it provides clarification of the job requirements, the employer's expectations, and the employee's benefits.

39. Article 5186a of the Small Business Assistance Act of 1975 establishes the Small and Minority Business Enterprise Division of the Texas Industrial Commission for the purpose of carrying out these duties.

40. Texas Sunset Advisory Commission, Final Report, vol. 1 (Austin, Tex., January 1983), p. 183.

41. Susan Goodman and Vic Arnold, "The State of Small Business in Texas," Texas Business Review 37, no. 5 (September-October 1983): 204-5.

42. Texas Sunset Advisory Commission, Final Report, vol. 1, p. 188.

43. Ibid., pp. 188-9.

44. Ibid., p. 188.

45. Data furnished by Jean Talrico, Administrative Assistant, Texas Economic Development Commission, Austin, Texas, November 1983.

46. Texas Sunset Advisory Commission, Final Report, vol. 1, p. 191.

47. John M. Kline, State Government Influence in U.S. International Economic Policy (Lexington, Mass.: D. C. Heath and Co., 1983), p. 24.

48. Ibid., pp. 53-55.

49. Ibid., p. 41.

50. Lyndon B. Johnson School of Public Affairs, The Promotion of Exports from Texas, Policy Research Project Report Series no. 46 (Austin, Tex., 1981), p. 187.

51. Texas Sunset Advisory Commission, Final Report, vol. 1, pp. 174, 177.

52. "Texas Working to Boost World Trade," Port of Houston Magazine 27, no. 9 (September 1983): 36.

53. LBJ School, Promotion of Exports, p. 187.

54. Kaye Northcutt, "Texas and Mexico: Two Nations, Indivisible," Texas Business 8, no. 5 (November 1983): 32.

55. Alan R. Posner, "Export Promotion in Texas," Texas Business Review 55 (July-August 1981): 153.

56. LBJ School, Promotion of Exports, p. 183.

57. Lifson, Wilson, Ferguson, and Winick, A Study of The Texas Industrial Commission (Austin, Tex., April 1974), p. 24. This is a study done by the management consultant firm Lifson, Wilson, Ferguson, and Winick on the Texas Industrial Commission for Sunset Advisory Commission review hearings held in 1974. The study was obtained from TEDC files.

58. Interview with Texas Economic Development Commission Staff: Jean Talrico, Administrative Assistant; Charles B. Wood, Executive Director; Bob McKay, Director, Department of Research; and others, Austin, Texas, February 1, 1984.

59. U.S. Department of Commerce, International Trade Administration (ITA), "Texas Exports Means Jobs" (Dallas, Tex., 1983), p. "doc #10f." This is a study prepared by ITA staff in Dallas, Texas. It was obtained during an interview and document search at the ITA.

60. U.S. Department of Commerce, Bureau of the Census, Annual Survey of Manufacturers (August 1983), Table E-4, p. 35. This was obtained from ITA files in Dallas.

61. Ibid.

62. National Association of State Development Agencies, 1981-1982 Expenditure and Salary Survey for State Development Agencies (Washington, D.C., September 1982). Forty states and Puerto Rico responded.

63. Diane E. Downing, "Thinking for the Future: The Promise of MCC," Austin 25 no. 8 (August 1983): 105-10.

64. Austin American-Statesman, February 24, 1984, p. A-1.

65. Interview with Meg Wilson, Coordinator of Science and Technology, Governor's Office of Economic Development, Austin, Texas, January 20, 1984.

66. Goodman and Arnold, "Small Business," pp. 201-2.

67. Office of the Governor, Texas 2000 Commission Report and Recommendations (Austin, Tex., March 1982), pp. 13-40.

68. Ibid., pp. 3 and 5.

69. Goodman and Arnold, "Small Business," pp. 205-6.

70. Ibid., p. 202.

71. Interview with Meg Wilson, Coordinator of Science and Technology, Governor's Office of Economic Development, Austin, Texas, February 24, 1984.

72. Interview with Meg Wilson, April 11, 1984.

73. Interview with Meg Wilson, February 24, 1984.

74. Office of the Governor, "Governor White's Economic Development Program," Austin, Tex., January 30, 1984 (Draft).

75. Governor White Press Release, January 24, 1984. The Council consists of the chairmen of the Texas Economic Development Commission, Texas Employment Commission, State Department of Highways and Public Transportation, Good Neighbor Commission, Texas Department of Parks and Wildlife, Texas Tourist Development Agency, and Texas Department of Water Resources.

76. C. G. Alexandrides, "The Case for Export Development of States: A Comparative Analysis with Recommendations," Southern Consortium for International Education, p. 2. This is a paper by Dr. Alexandrides, who is the Director of the International Market Information System, South Consortium for International Education. It was obtained from TEDC files.

77. Meg Wilson, Coordinator of Science and Technology, Governor's Office of Economic Development, in address to Policy Research Project, Lyndon B. Johnson School of Public Affairs, Austin, Texas, September 20, 1983.

78. Gregory Mignand, "California: Gateway for Trade," Business America 7, no. 3 (February 6, 1984): 11.

79. Office of the Governor, Governor Mark White Reports, Governor's Column Series no. 16, Austin, January 12, 1984.

80. Diana Claitor, "Special Report: Texas," Hollywood Reporter, August 9, 1983, p. T-6.

81. Office of the Governor, Governor Mark White Reports, no. 16.

82. Ibid.

83. Data furnished by Tom Copeland, Texas Film Commission, Austin, Tex.

84. Claitor, "Special Report," pp. T-10 and T-11.

85. Ibid., p. T-6.

86. Ibid.

87. Don Umphrey, The Economic Impact of the 1980 Film/Tape Industry in Texas (Austin, Tex.: Texas Film Commission, January 1982), p. 6.

88. Robert J. Reinshuttle, Economic Development: A Survey of State Activities (Lexington, Ky.: Council of State Governments, 1983), p. 46.

89. Ibid., and Umphrey, "Economic Impact," p. 6.

90. Texas Economic Development Commission, Small and Minority Business Report, FY 83 (Austin, Tex., 1983).

91. Ibid. Thirty percent of total state procurement for FY 1983 was handled by the State Purchasing and General Services Commission.

92. Tex. Rev. Civ. Stat. Ann., art. 5190.3, sec. 10(b) and sec. 11 (Supp., 1984). Small business, as defined by the Act, "means a corporation, partnership, sole proprietorship, or other legal entity formed for the purpose of making a profit, which is independently owned and operated, has either fewer than 100 employees or less than $1,000,000 in annual gross receipts." Also, progress reporting by each state agency (sec. 10 (c)) is to be done on an annual basis and submitted to TEDC, where all reports are consolidated and copies sent to the Governor, Lieutenant Governor, and Speaker of the House of Representatives.

93. Tex. Rev. Civ. Stat. Ann, art. 601(b), sec. 3.28 (Supp., 1984).

94. Tex. S.B. 179, 68th Leg., reg. sess. (1983). A minority business is defined as "a business enterprise that is owned or controlled by one or more socially or economically disadvantaged persons. Such disadvantage may arise from cultural, racial, or chronic economic circumstances or background or other similar cause. Such persons include, but are not limited to, Blacks, Puerto Ricans, Spanish-speaking Americans, American Indians, Eskimos and Aleuts."

95. Data provided through U.S. Travel Data Center, Washington, D.C. The 1982 total travel expenditures figure represents a 9 percent increase over 1981 expenditures, when Texas ranked fourth nationally behind California, Florida, and New York, and was capturing 7 percent of the nation's travel market.

96. Pauline Neff, "The Ambush of the Urban Cowboy," Texas Business 8, no. 8 (February 1984): 32. However, this was not always the case. In 1958, Texas was ranked twenty-third among the states in visitor revenues. The Texas Tourist Development Agency attributes this low ranking to the "carpetbagger clause" of the Texas Constitution, inserted in the original constitution in 1876. The clause prohibited the State from spending tax dollars to attract immigrants, which was interpreted to include any visitors (tourists) from outside the state borders. This clause, written into the constitution as a backlash to Reconstruction "carpetbaggers," was eliminated through a constitutional amendment passed by Texas voters in 1958.

97. Interview with Phil Davis, Director of Community Relations, Texas Tourist Development Agency, Austin, Texas, March 30, 1984.

98. Ibid.

99. Ibid.

100. Interview with Don Clark, Assistant Director of Travel Services, Texas Travel and Information Division, State Department of Highways and Public Transportation, Austin, Texas, April 11, 1984.

101. Ibid.

102. National Association of State Development Agencies, 1981-1982 Expenditure and Salary Survey. Per capita figures were derived using 1980 U.S. Census data.

103. Neff, "Urban Cowboy," p. 32.

104. Ibid., p. 34.

105. Ibid., pp. 34 and 36.

106. Texas Sunset Advisory Commission, Final Report on Cultural and Advisory Agencies, vol. 2 (Austin, Tex., January 1983), pp. 263-64.

107. Ibid., pp. 175 and 185.

108. Ibid., p. 191.

109. Mildred J. Little, Camper's Guide to Texas Parks, Lakes and Forests (Houston, Tex.: Gulf Publishing Co., 1978), pp. 1-2.

110. Texas Parks and Wildlife Department, Sunset Commission Report, Self-Evaluation Report, vol. 2 (Austin, Tex., 1983), p. 85.

111. Texas Parks and Wildlife Department, Sunset Commission Report, Administrator's General Statement (Austin, Tex., 1983), pp. 1-3.

112. Ibid.

113. Ibid., p. 23.

114. Interview with Tim Hogsett, Program Section Leader, Grants-in-Aid Branch, Texas Parks and Wildlife Department, Austin, Texas, October 11, 1983.

115. Tex. Rev. Civ. Stat. Ann., art. 601b (Supp., 1984).

116. Terry L. Anderson, "Institutional Underpinnings of the Water Crisis," CATO Journal 2, no. 3 (November 1979): 126.

117. Ibid.

118. Ibid., p. 127.

119. Ibid.

120. Interview with Dr. Jerry Higgins, Director of Economic Section, Planning Division, Texas Department of Water Resources, Austin, Texas, November 10, 1983.

121. Texas Department of Water Resources, Water for Texas - Planning for the Future (Austin, Tex., February 1983), p. 17.

122. Ibid., p. 2.

123. Ibid.

124. Ibid.

125. Ibid.

126. Ibid.

127. Interview with Dr. Jerry Higgins, November 10, 1983.

128. Lyndon B. Johnson School of Public Affairs, "Financing Texas Water Resources," Draft Policy Research Project Report, Austin, Tex., 1983, p. 25.

129. Ibid.

130. Charles River Associates, The Role of Transportation in Regional Economic Development (Lexington, Mass.: Lexington Books, 1971), p. 1. This is a study done by Gerald Kraft, John R. Meyer, and Jean-Paul Valette for Charles River Associates.

131. Ibid.

132. Curtis C. Harris, Jr., Regional Economic Effects of Alternative Highway Systems (Cambridge, Mass.: Ballinger Publishing Co., 1974), p. 1.

133. William E. Claggett, "Planning for Infrastructure Needs in Texas: The Scope of the Problem," University of Texas at Dallas, August 1983, chap. 3 (draft).

134. Texas Good Roads/Transportation Association, Texas Mobility Crisis: Deteriorating Highways and Lagging Revenues (Austin, Tex., March 1982), p. 13.

135. Claggett, "Planning," chap. 3.

136. Texas Good Roads/Transportation Association, Mobility Crisis, p. 2.

137. State Department of Highways and Public Transportation, Operational Planning Document Study (Austin, Tex., 1982), pp. 5-9.

138. Ibid., p. 22.

139. Ibid., p. 95.

140. Texas Good Roads/Transportation Association, Mobility Crisis, p. 4.

141. U.S. Department of Commerce, Bureau of the Census, United States Census of Population: 1980, vol. 1, General Social and Economic Characteristics, pt. 55, Texas (August 1983), pp. 3-5.

142. U.S. Congress, House, Job Training Partnership Act, 97th Cong., 2d sess., 1982, H.R. 97-889, p. 83.

143. Job Training Partnership Act of 1981, PL 97-300, 96 Stat. 1358, sec. 201 (1981) (hereafter cited as JTPA).

144. State Job Training Coordinating Council (SJTCC), "Minutes of Council Meetings," Austin, Tex., 1983 (mimeographed). The SJTCC is comprised of representatives from business, industry, the state legislature, local governments, relevant state agencies, the state employment commission, organized labor, community-based organizations, and education agencies.

145. Texas Employment Commission, A Labor Market Information System (Austin, Tex., May 1983), p. 8.

146. JTPA, pp. 1323-24.

147. Each PIC is composed of private sector representatives from area businesses and industry.

148. SJTCC, "Minutes."

149. JTPA, p. 1328, sec. 101. A labor market area is defined as an area where people live and work and can change jobs without having to change their place of residence.

150. SJTCC, "Minutes."

151. JTPA, p. 1358, sec. 201.

152. SJTCC, "Minutes."

153. JTPA, p. 1361, sec. 204.

154. Ibid., p. 1359, sec. 202; p. 1341, sec. 124; and p. 1342, sec. 125.

155. Ibid., p. 1360, sec. 202.

156. Ibid., p. 1364, sec. 251.

157. Ibid., p. 1333, sec. 106.

158. Ibid., p. 1334.

159. Ibid., p. 1365, sec. 302.

160. Ibid., sec. 301.

161. SJTCC, "Minutes."

162. Interview with Rik Makay, Associate Director, Employment and Training Division, Texas Department of Community Affairs, Austin, Texas, February 22, 1984.

163. Texas Department of Community Affairs, <u>Planning Guidelines for Title IIA, Job Training Partnership Act, July 1, 1984- June 30, 1986</u> (Austin, Tex., January 1984), sec. 2, p. 12.

164. Ibid.

165. Ibid.

166. Interview with Rik Makay, February 22, 1984.

167. Texas Department of Community Affairs, "Employment Generating Services Plan," Austin, Tex., 1984 (mimeograph).

168. Interview with Rik Makay, February 22, 1984.

169. U.S. Chamber of Commerce, <u>Nation's Business</u> 71, no. 1 (January 1983): 37.

170. Research Triangle Institute, <u>Final Technical Report - A Study to Make Recommendations Regarding a Cmprehensive State Occupational Education Program</u>, submitted to the Texas Education Agency, October 31, 1982 (Research Triangle Park, N.C., October 1982), p.5.

171. Bernard L. Weinstein, "Future of Texas High Tech," <u>Dallas Morning News</u>, January 20, 1984.

172. Bernard L. Weinstein, "No High-Tech Texas without High Education Standards," <u>Houston Chronicle</u>, February 14, 1984, p. 45.

173. Ibid.

174. Advisory Commission on Intergovernmental Relations, <u>State Aid to Local Governments</u>, chap. 3, "Financing Local Schools - A State Responsibility" (Washington, D.C., April 1969), p. 40.

175. Ibid.

176. Tex. Educ. Code Ann., chap. 16, subchap. A, sec. 16.001, from <u>Texas School Law Bulletin</u> (Austin, Tex.: Texas Education Agency, 1982).

177. Richard Musgrave and Peggy Musgrave, <u>Public Finance in Theory and Practice</u> (New York: McGraw-Hill, 1980), p. 578.

178. Texas Legislative Budget Board, <u>Fiscal Size-Up, 1982-83 Biennium</u>, Annual Report, Austin, Tex., 1983, p. 46.

179. Tex. Educ. Code Ann., title 3, subtitle 6, sec. 130(e), from <u>Texas School Law Bulletin</u>, p. 301.

180. Texas Legislative Budget Board, <u>Fiscal Size-Up, 1982-83</u>, p. 46.

181. Ibid.

182. Ibid.

183. Advisory Council for Technical-Vocational Education in Texas, <u>Vocational Education in Texas - Unified Report to the State Board of Education for Vocational Education</u>, Austin, Tex., December 1982, p. 11.

184. Texas State Technical Institute, <u>Report to the 68th Session of the Legislature</u> (Austin, Tex., March 1983), p. 2.

185. Ibid., p. 18.

186. Ibid., p. 5.

187. Ibid., p. 6.

188. Texas Legislative Budget Board, <u>Fiscal Size-Up, 1982-83</u>, p. 52.

189. Texas Rehabilitation Commission, <u>Self-Evaluation Report to the Sunset Advisory Commission</u> (Austin, Tex., 1983), p. 6.

190. Texas Legislative Budget Board, <u>Legislative Budget Board Estimates</u> (Austin, Tex., 1980), p. II-4; and interview with Charles Schnaebel, Executive Assistant Commissioner, Texas Rehabilitation Commission, Austin, Texas, December 15, 1983. The Texas Rehabilitation Commission (TRC) provides specific training services for the physically disabled for preparation of employment in suitable occupations through the acquisition of appropriate work skills and/or personality traits necessary for obtaining and retaining employment. The vocational rehabilitation program is funded on a 80:20 federal-to-state match base. Of the total $113.7 million appropriated to the vocational rehabilitation program in 1982-83, $16.8 million was spent on training programs.

191. Texas Rehabilitation Commission, <u>Annual Report, 1982</u> (Austin, Tex., 1982), p. 9.

192. Texas Rehabilitation Commission, <u>Self-Evaluation Report</u>, p. 6.

193. Ibid.

194. Texas Legislative Budget Board, <u>Fiscal Size-Up, 1982-83</u>, p. 65.

195. Texas Department of Human Resources, <u>Annual Report, 1982</u> (Austin, Tex., 1982), p. 13.

196. Texas Department on Aging, <u>Self-Evaluation Report to the Sunset Advisory Commission</u> (Austin, Tex., 1983), p. 68.

197. General Appropriations Act, Tex. H.B. 656, 67th Leg., reg. sess. (1981), p. I-8; General Appropriations Act, Tex. S.B. 179, 68th Leg., reg. sess. (1983), p. I-9.

198. Texas Comptroller of Public Accounts, Education Workpapers, vol. 1, Texas and U.S. Education: Facts and Figures (Austin, Tex., June 1984), p. 12.

199. Texas Legislative Budget Board, Fiscal Size-Up, 1984-85 Biennium (Austin, Tex., 1984), p. 34.

200. U.S. Department of Education, State Education Statistics (Washington, D.C.: G.P.O., January 1984).

201. C. Emily Feistritzer, The Condition of Teaching (Princeton, N.J.: Carnegie Foundation for the Advancement of Teaching, Princeton University, 1983), p. 54.

202. U.S. Department of Education, State Education Statistics.

203. Feistritzer, Teaching, pp. 10-12.

204. Raymon L. Bynum, Commissioner of Education, "Remarks to the Mid-Winter's Conference of School Administrators," Austin, Texas, January 19, 1981.

205. Texas Legislative Budget Board, Fiscal Size-Up, 1982-83, p. 42.

206. U.S. Department of Education, State Education Statistics.

207. Texas Education Agency, "Texas Public School Statistics," Austin, Tex., 1982 (mimeograph).

208. Ibid.

209. Texas College and University System Coordinating Board, Office of Postsecondary Education, "Postsecondary Educational Supply and Occupational Demand," published report, Austin, Tex., Spring 1983, pp. 4-5.

210. Ibid.

211. Research Triangle Institute, Final Technical Report, p. 63.

212. Ibid.

213. Ibid.

214. Feistritzer, Teaching, Table 54.

215. Ibid.

216. Ibid.

217. Tex. H.B. 246, 66th Leg., reg. sess. (1979).

218. Tex. S.B. 50, 66th Leg., reg. sess. (1979).

219. Tex. H.R. Con. Res. 275, 68th Leg., reg. sess. (1983).

220. Eva C. Galambos, Issues in Vocational Education (Atlanta, Ga.: Southern Regional Education Board, 1984), p. 13.

221. Office of the Governor, Report of the Governor's Task Force on Emergency Jobs and the Unemployment Trust Fund (Austin, Tex., 1983), p. 26.

222. Texas State Technical Institute, Techline 1, no. 2 (Winter 1984): 3.

223. Advisory Council for Technical-Vocational Education in Texas, Vocational Education in Texas, p. 22.

224. Ibid., p. 23.

225. "Employers Lead in Job Training, Study Suggests," Education Week 4, no. 2 (July 2, 1983), p. 3.

CHAPTER 4:
STATE DERIVED POWERS OF LOCAL GOVERNMENT

Local governments, as subdivisions of the state, derive most of their powers from specific delegations of authority contained in state statutes. In addition to summarizing the types of authority which have been granted to Texas localities, this chapter focuses on the extent to which these powers either facilitate or constrain the ability of these governments to influence economic development, as well as the degree to which local governments use these powers.

Divided into two major sections, the chapter begins with a discussion of the relationship between economic development and the powers of municipal government in the areas of of taxation, provision of infrastructure, bonding authority, land-use incentive tools for growth, foreign trade zones, and employment and training. The second section deals with the powers and activities of the two most important nonmunicipal government entities: water districts and counties.

I. MUNICIPAL GOVERNMENT

A. Taxation

To understand the importance of the impact of local government revenue-raising powers upon economic development in Texas, it is necessary to appreciate two essential points. The first is that in addition to revenues specifically set aside for development, many other local taxes and fees may also have important indirect effects upon development. The second is that municipal governments in Texas rely on their own fiscal resources to a much greater degree than do most local governments in the United States.

Dennis W. Carlton, in a recent econometric study of the effect of local government taxation on firm location decisions, noted that municipal taxes and fees provide many indirect benefits to development. He noted that taxes have a positive effect for firms because they are used to purchase new services. This effectively cancels adverse tax costs by providing benefits of new infrastructure and services to the public and to firms. He suggested that a community which offered a number of high-quality public goods funded by taxes would attract a large number of workers, resulting in falling wages, which would in turn make an individual community more attractive to new firms. Of course if tax revenues are not effectively utilized, there would be no attraction to workers or firms.(1)

Funding efforts of municipal governments in Texas are characterized by a high degree of self-reliance and by a tendency toward low tax effort and tax limitation. These seemingly contradictory characteristics are the result of a long period of prosperity in the state that has permitted a steady growth in local tax revenues despite limitations.

The State of Texas provides some direct aid to local governments, as described in chapter 3, but this accounts for only 1 percent of total municipal revenue. This aid has declined by 19.2 percent between 1982 and 1983, largely in response to a decrease in anticipated state revenue that affected all state spending.(2) Further participation by the State in the fiscal activities of municipal governments is limited to administration of optional sales and hotel occupancy taxes, and a limited sharing of revenue from the state gross receipts tax on liquor. As a consequence, the most important effects of state government on economic development are a result of the revenue powers the State grants to municipalities through the Texas Constitution and the General Laws of the State of Texas.

B. Economic Development Aspects of Local Taxation

In examining the role of local taxation in economic development, several issues must be addressed. First, the State grants authority to local governments permitting the collection of several types of taxes. Some, such as the local sales and property taxes, have indirect effects on development, since they are used as general revenue sources to fund public goods and services.(3) Other taxes, including the Metropolitan Transit Authority Tax and the Hotel Occupancy Tax, are applied specifically for economic development purposes.(4) A third category, which includes the Alcoholic Beverage Gross Receipts Tax, consists of state taxes shared in part with local governments for general revenue purposes.

Second, limitations on the taxing power of local government are also important to economic development. Texas places constraints on local taxation, including maximum limitations on tax rates based on the size and type of government of a municipality.(5) Property taxes are also limited by exemptions for homeowners, the elderly, and the disabled(6) and by provisions permitting citizens to reduce tax increases approved by local governments.(7) Municipalities, using powers granted to them by the State, have also limited their own taxation powers; ten municipalities have enacted such limitations since 1979.(8) Local tax efforts in Texas tend to be comparatively low; municipal tax rates were $331 per capita in 1980, somewhat below the national average of $381 per capita.(9)

A third issue in municipal taxation is the local option nature of many taxes. Several types of taxes permitted by state law may be adopted by individual towns and cities only by voter approval. Municipalities with charters granted by the State have the power to impose taxes on specific businesses and occupations.(10) Transit and hotel taxes may be applied at varying rates, at the discretion of individual communities, or they may not be adopted at all. In addition, municipalities levy a variety of fees and charges for services; indications are that user charges will represent an important source of revenue in the future.

Finally, sales taxes, the source of over 30 percent of municipal revenue in Texas, not only affect economic development but are themselves highly sensitive to local economic conditions.(11) After three years of steady growth, sales tax collections suffered a noticeable decline in

Houston and El Paso in 1983, as a result of economic conditions. Houston was adversely affected by the recession conditions in the oil industry, while El Paso lost significant trade with Mexico because of peso devaluations and continuing economic problems.

Statewide, sales tax revenue dropped by $21.7 million between 1982 and 1983, according to the State Comptroller of Public Accounts.(12) Such decreases reduce the ability of local governments to respond to service needs within their communities, and thus contribute to the unattractiveness of the local business climate of a depressed community.

1. Local Taxation Authority. The basic authority for the taxation powers of local government is found in the Texas Constitution.(13) Local governments are permitted to levy and collect taxes so long as they are equal and uniform within the jurisdiction.

2. The Local Property Tax. This tax is the most significant local revenue source in Texas, accounting for 84 percent of all local government tax collections in 1982.(14) The Texas Constitution and state statutes permit municipal use of property taxes, and limit the tax bases and rates for ad valorem taxes in several ways.(15) Some of these tax limitations are based on the size of the municipality.(16)

The so-called "Truth in Taxation" provision of the Constitution(17) and the Property Tax Code forbid municipalities from raising taxes without first giving notice and holding public hearings on the proposed increase.(18) The Code also contains a provision permitting citizens to petition for referendum elections to repeal any increases approved by the municipality in excess of 8 percent of the previous year's tax rate.(19)

Some local officials have expressed concern that this provision could represent a significant constraint upon their ability to meet future revenue needs. A number of municipalities have enacted their own tax limitations, however, and some tax limitation referenda were held under local charter provisions even before the terms of the state law went into effect. In all, ten Texas cities have enacted local tax limitations under the provisions of individual municipal charters since 1979, although one of those limits was overturned by the courts.(20)

3. The Local Sales Tax. The second major source of municipal tax revenue in Texas is the optional 1 percent retail sales tax, which accounted for 30 percent of local tax revenue in 1982.(21) Authority for the tax is found under the General Laws of the State of Texas, which permits adoption of a 1 percent retail sales tax by municipalities with approval by a majority vote of local citizens.(22) The law restricts expenditures of funds raised by the tax to general revenue purposes only. Consequently, the impact of the sales tax on economic development is an indirect one, since revenue is used to pay for the operating expenses of municipal governments. To the extent that high sales tax revenues help municipalities to maintain services at a level conducive to development, the sales tax may produce some incentives to development.

In such cases, though, other factors are likely to be more important as growth incentives or disincentives than the volume of sales tax revenue. Depressed areas are less likely to attract new business than prosperous communities, no matter what the level of tax collection happens to be. For example, according to an analysis of city sales tax trends by the State Comptroller of Public Accounts, communities in regions most affected by negative economic conditions--including the slump in the oil industry, the devaluation of the Mexican peso, and problems in the agricultural sector caused by falling farm prices--suffered decreases in sales tax revenue.(23) Revenue dropped by 15.9 percent among municipalities along the Mexican border between 1982 and 1983. Tax collections in the oil-industry-dominated Gulf Coast municipalities dropped 4 percent during the same period.(24)

By contrast, those areas of the state experiencing the most economic growth, the Dallas-Fort Worth area and the corridor between San Antonio and Waco, experienced increases in city sales tax collections in 1983 over 1982 levels.(25) The volume of sales tax revenue reflects rather than causes the economic vitality (or lack thereof) of a city.

Because the 1 percent city sales tax is piggybacked on the universally administered state tax, the importance of the sales taxes as a determining factor in economic development is limited. In other states which have a large proportion of cities which have not adopted the sales tax, retailers in jurisdictions with the tax are at a notable economic disadvantage in relation to enterprises in neighboring areas which do not impose the tax.(26) In Texas, the municipal sales tax has been adopted so widely that such an advantage scarcely exists, and the difference between a total sales tax of 4 percent and of 5 percent is so negligible as apparently to have no significant economic impact.

Despite the inherently regressive nature of sales taxes (which in Texas is mitigated somewhat by exemptions for food, prescription drugs, and other items), the general public does not appear to object greatly to paying a tax at the point of sale. The United States Advisory Commission on Intergovernmental Relations surveyed public attitudes on taxation in forty-five states and found very little public resistance to sales taxes. In southern states including Texas, the Commission found that citizens polled indicated by a three-to-one margin that they would prefer to pay higher sales taxes than to pay higher property taxes, regardless of the degree of regressivity of either tax.

4. Metropolitan Transit Authority Taxes. The State permits Metropolitan Transit Authorities, which are organized as subdivisions of municipal governments, to levy an optional sales tax of up to 1 percent, subject to voter approval.(27) At present, the San Antonio Metropolitan Transit Authority levies a 0.5 percent tax, and the Houston Metropolitan Transit Authority imposes a 1 percent tax. The newly authorized Dallas Area Rapid Transit Authority was funded by a 1 percent tax, effective January 1, 1984.

The transit taxes function as piggybacked sales taxes in the same manner as the municipal sales tax, with the same apparent lack of indirect effects on economic development. Nevertheless, as one of the few taxes dedicated directly to an activity strongly linked to economic development, the transit tax represents an important financial contribution to the public goods offered by Houston and San Antonio, since it is a major source of funds for their transit authorities. Houston's transit tax revenue grew from $129.8 million in 1980 to $166.7 million in 1982, before dropping to $157.8 million in 1983 (a reflection of local economic conditions). San Antonio's transit tax collections have enjoyed steady growth from $16.9 million in 1980 to $23.5 million in 1983.(28) The major problem with the transit tax, as demonstrated by Houston's 1983 collections, is that it is sensitive to shifts in the local economy. Nevertheless, even with a drop in collections, the revenue available from the tax to the Houston Transit Authority is still substantial.

5. The Hotel Occupancy Tax. This state tax is collected by the Comptroller of Public Accounts and shared with municipalities.(29) The tax is currently set at 7 percent on room charges for accommodations at hotels and motels, with an additional 3 percent permitted on a local option basis by an act of the Sixty-eighth Legislature. Revenues from the existing 7 percent tax are shared, so that effectively a 3 percent tax on rooms is allotted to the State for tourist development purposes and a 4 percent tax is allotted to municipalities for local development of tourist and visitor facilities. At the local level, state law permits use of the tax to furnish public facilities, to develop tourist activities, and to promote the arts. The tax raised a total of $40.6 million statewide in 1983, a drop of 4.8 percent from the 1982 total of $42.4 million.(30) Collections from the tax are relatively small, even in the large Texas communities that encourage the tourist and convention industries, but are more than adequate as a source of funds for promotional purposes.(31)

The tax functions almost as a user fee, since it uses a portion of the hotel and motel revenue of a community to promote activities aimed at attracting more visitors to the community. Collections have a direct relationship to tourist development, since the highest collections are from communities with the highest volume of visitors.

6. Alcoholic Beverage Tax. Another state tax shared with municipal governments is the 12 percent gross receipts tax on alcoholic beverages.(32) Fifteen percent of the total collection from this tax is returned to local governments for general revenue purposes. The effect, if any, on economic development efforts is of an indirect nature.

7. Municipal Occupation Taxes, Fees, and Charges. Local charters permit municipalities to pass ordinances levying fees and charges for municipal services and utilities. The State of Texas also permits municipalities to levy occupation taxes on certain businesses and individuals in the form of licensing fees.(33) The latter form of tax provides a small portion of municipal revenue, and is something of an anachronism. Fees and charges are used more widely, and are an important and growing source of revenue in municipalities that provide an array of services. Fees may become a more important revenue source in the future, particularly as municipalities reach the limits of their taxing capacity. In terms of economic development, the ability to levy fees and charges will tend to favor those communities such as Austin and San Antonio that operate their own utilities and provide an array of services upon which to base charges.

Texas has traditionally had a structure of municipal taxation that has encouraged communities to stand on their own in meeting their revenue needs. Direct state aid has always been limited and has declined in the past several years because of current economic conditions. State participation in meeting the revenue needs of local governments has been largely restricted to a limited sharing of the revenue and the administration of some taxes. Local taxes--ranging from the major sources of local revenue, property, and sales taxes, to the more minor taxes such as the hotel tax--have proved more than adequate to meet the fiscal needs of the state's communities.

The near future, however, presents some challenges to this system. The Texas economy has become very complex, with some communities experiencing recession conditions while others are straining under unprecedented economic growth. The present tax system may be unsatisfactory for communities that seek to meet the fiscal problems posed by these challenges.

Property taxes are limited by the constitution and by laws including a system of citizen-initiated controls that provide an incentive for local governments to keep taxes low; and a system of exemptions for the elderly, disabled, and all homeowners. As the major source of local taxes, the property tax may soon be affected by a conflict between the pressure to limit tax increases and the pressure to increase revenues to meet the needs of rapid development. When that happens, municipalities may need to look elsewhere for fiscal resources, or they may have to restrict their levels of service. Thus, the powers and limitations of cities with regard to property taxes play an indirect role in the development of the Texas economy.

Similarly, local sales taxes, while acceptable to citizens and a reliable and growing source of tax revenue during much of the past decade, have shown an acute sensitivity to local economic conditions. The irony of sales taxation is that when conditions are depressed and revenue is needed to maintain infrastructure and public goods in order to promote economic recovery in a community, sales tax revenue is likely to drop precipitously. A positive feature of sales taxation is that as a community experiences rapid growth, tax revenue is likely to grow proportionately, providing a revenue source that has the potential of keeping pace with expanding community demands for services.

The use of fees and charges shows promise for local governments in helping to maintain public goods and--in the cases of communities (such as Austin) that operate their own utilities--in generating considerable revenue. Fees, however, present several problems in meeting the revenue needs of communities. Not all communities are capable of operating some services in such a way as to subsidize other city operations. Should local taxes prove inadequate to meet future needs, then the ability to levy fees and charges will tend to favor the development of those communities that can provide services most efficiently. Fees alone cannot replace tax revenue but can act as a supplement, unless fees for services are raised to such a level that they either bring about citizen resistance or act to deprive the economically disadvantaged of access to services.

Taxes that are related directly to economic development, such as the Hotel Occupancy Tax and the Transit Tax, are significant sources of revenue for developing communities. They are, however, limited in their effectiveness to those communities that are either large enough to maintain a mass transit authority, or to those communities that have a significant tourist trade. They do not represent a complete answer to the revenue needs of all Texas municipalities.

In the near future, Texas towns and cities may be forced to turn to state government for revision of their revenue powers in order to deal with their complex economic conditions, and perhaps to play a more direct role in meeting their fiscal needs. The impact of state laws on one of the responsibilities of municipal government which gives rise to a major part of these fiscal needs--the provision of infrastructure--will be examined in the next section of the report.

II. INFRASTRUCTURE and BONDS

A. Infrastructure

Provision of infrastructure is an important component of local governments' economic development efforts. In order to determine whether Texas municipalities are able to provide adequate infrastructure, it is necessary first to determine whether state laws have influenced the development of local infrastructure. The second aspect involves evaluating the development of Texas's infrastructure system, and the final part of the analysis involves the determination of other factors that influence infrastructure development. These considerations are important because the extent to which a municipality can provide infrastructure is a factor that firms take into account when deciding where to locate or expand production. Therefore, a municipality's ability to provide for infrastructure is a vital element in its economic development.

1. State Laws. The Texas Constitution and civil statute provisions regarding infrastructure determine what types of finance mechanisms should be used for specific infrastructure purposes and the procedures for issuing bonds, including specifications of voter approval, state approval, and registration procedures.

These statutory provisions differ depending on the type of infrastructure: highways, roads, and streets; bridges; transit systems; airports; ports and harbors; sewer systems; water and drainage systems; solid waste disposal; utility systems; public improvements, parks, and public works.(34) There are four primary distinctions regarding these ten infrastructure categories. Four categories are considered components of basic infrastructure: highways, roads, and streets; sewer systems; water and drainage systems; and solid waste disposal. Four categories are transportation related: bridges; transit systems; airports; and ports and harbors. Utility systems, although basic to a city's needs, are not always municipally operated; therefore, they are considered a separate category. The last category is related to quality of life projects: public improvements, parks, and public works.

Infrastructure laws distinguish between three types of local governments: general law cities, home rule cities, and counties. General law cities are incorporated cities that have more than six hundred inhabitants or that have one or more manufacturing establishments within the corporate limits. Home rule cities are incorporated cities that have a population over five thousand inhabitants and have adopted a city charter.(35) Counties, the largest territorial division of local government within the state, will be addressed in another section of the report.

Laws regarding highways, roads, and streets; water and drainage systems; bridges; and utilities allow home rule cities more freedom than general law cities in financing mechanisms for these types of infrastructure. The primary means of financing infrastructure for both types of cities is the same--the issuance of bonds. Statutes regarding infrastructure do not appear to have restricted the economic development of Texas cities. The greater latitude given home rule cities derives largely from the practical consideration that these more highly populated municipalities have stronger infrastructure needs than general law cities.(36)

2. Infrastructure Systems. Attempts to evaluate the adequacy of Texas municipalities' provision of infrastructure have fallen short; in spite of isolated efforts, Texas lacks a comprehensive inventory of the infrastructure needs of municipalities. <u>Planning For Infrastructure Needs in Texas: The Scope of the Problem</u> by William Claggett of the University of Texas at Dallas is apparently the only statewide overview of both state and local infrastructure needs.(37) Claggett's analysis of Texas local government infrastructure is based on a direct poll of seventy-four small cities (under ninety thousand population) and twelve large cities (over ninety thousand population). The following is a summary of the major points in this municipal infrastructure inventory.(38)

The small-city survey results assessed past and anticipated expenditures (FY 1982, FY 1987, and FY 2000) for those types of infrastructure for which cities are primarily responsible: streets, water distribution systems, wastewater facilities, and drainage systems. In general, small municipalities indicated stronger spending projections for FY 1987 and FY 2000 for water distribution systems, drainage systems, and new street construction, but were unable to indicate future budgetary commitments for wastewater facilities. Anticipated revenue sources for new construction of water distribution systems, drainage systems, and wastewater facilities repair indicated increased user fee financing. This finding points to the strong likelihood that the costs of future expansions of underground water systems will be borne primarily by new users who will generally be served by Municipal Utility Districts (discussed more fully below).(39)

The survey indicated that smaller cities were either simply not planning for growth or were not aware of the magnitude of their infrastructure problems. Claggett found that cities not planning for growth were well under twenty-five thousand in population (28 percent), while cities planning for growth had populations of twenty-five thousand to ninety thousand (68 percent).(40)

The large-city survey provides a stronger assessment of past and anticipated expenditures. In general, large cities realized the need for substantial infrastructure investments, but the full extent of this need was not known. Survey responses were inconsistent and incomplete. They failed to explain spending increases and decreases. For this reason, a more concerted inventory-planning program is needed to avoid random and inadequate need projections. Claggett summarized the local government survey as follows:

> The collective inability among local officials to respond to questions concerning their current and future infrastructure needs--particularly among smaller cities and towns--demonstrates a local information gap every bit as large as and perhaps more significant than the revenue gap. Yet much of the brunt of infrastructure planning and provision is the responsibility of local government.(41)

Although Claggett recognized that local government spending accounts for over half of total government spending on infrastructure systems, he recommended that regional councils of government assist in planning and management of infrastructure systems. The intent of regional council coordination is elimination of data-gathering difficulties. The low city response rate (20 percent), coupled with inexplicable fluctuations in large-city spending, made the interpretation of the data difficult, particularly in attempting to form generalizations. Nevertheless, extrapolation of the county and city data indicated that Texas local governments will need to finance $80 billion in infrastructure costs.(42) Given that state government will only have to finance $70 billion during the same period and that the State relies primarily on current revenue, it is clear that local governments (relying largely on bond finance) are in a more precarious position than the state government with regard to meeting future financial needs.

3. Other Factors Influencing Infrastructure Development. A study conducted by Peter Wilson, The Future of Dallas's Capital Plant, which assessed Dallas's infrastructure condition over a three-year period--(1976-78), found that the street, sewer, water, and transit systems in Dallas were in good condition because of the high quality of maintenance.(43) Other factors contributing to this high rating included the relatively young age of the systems, heavy capital investment, and a favorable weather climate. In addition, the City of Dallas financed most capital investment by issuing voter-authorized bonds, which were favorably received because of the following factors:

- Voters were willing to approve most proposed bond issues.

- Both of the national bond rating services assigned Dallas the highest possible ratings for its general obligation debt.

- State-imposed debt limits were not tight enough to constrain debt issuance.

- Nearly all public investment was in new facilities with long service lives, and was thus appropriate for bond financing.

Wilson determined that Dallas demonstrated that public infrastructure could be developed, built, and maintained well with reasonable debt and tax burdens. This success, however, would not be possible without an expanding tax base, public support for capital projects, and the ability to take advantage of new technology for maintenance and the monitoring of plant conditions. Interviews with public works finance managers in eight other Texas cities revealed that these managers also considered voter approval and bond ratings to be extremely important in the provision of an adequate infrastructure. The foremost difficulty in suggesting that Texas cities emulate Dallas's infrastructure development practices involves financial constraints. Most Texas cities do not have an expanding tax base comparable to that of Dallas. Cities could, however, implement sound planning and financial management practices by degrees, depending on their financial condition.

B. Bonds

As indicated in the previous section, bonds provide a primary means of financing infrastructure expenditures and account for a major portion of municipal borrowing. Most municipal infrastructure needs are for expensive, durable facilities which are basic to the economic growth of cities, and demand considerable financing that is best met on a long-term basis.

1. State Laws. The Texas Constitution and civil statutes determine, to some extent, a municipality's ability to incur debt.(44) Texas municipalities face few debt restrictions, while counties are authorized to issue debt up to 25 percent of the locally assessed value (LAV) of property.(45) The state constitution and statutes authorize cities and counties to issue bonds, stipulate procedures for bond issuances by setting interest limits, state whether voter authorizations are necessary, and prohibit cities and counties from financing private ventures. Although general law cities face more restrictions, they do not require the same powers as larger, often growing, communities whose homerule charters allow them to plan and direct growth.

A significant statutory change occurred during the Sixty-seventh Legislative session; Article 717k-2 was amended to increase the interest rate ceiling from 10 percent to 15 percent in response to national bond market pressures that restricted the economic growth of Texas municipalities. When national bond interest rates rose above 10 percent, Texas experienced an inability to market municipal bonds competitively. This caused the Texas legislature to increase the statutory limitation on interest rates thus allowing Texas municipalities to compete in the national bond market.(46)

2. Assessment of Bond Market. Trend data on local government debt are generally aggregated on a statewide basis by the State Comptroller's Office. This agency's June 1981 issue of <u>Fiscal Notes</u> provided a succinct summary of municipal bond activity in Texas during 1973-80:

The high interest rates that prevailed from calendar year 1974 through the first half of 1976 helped keep a lid on bond activity. When interest rates began to fall in late 1976, bond sales increased but tended to stay at steady levels. This trend changed markedly beginning with fiscal 1979 as sales levels began to fluctuate wildly from month to month. This phenomenon resulted from two competing market pressures. On the one hand, rising interest rates made the use of debt financing less attractive, and many Texas governments attempted to stay away from the bond market. On the other hand, the continued influx of people and businesses into the state made it necessary for many jurisdictions to enter the bond market to fund capital improvements.(47)

A report recently authored by Arthur Ziev provides a more detailed account of debt trends among Texas cities and is apparently the only study thus far which has analyzed municipal debt by size of city in Texas.(48) The three categories of municipalities include small cities (less than 50,000 population), medium-size cities (50,000-250,000 population), and large cities (over 250,000 population). The analysis of small cities is based on a random sample of twenty-five cities, while the medium- and large-city analysis is based on all Texas cities in those population categories.(49) The data source on outstanding debt is the Texas Municipal League's annual survey of local government debt.

Ziev found that the financial condition of small cities appeared sound. Medium-size cities, in general, managed debt properly and could increase their debt levels without adverse effects to their financial health. These encouraging findings were, however, tempered by several potential problems. Data for twenty-seven cities indicated that a raised debt level could be imprudent; two of these cities indicated possible financial difficulty with present debt levels. Large cities did not appear to be in financial trouble. Two of the six cities indicated, however, that potential financial problems could be associated with high or unusual debt indicators.

The significance of credit ratings also relates to Ziev's three categories of cities.(50) Texas's smaller local governments with lower credit ratings and weaker financial bases faced higher interest costs as interest rates rose, resulting in less bond activity by municipalities under fifty thousand population. Medium-size-city and large-city credit ratings were generally stable and had increased bond activity: thirty-three medium and large cities found it necessary to enter the bond market to fund capital improvements for growth.

Large cities may soon be faced with an added rating variable: the establishment of an emergency fund to cover unexpected crisis situations that may be encountered by cities when recovering from the financial pressures caused by natural disasters.(51) Dallas and Fort Worth were able to recover from the financial pressures caused by the effects of the 1983 severe winter because of the existence of an emergency fund. This fund provided for emergency street and waterline repair that would otherwise have required increased local taxes (or possibly state or federal assistance). Emergency funds should be built by degrees, in a logical and planned fashion, rather than rapidly at the expense of other programs.(52)

3. Bonds and Infrastructure Development. Because local government infrastructure development is heavily reliant on municipal bonds, the analysis of these two topics is combined. Firms considering new locations will assess a municipality's ability to provide infrastructure services. Hence, those cities which have tended to provide these services adequately are more attractive to firms and more likely to experience growth. In this sense, bond ratings are an element of economic development. Municipal ability--or inability--to finance a a collective $80 billion future infrastructure debt will depend on financial determinants related to municipal bonds rather than on state laws.

Cities most likely to plan for infrastructure development are those receiving population inflows. Cities least likely to expand or improve infrastructure are those with dwindling populations or little change in population, a characteristic of general law cities. The Ziev and Claggett reports, which provide the most conclusive data to date, suggest that cities with populations over 250,000 are in the most favorable position to increase debt. These cities are also more likely to have capital investment plans for the purpose of projecting infrastructure needs. In contrast, smaller cities between 25,000 and 90,000 also plan for infrastructure development, but those with populations between 25,000 and 50,000 have better financial positions than those between 50,000 and 90,000 in population because the latter's growth demands may already have strained financial resources.

The extent to which cities may want to encourage growth will obviously depend somewhat on the degree to which development has already overburdened their infrastructure system and on their financial condition. For those localities which want to encourage growth, however, numerous mechanisms for stimulating such development are legally permissible. In the next section of this report, some traditional activities of cities which have the potential to facilitate economic growth are examined.

III. STATE-DERIVED POWERS RELATING TO ZONING, ANNEXATION AND EMINENT DOMAIN

Texas cities have been delegated the legal authority to pass zoning ordinances, annex land, control development, establish industrial districts, and exercise eminent domain in order to manage and control patterns of land use within their sphere of authority. Such control can impede or accelerate economic development depending on how it is exercised, or it can have no influence whatsoever. In order to assess the utilization of these potential tools for economic development, the nature of their statutory authority was examined. The ways in which Texas cities exercise these powers either to promote or retard economic development was explored by interviewing city planners in nine major Texas cities. The cities selected represent a diverse group geographically and in terms of fiscal capacity.(53)

A. Zoning

Zoning ordinances in Texas permit cities to regulate the purpose of land use by designating districts as residential, office, commercial, and industrial, and by specifying varying levels of intensive use within each type. They also permit cities to regulate within zoning districts the height, number of stories, and size of buildings; the percent of a lot that may be occupied; the size of yards, courts, and other open space; the density of population; and historic preservation. Also, they permit cities to restrict or prohibit development.(54) Thus, every aspect of the power to zone has the potential to affect economic development. For example, the imposition of restrictive residential zoning throughout the undeveloped areas in a community would prohibit the construction of a commercial or industrial facility. Conversely, the effective use of commercial and industrial zoning for districts near good transportation facilities enhances economic development.

The only city in Texas without a zoning ordinance is Houston, the state's largest city. Of the other eight cities surveyed, city planners in slightly more than half tended to view their ordinances as promoting office, commercial, and industrial development. Only three of the eight cities reported ever having rezoned land for commercial or industrial purposes, however, and only two of these (one-fourth of the eight cities) said they actively recruited these projects in joint efforts with other groups (such as the chamber of commerce or the Governor's Office). Moreover, few jobs were created by this rezoning. Certainly, most Texas cities are not actively using their zoning powers to recruit businesses and promote economic development.

B. Annexation and Control of Extraterritorial Jurisdiction

The Texas Constitution is extremely specific with respect to annexation, that is, the incorporation of land formerly outside the city limits into the city. A city may annex up to 10 percent of its area each year. If it does not annex the entire 10 percent in a given year, the amount can be accumulated up to a maximum of 30 percent in one year.(55) Areas to be annexed must lie within the city's extraterritorial jurisdiction (ETJ) and be continuous to the existing city limits.

Before the adoption of the 1963 annexation act, a city could annex land up to the city limits of another city. In 1963 the Fifty-eighth Legislature tied annexation to the concept of extraterritorial jurisdiction. The 1963 law specifies the ETJ of cities of various sizes, ranging from one-half mile for cities of less than 5,000 to five miles for cities over 100,000.(56) Provisions for overlapping ETJs were also made. They are apportioned in the same ratio as the cities' respective populations.

Just as the city's powers to annex are clearly defined, the responsibilities which accompany annexation are equally clearly defined. All areas annexed by a city must receive urban municipal services within two and one-half years of annexation.(57) Thus, in deciding whether or not to annex a developing or undeveloped area within its ETJ, the city must examine the benefits in terms of increased tax base and land use management controls against the costs of providing fire and sanitary services, street maintenance, police protection, utilities, and urban amenities such as parks and libraries. It is clear that annexation is not always economically advantageous.

Annexation theoretically provides cities with a way to grow, expand their tax base, and attract new development by providing urban services. However, in terms of the relationship between the power to annex land and economic development, annexation does not seem to be used as a tool for economic development at the present time. Only seven of the nine cities surveyed had sizable ETJs. Two cities, Dallas and Irving, are already surrounded by other communities and therefore have limited annexation powers. Only two of the remaining seven cities with ETJs annexed more than one square mile of land in any one year, and only one of these reported an aggressive and positive annexation policy. The others annexed very small amounts. In all seven cities, the purpose of annexation was unclear. Most of the land annexed in the last five years was either undeveloped or of mixed use.

One-third of the cities specifically annexed land for commercial or industrial development. In each case, annexation was sought by the project developer in order to obtain municipal utilities rather than being actively initiated by the cities themselves in order to promote economic development. Perhaps somewhat significantly in terms of assessing the relationship between annexation and economic development, none of the planning officials in any city knew how many new jobs had been or would be created by these projects. This suggests that city planners do not perceive much relation between annexation and job development and that annexation is not being utilized to promote economic development in a majority of the cities.

All Texas cities have the power to designate industrial districts in their ETJs that are free of taxation for seven years.(58) Creation of such districts is another way cities could stimulate economic development. This seems to be the most underutilized tool of all. A planning official of one of the largest cities in Texas did not even know that such a practice was legally possible. Of the seven cities surveyed which had ETJs, only one city has actively pursued this technique. Its purpose was to permit development outside its city limits in order to stimulate industrial development. These districts will result in the creation of over fourteen hundred new jobs in this city. A second city has utilized this device in lieu of annexation in order to provide fire protection in its inner harbor to businesses already in existence. A third city designated an industrial district, but it was never used. The remaining cities have never attempted to use this tool for economic development.

C. Eminent Domain

The use of eminent domain as a tool for economic development is cumbersome, time consuming, and expensive. Eminent domain gives Texas cities the power to acquire property from individuals for various public purposes through specific legal procedures.(59) Cities may only act to acquire property by eminent domain proceedings (condemnations) after they have attempted and failed to reach an agreement with the landowner.(60) Because of the lengthy and expensive nature of the eminent domain process, its relationship to economic development was thought to be a weak one. This proved to be the case. None of the nine cities examined used this tool to obtain parcels of land for central business district development. Their use of eminent domain was restricted to utility easements, street rights-of-way, site selection for facilities, and other infrastructure improvements outside the central business districts.

To summarize these findings, there appears to be little or no relationship between the use of zoning, annexation, designation of industrial districts, and utilization of eminent domain and the promotion of economic development in the nine cities surveyed. In the absence of a strong positive relationship between economic development and the powers granted to Texas cities by the Texas Constitution to regulate land use, there is a strong inference that few Texas cities are utilizing the powers they now possess to regulate land use in order to promote economic development. It is not clear whether this has happened because these tools are unnecessary, or whether they represent untapped and overlooked resources.

Mechanisms available for the stimulation of economic development at the local level are not limited to these traditional powers of Texas cities. The following section will focus on options which have become available to municipal governments in the past few years.

IV. LOCAL ECONOMIC DEVELOPMENT INCENTIVE TOOLS

A. Recently Created Local Economic Development Incentive Tools

Since 1979, the Texas legislature has passed several pieces of legislation which have a potential effect on local economic development. These acts have enabled Texas cities to provide various incentives to promote the development and/or redevelopment of targeted areas in the community. Below, four mechanisms through which cities may offer financial incentives to encourage development are discussed: industrial development corporations, tax abatement, tax increment financing, and enterprise zones.

1. Industrial Development Corporations. In June 1979, the Texas legislature passed the Industrial Development Corporation Act. This Act granted cities the authority to create nonprofit industrial development corporations (IDCs) which can issue tax-exempt revenue bonds to finance commercial and industrial projects. As of July 1983, the Texas Economic Development Commission had 359 IDCs on file, most of which have issued bonds.(61) Three issues currently surround the use of industrial revenue bonds (IRBs): (1) what type facilities should have access to them, (2) whether their use is being abused, and (3) whether the use of such bonds attracts industry.

The intent of this legislation was to limit the IDC to the role of conduit for financing of projects which benefit the public purpose of the authorizing entity.(62) The proceeds of IRBs issued by the corporation may be loaned directly to the user or may be used by the corporation to build or finance a project which will then be leased or sold to the user. The IDC may not own and operate a project.

The IRBs issued by the IDCs are typically sold to banks, savings and loan institutions, mortgage companies, and other conventional lenders.

Since the bonds are issued by an eligible nonprofit corporation, the buyers pay no income taxes on the interest earned. Hence, the corporation is able to borrow money at below-market rates. Subsequently, companies using an industrial development facility pay interest rates substantially below non-tax-exempt, long-term lending rates.

The concern over what type firms should have access to IRBs stems from the argument that the public purpose is not served by nonindustrial (commercial) uses of the bonds.(63) The federal law allows each state to determine eligibility for financing, and the degree of restrictiveness varies among the states. In Texas, commercial issues are reserved for city-designated blighted areas, or federally designated economically distressed counties with populations under fifty thousand.(64)

Although manufacturing facilities are still the most widely eligible projects, the use of commercial projects is on the rise. "The trend toward commercial usage is largely explained by the increasing potential for job creation in that sector. . . . In contrast, manufacturing enterprises, in general, have shown a decrease in labor intensity because of the greater reliance today on technological advances to increase production."(65) Thus, the argument that commercial IRBs do not serve a public purpose may be incorrect.

An analysis done by TEDC in 1983 indicated that the net taxes generated by a typical project in each of the four major commercial categories are substantial.(66) TEDC also estimated that these projects will produce in excess of 4,500 permanent jobs and an additional 4,500 jobs in supporting industrial and commercial enterprises.(67)

The second issue to be addressed, then, is abuse of the law. Critics often cite the use of IRBs by large, highly profitable firms that could obtain financing through conventional means. Of course, it could be argued that such deviations from the spirit of the law are not really detrimental to society, since prices of the products produced by these firms may be lower as a result of the cheaper financing, although there is a loss of federal tax revenues. Such abuse, however, may not be a real concern in Texas. Eleven of eighteen (61 percent) firms responding to a TEDC survey of commercial projects indicated that the project would not have been started without the use of IRB funds; 74 percent agreed that the project would have taken longer to complete without IRB financing; and about 36 percent of the firms used a combination of financing.(68)

Another concern related to abuse or, more precisely, overuse of IRBs is that the foregone federal tax dollars may eventually lead to increased taxes for others. Similarly, some worry that the loss of revenue at the federal level threatens all tax-exempt bonds, which if curtailed would increase the debt service levels of municipalities. IRBs also are perceived by some as a threat to municipal borrowing power. The fear is that municipal bonds will be crowded out of their communities' bond markets. In response to such worries, proposed changes in the federal law include a sunset provision for the tax exemption of all small issues.(69)

The final concern is whether IRBs attract new industry. A survey of fifty IDCs conducted by TEDC found that 30 percent of the thirty responding IDCs were formed to attract new business. Since formation, however, over 85 percent view their function as providing incentives to the location of new businesses and assisting growth in their area. Moreover, 17 percent reported that the potential for IRB financing gave their community a competitive edge.(70) Of course, if all communities utilized this incentive, a competitive advantage would not accrue to any city.

2. Tax Abatement. In 1981, the Sixty-seventh Session of the Texas Legislature ratified the Property Redevelopment and Tax Abatement Act. The voters of the state later approved an amendment to the Texas Constitution which granted cities, towns, and other taxing units the power to abate ad valorem property taxes in certain instances.

Under the Act, the governing body of any incorporated city or town may designate an eligible area within its boundaries as a reinvestment zone.(71) The governing body is then authorized to enter into contractual agreements with the owners of taxable property in that zone to exempt all or part of the value of the property from taxation. This is done on the condition that the property owner make specified improvements or repairs to the property, in conformance with the comprehensive plan of the city. The designation period may not exceed fifteen years, at the end of which the property returns to the tax rolls at its full appraised value and at the full tax rate.(72)

Since no property taxes have been abated in Texas pursuant to the enabling legislation, one must examine this incentive's effectiveness in other states. Abatement legislation has been passed in several states including Ohio, Massachusetts, Wisconsin, New York, Pennsylvania, Michigan, and Missouri. Like Texas, however, there is no requirement for a reviewing agency to approve abatement contracts in these states. Hence, much of the information available deals only with the major legislative provisions in each state.

One study of tax abatement was conducted in the City of St. Louis, Missouri. The real estate property tax in St. Louis is a relatively minor source of income to the City. Its receipts represented only 8.1 percent of the City's total revenue for FY 1977-78.(73) As a result, St. Louis's revenue base is sufficiently diverse to recoup, through nonproperty taxes, the revenue foregone through property tax abatement. Largely for these reasons, property tax abatement in St. Louis has resulted in positive net gains to the City's revenue. The structure of the revenue base in St. Louis is, however, such that its findings may not be applicable to Texas cities.

It is argued that even if abatement benefits do not result in positive net revenue gains, the probable alternative for most cities is to buy the land, clear it, and sell it at a loss. Thus, proponents contend that cities have little to lose by granting abatements in blighted areas. Dollars invested are not the sole criterion for measuring effectiveness, however. Tax abatement as a development incentive must also be considered.

Many critics argue that tax abatements do not cause development; they contend that the same development would have occurred with or without tax abatement. This theory is illustrated by the findings of the Council of

State Planning Agencies of the National Governors Association, which concluded that "tax incentives have had little effect in attracting commercial development."(74) Numerous other studies have found that factors such as the availability of raw materials, proximity to markets, transportation access, and labor pools dominate the location decision process, and that local taxes are generally of little significance in comparison with these overriding cost considerations.

The significance of the tax cost element is reduced further by the deductibility of state and local taxes from federal corporate income taxes. Thus, higher property taxes reduce federal income tax liability. This fact also takes credence from the argument that property tax abatement addresses an inherent deficiency in the property tax itself--the tendency to discourage reinvestment in new improvements. Nevertheless, studies do suggest that local property tax differentials can be a swing factor in favor of one location over another, once a particular metropolitan area has been selected.(75)

While it is clear that the City of St. Louis has had success with its tax abatement efforts, we cannot draw a sound inference as to the effects the same efforts would have on Texas cities since they rely much more heavily on the property tax for municipal revenues. It is not clear whether this economic development tool has not been used in Texas because of expected negative consequences or because economic conditions have made it unnecessary in most areas in the past.

3. Tax Increment Financing. Along with the Property Redevelopment and Tax Abatement Act, the Tax Increment Financing (TIF) Act of 1981 became law in November 1982 after passage of a constitutional amendment. Under this incentive, a city can finance certain public projects in targeted areas. The assumption is that these projects will make the area attractive enough to induce private investors to improve their property.

To finance these projects, municipalities freeze property tax assessments for all overlapping districts at the value for the year in which the zone was designated a tax increment district (TID). The value of this assessment forms the tax increment base for the zone. Each taxing authority continues to collect revenues on the base amount. Any increase in the ad valorem tax then accrues to the municipality, and is earmarked for the tax increment fund. Money in the tax increment fund may be used for direct financing of renewal projects (the "pay as you go" method), or it may be used to service bond debt and interest.(76) This amount is known as the captured appraised value. The bonds, which are tax exempt, are payable only out of the tax increment fund.

One important aspect of tax increment financing projects is that they are market oriented; the marketability of tax increment bonds depends on the likelihood of their becoming profitable. This has led to a controversy over whether only blighted land should be included in TIDs. Designing zones to include some expensive property virtually assures an increase in the value of the district, and thus makes the bonds more marketable.(77)

Such deviation from the spirit of the 1981 law was one of several factors which led to the passage of Senate Bill (S.B.) 641 by the legislature in 1983, which imposed numerous reforms on the 1981 Tax Increment Financing Act. The most significant was the addition of a "but For" clause, which states that tax increment financing development may only occur if a city finds "that [growth in a TID] would not [otherwise] occur solely through private investment in the reasonably foreseeable future."(78)

No tax increment financing projects are now under development, but several cities have created tax increment districts.(79) These include Houston, Galveston, Waco, Corpus Christi, Beaumont, and Bellaire. Port Arthur created two TIDs in 1981, rescinded each of them under county and school district pressure, and has since recreated them. In 1980, Laredo also established a TID, but no final project plan was ever formally adopted. Finally, El Paso was one of the first Texas cities to establish a TID in 1979. The use of school taxes in tax increment financing, however, is currently in litigation there.(80)

Many of the issues important to our analysis of tax increment financing are similar to those surrounding tax abatement. Since the use of TIF has been more widespread, however, several additional controversies have arisen. These will be the focus of this section.

Two areas that have become of particular concern involve jurisdictional equities and abuses of the law. With reference to the latter, the Wisconsin Legislative Audit Bureau found two major types of abuse of the law--TIF was used where growth would have occurred anyway, and was used to fund projects not directly related to economic development.(81) The Bureau also found several instances of abatement being used where it was not necessary. Most of these dealt with the inclusion of vacant land in TIDS.(82) Abuse of this sort has been evidenced in Texas as well. For example, the newly recreated TIDs in Port Arthur consist largely of vacant land.

No abuse of TIF by including unrelated projects has been identified in Texas, since no project plans have been implemented to date. The reason for this inactivity is related to the other concern--jurisdictional equity. While cities claim that any jurisdiction that will benefit from increased property values ought to share in the improvement costs, school districts (as well as other jurisdictions) are more dependent on property taxes than cities, and fear that a freeze on such taxes could damage their financial integrity. Furthermore, the law grants the authority to create TIDs solely to cities. Yet it is school districts, who often have higher tax rates than cities, that become the major contributor to TIF funds.

As previously mentioned, this potential inequity has resulted in litigation in El Paso. Subsequently, bond counsels have advised several Texas cities against implementing their project plans until a decision has been made in the El Paso case since the outcome may adversely affect the marketability of the TIF bonds.

Another situation which could hamper the use of TIF involves inflation and tax limitations. Since inflation directly affects property values, a drop in the inflation rate may mean that incremental increases in tax receipts will depend to a greater extent on increases in property tax rates. However, limitations on tax levies, which have already been imposed in a number of Texas cities, could severely restrict the use of TIF.

One further criticism of TIF is that cities may be forced to create TIDs to "keep pace" with neighboring cities. Taxes paid by property owners do not necessarily change under TIF, but the loss of revenue increases from a TIF could cause tax rates to increase across the jurisdiction. Although studies have established that local tax considerations play only a minor role in location decisions, officials from four of fourteen states surveyed felt that competition, regardless of need, motivates TIF in their cases.(83)

Despite each of these concerns, TIF has proven a more popular tool than tax abatement. Although TIF requires bond counsel services and a bigger investment of staff time, the actual tax-dollar cost to a city is about the same under both incentives. However, TIF may be more advantageous to developers because the federal tax deductibility of the property tax reduces its impact as a cost factor while the city provides more facilities or amenities in the TID than could be provided if taxes were abated and thus not available for TID use.

4. Enterprise Zones. In May 1983, the Sixty-eighth Regular Session of the Texas Legislature approved the Texas Enterprise Zone Act. This gave local governments the authority to nominate qualified areas as enterprise zones, create a state Enterprise Zone Board, allow state and local tax and regulation exemptions for businesses locating in the zones, and promote neighborhood self-help associations.

Under the Act, two types of zones, urban and rural, and two levels of zones, local (Level I) and state (Level II), were established.(84) Authorization of the Level II zone, in which federal and state tax exemptions would be authorized, has not yet been approved by Congress.(85) State participation in local zones is limited to authorizing lower city taxes and fees and lifting state regulations to increase local autonomy. Local governments can refund local sales and use taxes to retailers to purchase equipment, machinery, or materials for remodeling, rehabilitation, or construction within the zone. In addition, local governments can suspend zoning, licensing, or building codes, subject to restrictions set by statute.(86)

Both Level I and Level II zones qualify for tax increment financing and tax abatement, and businesses qualify for industrial development bonds. Enterprise zones also double as foreign trade zones, where businesses can assemble, store, process, and display goods from abroad without paying tariffs. (These are discussed more fully below.) Having only become effective September 1, 1983, however, no enterprise zone designations have been made yet in Texas.

Great Britain pioneered the concept of enterprise zones in 1981 with the designation of thirteen zones. What the British experience seems to suggest, as reported in the Urban Lawyer, is that "substantial federal aid is the sine qua non of a successful enterprise zone program. Tax breaks and regulatory simplification alone are not enough."(87) Yet, the United States federal government is offering no new money to provide for new or increased services and infrastructure in these zones.

Moreover, the accounting firm of Coopers and Lybrand recently performed a study of incremental effects of federal enterprise incentives on the cash flow of various firms. They found that although the incentives generate cash flow benefits for all firms studied, incentives have their greatest impact during the third to sixth years of a firm's existence.(88) This is so because the relevant features of the administration's proposal are wage and investment credits, which could not be used during the first year for any of the firms analyzed.(89)

According to National Journal, regulations are probably more relevant to location decisions than federal taxes, but state and local regulations are far more important than those at the federal level.(90) Furthermore, cities can provide other tax (property and sales) incentives, which can be taken advantage of sooner. Thus, one begins to question the need for, and appropriateness of, federal enterprise zone legislation.

In conclusion, it appears that tax incentives alone may not have much of an effect on firm's location decisions. Moreover, the effect that is realized by such incentives is extremely hard to determine. Thus, tax abatement and tax increment financing may not be appropriate tools to encourage economic development. Enterprise zones, on the other hand, are more comprehensive. It appears, however, that both the proposed federal legislation and the existing Texas legislation are geared toward large businesses which provide relatively fewer jobs per dollar of investment than small businesses. Therefore, although the enterprise zone concept may be more favorable than tax incentives alone, it is important that the incentives offered be attractive to the firms that have the greatest effect on economic development.

Finally, it appears that of the four tools discussed, industrial development corporations have the most to offer a community in terms of net taxes generated and employment. Although there are some valid concerns, it is not clear that the use of IRBs will actually have any detrimental effect on federal tax revenues, municipal borrowing power, or on economic development in Texas communities. But in any event, the tool effecting capital seems to be more effective than the other tax-related tools.

Below, we examine a development tool whose effects extend beyond the local community to international trade and commerce. This tool, the foreign trade zone, may contribute significantly to employment and production of goods outside as well as within a local economy.

V. FOREIGN TRADE ZONES IN TEXAS

On June 18, 1935, the Seventy-third United States Congress passed the Foreign Trade Zones Act "to encourage foreign commerce." The Act was designed to stimulate international trade and thereby create jobs in the United States by relaxing import/export levies and regulations in designated areas called foreign trade zones (FTZs). To provide more flexibility for the FTZs, an amendment to Public Law 397 passed by the Eighty-third U.S. Congress in 1950 permitted manufacturing in the FTZs, increasing their potential for contributing to the national economy.(91)

Foreign trade zones are secured areas legally outside a nation's custom territory. The zones are operated as public utilities chartered by states, political subdivisions, or corporations for the purpose of attracting and promoting international trade and commerce. FTZs are usually located in or near customs ports of entry, industrial parks, or terminal warehouses. Until the past decade, there were only about fifteen FTZs devoted mainly to seaport terminal operations. In the past few years, however, as costs of production in the United States have become more comparable to those in other industrialized countries, and with the containerization of cargo on shipments to inland ports, FTZs have become more versatile and widely available. By 1983 the United States had approximately ninety-four FTZs, although more than half of these were inactive.

Substantial economic activity takes place in these FTZs. In 1983, FTZs served approximately fifteen hundred companies, handled seven billion dollars in merchandise, and provided twelve thousand to sixteen thousand jobs. Some of the more notable FTZs include the Volkswagen plant in Pennsylvania, the Nissan plant in Tennessee, and the Zenith plant in Texas. These firms are both import substituting and export generating.(92) On the average, the siting of a new plant with one hundred workers means over $1 million in personal income and the creation of an additional seventy nonmanufacturing jobs.(93)

The purpose of an FTZ is to provide greater flexibility in the customs system in order (1) to assist firms exporting from the United States and (2) to encourage the value-added processing of goods here in the U.S. that might have otherwise been imported into the United States as finished goods. In this manner, the United States can capture the added income and the employment from FTZ activity that might have gone to overseas competitors. Foreign or domestic merchandise may be brought into the FTZ without a formal customs entry or the payment of customs duties or government excise taxes, or a thorough examination. Merchandise brought into the FTZ may be stored, tested, relabeled, repackaged, displayed, manipulated in some manner, mixed with domestic and/or foreign materials, and used in an assembly or manufacturing process.(94)

Since 1965, the State of Texas has authorized sixteen public corporations to apply for FTZ licenses.(95) Of these sixteen, five--Amarillo, San Angelo, Harlingen, the Southeast Texas Foreign Trade Corporation in the Beaumont-Orange-Port Arthur area, and Midlothian--do not actually operate FTZs at present, although several will probably initiate operations in the near future.

Eight of Texas's FTZs are found along or near the Mexican border (McAllen, Laredo, Del Rio, Eagle Pass, Harlingen, El Paso, Brownsville, and Starr County). Not including the Port of Brownsville FTZ, two Texas FTZs are located at seaport sites, Houston and Galveston, and the Beaumont-Orange-Port Arthur site is pending. Texas has three FTZs at airport facilities--the Dallas-Fort Worth Regional, El Paso International, and Laredo International airports--and the Jefferson County Airport site is pending. The San Antonio, Dallas-Fort Worth, and pending Midlothian and Amarillo FTZs are the only sites that can be considered inland.

Of the Texas FTZs now in operation, the biggest in terms of income generated, tonnage shipped, and employment is the McAllen FTZ. In 1982, the McAllen FTZ received the "E Award" from the U.S. Secretary of Commerce for generating the nation's largest dollar volume of merchandise handled in an FTZ. For FY 1983, it accounted for $1.1 billion in volume of goods. (The nation's second largest FTZ is Miami, Florida, with a volume of $350 million.)(96) After the McAllen FTZ, the state's second largest dollar-volume FTZ was the El Paso FTZ at $30 million, followed by Dallas-Fort Worth at $8.1 million, Brownsville at $4.2 million, and Galveston at $1.4 million. The Houston, San Antonio, Laredo, Eagle Pass, Del Rio, and Starr County FTZs have reported no income or employment figures because they were only opened in late 1983.(97)

A. The Border

The best example of the potential expansion of trade and manufacturing in Texas through FTZs is in McAllen. The success of this FTZ stems from several factors: its proximity to the Mexican border, a twenty-year effort by area leaders, the presence of maquilladora plants across the border, and the presence of General Electric and Zenith Radio corporations' facilities in the McAllen FTZ. Capital investment in the zone to date is $3.0 million on a forty-acre site with a planned expansion of $621 thousand to double the zone's present acreage. This zone was originally developed by a federal Economic Development Administration (EDA) grant and local funds. Manufacturing and other activities in the zone employ 1,725 people as of 1984. About twenty-five clients utilize the zone, the priority users being Mexico, Japan, Taiwan, and Hong Kong. Despite the zone's proximity to Mexico, in 1983 imports from Japan and Taiwan actually exceeded those from Mexico in merchandise.(98)

One of the ten most productive FTZs in the United States, the El Paso FTZ handles more than $2 million in merchandise monthly. New capital investment in this zone has been minimal because of the availability of existing plant facilities adjacent to the zone. The chief country clients are Mexico and Japan. Almost all of this zone's goods, primarily consumer electronic components and automotive parts, are re-exported. The potential for expanded economic development is enhanced by the presence of about 150 twin plants in the El Paso-Juarez area.(99)

In 1983, the Brownsville Navigation District received approval to expand its FTZ operation to encompass the entire Port of Brownsville and a 300-acre site at the airport. At present, however, the FTZ consists of one warehouse that has been used for general purpose storage. The chief clients are Mexico, Guatemala, Hong Kong, West Germany, and the United

States. Of the zone's $4.2 million volume, $3.4 million was re-exported. Like other border locations, expansion in this FTZ will be favored by the presence of thirty-five twin plants, or maquilladoras, in this border area and the port's extensive land holdings.(100)

In 1965, state legislation enabled the City of Laredo to apply for FTZ status. Although Laredo enjoyed a trade that allowed more tonnage through its city than any other Texas port of entry ($3.1 billion for 1982), FTZ status was not granted until November 1983. This occurred after the State intervened in the authorization process as part of its efforts to bring economic relief to the area after the peso devaluation.(101)

Del Rio, Eagle Pass, and Starr County were all authorized in November 1983 as a part of state development efforts to offset the negative impacts of the Mexican economic crisis, but these three FTZs are not yet in operation.

B. The Gulf

In operation since September 1978, the Port of Galveston FTZ consists basically of warehousing activities for West Germany, England, Israel, Japan, France, and Belgium. The top commodities imported into this zone are chemicals, clothing, and gas turbine generators. No manufacturing, assembly, inspection, or inventory repacking occurs at the zone.(102)

The FTZ at the Port of Houston, the second largest U.S. port, has been operating since November 1983. First-quarter 1984 figures for trade volumes indicate that within three years this FTZ may be handling an estimated $500 million value of foreign goods yearly, which would make it the second largest zone in the state and the United States. Of a designated thirty-three sites at the port, only seven are now being utilized for warehousing and storage by FTZ clients. The zone's marketing strategy is to recruit the many multinational corporations with Houston branches to conduct their manufacturing operations at the zone, including petrochemicals, steel, and heavy machinery industries.(103)

C. Inland

Located at an international port of entry, the Dallas-Fort Worth Regional Airport FTZ has been in operation since March 1981. The chief activities at the zone are warehousing, computer testing, and repair. Its marketing strategy is geared toward recruiting electronics and aircraft industries. In 1983 about one-fifth of all goods received were for export.(104)

Opened in May 1983, the San Antonio zone has no customers. The types of industry that are being recruited are machinery assembly, pharmaceuticals, and medical supplies and technologies to be used for U.S. import consumption.(105)

The Midlothian site is currently under application for FTZ status. To date, Mazda of America, a Japanese subsidiary, operates an automotive distribution center at the site, employing about eighty-five people.(106)

D. Legal and Political Factors Affecting FTZ Operations in Texas

The most commonly cited state law adversely affecting the operation of Texas FTZs is the county inventory tax.(107) This law has been applied to FTZs in a random manner. When it is applied, a rate of 5 percent is levied by Texas county assessors on all inventory in the zones at the taxation date, between January 1 and April 30.(108) The effect of this law is to cause shippers to eliminate their stocks of merchandise around the first of the year in order to avoid assessment of the tax. The long-run disincentive effect is not clear, but it appears that this inventory tax law may adversely affect Texas FTZs, as Texas and Michigan are the only two states that have such a law. This law may create inequities because of inefficient or unequal tax administration.(109) For example, the tax assessor-collector in one county may collect this tax from the local FTZ while the county officer for another FTZ may not collect it. It would seem that FTZs should be exempt from this law because the zones fall under federal jurisdiction and are for other purposes considered outside U.S. customs jurisdiction. At present, a federal law to correct this situation has been presented in the U.S. Senate.(110)

A second state law that has negative consequences for the operation of Texas FTZs is a lease taxation law on leasehold interests in land, buildings, or improvements owned in whole or in part by the state, a county, a city or cities, or any other governmental entity. Under this law, property held under lease for a term of one year or more is taxable. Property in an FTZ established by federal law is not exempt if the land size exceeds 250 acres. If the zone is less than or equal to 250 acres, an exemption from the leasehold law is made.(111) Therefore, large FTZs are penalized for their size. The law may be a constraint to the development and expansion of FTZs in Texas, although one might expect a proliferation of smaller FTZs around the state as a result of the law.

Another complaint of FTZ operators concerns the import licensing requirements of the state alcoholic beverage code.(112) Under state law, the holder of a state importer or branch distributor's license must also possess a manufacturer or general distributor's license; the required primary license has a residency requirement of six years. If alcohol is brought through a Texas FTZ, an import license is needed even if the bulk liquor products are only passing through the state. The residency requirement can be a hindrance to liquor importing through FTZs.(113)

In addition to the previous restrictions, Texas FTZs have had some difficulty in manufacturing activities that involve imported steel. For example, the FTZ Board approved restrictions on the Port of Houston zone for steel manufacturing at the request of area domestic steel producers and union leaders. The restriction requires the payment of duties on steel cargo prior to the production process if the steel products are for U.S. domestic consumption. If the final product is for re-export after the manufacturing, the restriction does not apply. The Houston zone is currently appealing to the FTZ Board in Washington, D.C., for removal of these restrictions.(114) Clearly, FTZs are vulnerable to political and economic interest groups whose livelihood is derived from import-sensitive products such as steel and textiles.

There are several benefits from the operation of foreign trade zones in Texas. First, the utilization of FTZs has increased the overall efficiency of international trade for the state and the nation. Given Texas's access to international waters and its common border with Mexico, FTZs in the state will play a greater role in facilitating increased trade levels from international sources. Second, FTZs in the state have provided a palpable measure of economic stimulation for manufacturers, importers, exporters, and consumers. The primary cause of this stimulation is reduced costs. A third advantage of the Texas FTZ system is its role in reducing high transportation costs through centralized industrial centers, in which production, assembly, and delivery activities occur simultaneouly. A fourth benefit to the state is increased investment in U.S. plants and equipment by foreign firms. This investment strengthens the industrial capacity of the state and contributes to increases in direct and indirect employment. It has been estimated that indirect employment created by one FTZ-related job ranges from 1.5 to 3.0 indirect jobs per direct jobs.(115)

Although FTZs have had a very positive influence on employment, it is obvious that this tool alone cannot meet the state's ever-increasing demands for jobs. The next section examines other local activity related to job development and training.

VI. EMPLOYMENT AND TRAINING

Despite the importance of well-developed employment and training programs to the success of business operations, no explicitly stated employment and training powers are given to local government by the Texas Constitution or civil statutes. Municipalities have traditionally operated employment and training programs but have relied primarily on federal and state employment and training funding, such as CETA funds, to do so. Since substantial funding is currently available to municipalities through the Job Training and Partnership Act (JTPA), it is doubtful that cities allocate significant local funds for this purpose.(116) Clearly, cities with relatively strong fiscal conditions would be in a better position to fund training programs to attract industry if they chose to do so.

A telephone survey of the city finance and personnel divisions of Texas's twenty-five largest cities revealed that no city used locally generated revenue to finance employment and training programs for the local labor force.(117) Cities did provide employment and training programs, however, for their own municipal employees. Training programs include police, fire, and maintenance certification in addition to management training and professional development programs.

A University of Texas at Austin Bureau of Business Research publication noted that employment and training programs are generally conducted at community colleges or on the premises of the firm offering a given program.(118) According to Kathleen Gamil, Manager of Training and Development for Houston Natural Gas, there is a growing need to use all levels of community educational institutions for training. Firms will continue to provide certain internal programs that focus on technical operations training; however, it will be more efficient for smaller firms to use the educational resources of the larger community. A former training director of Brown and Root, Inc., noted a growing relationship between construction-engineering firms and community colleges or vocational-technical institutes.

When interviewed for this project, Gamil stated that Houston Natural Gas was more inclined to conduct technical training for its employees, while relying on small universities and community colleges to conduct management training and specialized electronic data processing (EDP) training.(119) Weldon Holliway stated that Brown and Root's training philosophy is to capitalize on the skills of the local labor force, and they do so on both a national and international basis. If skills need upgrading, Brown and Root pays facility fees and instructor costs incurred through the training facility (generally a community college or high school), but employees pay training material expenses.(120)

It would seem, from the above results, that corporations are interested in developing employee skills through local education and training resources. These are limited to educational institutions such as community colleges and high schools rather than city governments, which are not expending local resources for labor force skills upgrading. Although such an expenditure may be in a municipality's interest, other factors such as availability of federal and community college programs forestall the need for local funding of employment and training programs. For this reason, city and county governments do not influence economic development through locally funded employment and training programs.

Economic development is influenced by the availability of water and related infrastructure, as well as by the local labor force. The next section examines the role of water districts, nonmunicipal providers of infrastructure, in economic development.

VII. WATER DISTRICTS

Water districts have been established in Texas to create, develop, and operate water-related services and facilities at the regional and local levels. The districts provide these services in response to the financial and administrative constraints placed upon local and county governments by the Texas Constitution. There are currently over one thousand water districts in the state. The districts can be divided into nine types : water control and improvement districts (WCID); water improvement districts (WID); municipal utility districts (MUD); fresh water supply districts (FWSD); levee and flood control districts (LFCD); drainage districts (DD); irrigation districts (ID); navigation districts; and river authorities. The districts are distinct units of local government with established organizations and operational autonomy.

For the purposes of this report, the activities of MUDs, river authorities, and navigation districts will be examined to assess their impact on the economic development of Texas cities. These districts have been chosen because they are the most common form of water districts providing services to urban areas. MUDs are the most numerous form of water district, and they have primarily been created to provide water, wastewater, and drainage services and facilities to residential subdivisions in suburban locations. River authorities are districts with planning authority over all or part of a river basin, and navigation districts are responsible for port development and operation in the state.

A. River Authorities

The Texas legislature has created river authorities, a special form of water districts, to facilitate the development, allocation, and preservation of water resources on a regional basis. There are currently twenty river authorities in Texas covering every major river basin. Each river authority has planning authority over all or part of a river basin.

The authorities are created under art. 16, sec. 59, of the Texas Constitution through a special act of the legislature. They are governed by a board of directors of six to twenty-four members who are appointed by the Governor and confirmed by the senate. River authorities are relatively autonomous units that function as regional governments in the state.

The authorities generally perform four functions: water supply and distribution, sewage treatment, flood control, and water quality control. In performing these duties they may provide contract services to local governments for technical assistance in flood control, water quality, and water resource development. They may also generate hydroelectric power and develop navigation and recreation facilities. They often develop and operate their facilities through contracts with municipalities or the federal government.

The fiscal powers of river authorities vary, but all have the power to issue revenue bonds based on the sale of water and/or hydroelectric power. Most of the authorities can issue these bonds without being constrained by a debt ceiling.

The operation of many river authorities may not significantly affect urban development because they have had a strong rural emphasis and have not been able to facilitate coordinated planning of water resource development. As the needs of metropolitan areas have increased, the State of Texas has chosen to create special districts to meet these needs rather than empower river authorities to provide services. "As a result, most river basins in Texas are divided up and partitioned out for administration by competing and overlapping districts with widely varying responsibilities."(121) River authorities lack the authority and financial power to either prevent the creation of or monitor the activities of other water districts. Therefore, the districts may not be prepared to plan for the future needs of metropolitan areas.

B. Navigation Districts

One of the Texas coast's greatest economic assets is its water transportation system. Economic growth in the state has been promoted by the development of ports along the Gulf Coast. "Historical statistics show that the seacoast towns of Texas were not dynamic centers of economic growth until they were opened to deepwater maritime traffic by the dredging of channels."(122) The development of Texas ports has facilitated the economic development of several sectors including manufacturing, petroleum production, and agriculture. Producers in these sectors depend upon port facilities for efficient cost-effective transportation of their products. For example, port-related economic activities in the Corpus Christi area include the production and export of chemicals, petroleum, primary metals, and fabricated metals.(123) Texas also contains two of the United States' largest port facilities: the Port of Houston and the Sabine-Neches waterways.

The Texas legislature has created navigation districts for the development of inland and coastal deepwater navigation, water channels, and water recreation. There are currently twenty-six districts in the state.(124) They are approved for development by special or general enabling acts of the Texas legislature, the commissioners' court, or the navigation board.

The districts perform a wide range of functions. Ten of the districts are concerned with the development of deepwater ports. Port development is undertaken in conjunction with the federal government and the U.S. Corps of Engineers since it is considered of national importance. The navigation districts work to assist development of port-related industries and of facilities on district-owned land that will enhance economic development in the area. These facilities generally include wharves, docks, bunkering facilities, and belt railroads. Other districts operate and maintain water channels that connect ports with the Texas Intercoastal Canal and the Gulf of Mexico. Some of the navigation districts have also been created primarily to develop water recreation and tourist facilities in an area.

Navigation districts, which are governed by a board of commissioners, utilize several mechanisms to generate funds. The districts may set rates and collect fees for use of port facilities and pilotage services. To finance capital improvement projects they may issue revenue and/or general obligation bonds without debt ceilings. They may also receive and utilize federal funds made available for the development of ports and facilities. To provide funds for the maintenance and operation of the ports and facilities, districts may establish a tax up to $.20 per $100 assessed valuation on all property within the district with voter approval.

The presence of navigation districts is advantageous for port development because it provides a mechanism to generate revenues and administer port operations with the oversight of the state and federal government. But the decisions influencing port development are substantially influenced by the market for water transportation and the goals set for port development by the federal government. The navigation districts appear to have responded well to these various influences since the districts provide a positive atmosphere for economic development in the coastal zone.

In seeking to meet the future needs of the industrial sector for water transportation facilities, navigation districts must continue to protect water resources utilized by other sectors of the economy. "Careful planning and management of the regional resources can assure continued growth and economic development by all sectors."(125)

C. Municipal Utility Districts

As economic growth generally means population growth with migration, it is essential for urban areas to provide an adequate supply of housing and basic infrastructure for their residents. Municipal utility districts (MUDs) are created primarily to provide water, wastewater, and drainage facilities and services to district residents, although they can perform other functions. MUDs facilitate residential development in suburban areas by providing an attractive financing mechanism, tax-exempt bonds, to pay for these services.

MUDs are governed by a board of directors elected by a majority of property owners in the district. They may issue tax-exempt bonds to finance their activities with the approval of a majority of property owners in the district, and they have unlimited authority to incur debt. A MUD may also impose charges, fees, and taxes to fund its facilities and services. Their taxing authority allows unlimited ad valorem taxation.

Of the currently active 529 MUDs in the state of Texas, over 400 are located in the Houston metrpolitan area, where they have been used to finance residential development. "In providing adequate housing for residents, developers of these utility districts have contributed to the rapid economic growth of the area."(126)

MUDs have proven to be an attractive development mechanism for several reasons.(127) They allow the use of tax-exempt bonds to provide advance funding for infrastructure development at favorable interest rates. This process can free land developers' available capital for other aspects of subdivision development. If MUDs are not used for infrastructure development and the subdivision is outside of a city's limits, the land developer is forced to secure funding in the private loan market. This requires a larger up-front capital contribution and places the developer in a disadvantageous position vis-a-vis the MUD developer.

The use of MUDs allows a metropolitan area to continue to grow without large capital outlays for infrastructure by the municipality, and subsequent increases in its debt. This process also does not obligate the city to provide other urban services including police and fire protection, health and human services, and park and recreation facilities to new development within its extraterritorial jurisdiction, as would be the case if the city annexed the area. These services are generally provided by county governments to MUD residents. The creation of MUDs also allows a city to annex areas after they have been developed and have repaid a substantial portion of the bonded indebtedness accrued for construction of their water, wastewater, and drainage facilities. In principle, a city can expand in terms of size, population, employment opportunities, and tax base without straining its finances. The development of a MUD reduces the need for an area to incorporate to receive services and increases the attractiveness of annexation in the future.(128)

Although there is limited empirical analysis on the effects of annexation on the fiscal capacities of central cities, a report on the annexation practices of southern cities indicates that annexation of suburbs has a neutral or positive effect on the revenues of central cities.(129) The effects of annexation on a city's revenues may be influenced by the quality and condition of infrastructure annexed by the city. For example, many MUDs utilize "package treatment plants" to treat wastewater within their districts. Package treatment plants are small facilities that serve a limited population size and generally last for ten years. If a city annexes MUDs on a seven-to-twelve-year schedule, most of these plants will probably be in need of repair or replacement, and, in such a case, the city may have to incur expenses for new infrastructure development in addition to those for extension of other city services to MUD residents.(130) The ratio of expenditures to revenues will indicate the impact of annexation on the city's fiscal condition.

The use of MUDs has quickened the pace of development by providing water-related infrastructure to undeveloped areas in a timely manner, but there has been substantial criticism of them as an urban development tool.(131) They have been characterized as inefficient service providers because of their small size and inability to take advantage of the economies of scale inherent in infrastructure development and operation. They may also promote functional fragmentation by duplicating administrative structures and services within each district that could be provided on a regional basis by the central city or a regional form of government in a more cost-effective manner.

There has been little question about jurisdiction and duplication of services related to county government, however. The role that counties play as governmental entities and, consequently, their influence in economic development have been greatly determined by the Texas legislature. This is discussed in the following section.

VIII. THE ROLE OF TEXAS COUNTIES IN ECONOMIC DEVELOPMENT

Because Texas counties are legal subdivisions of the state which do not enjoy the full legal status of municipalities, their role in the economic development of the state is primarily determined by the constitutional and political powers that have been granted by state government.(132) Though county powers are substantially more limited than those of municipalities, counties do have some discretionary power that is exercised by the commissioners' court. The court decides if the county will participate in activities authorized, but not required, by state mandate which might affect or influence the county's economic development, such as airport construction, creation of water districts, and plat approval for residential development. Thus, the ability of county government in Texas to manage, influence, and provide leadership for growth, development, and delivery of services varies drastically depending upon the interpretations and desires of the individual commissioners' court.(133)

The statutory authority for county economic development activity is not found under any one title of state law. Most statutory grants or prohibitions on counties are expressed in the form of duties and powers granted to the county commissioners' courts of the state. The commissioners' court has some authority in areas of economic development, although county powers are considerably weaker than the administrative and regulatory powers granted to Texas cities.

One major area of county responsibility that relates to economic development is transportation. Although the principal orientation of this function has traditionally been toward agricultural transport, that is, farm-to-market roads, urban growth in Texas counties has caused a demand for greater intercounty and intracounty road systems. The increase of residential and commercial users will continue to pressure counties into expanding their role as a provider of efficient and extensive transportation systems.

The county commissioners' courts in Texas have broadly prescribed powers in the construction and maintenance of all roads and bridges in the county that are not a part of the state highway system or within incorporated city limits.(134) To finance this activity, state law has provided that counties may issue bonds to purchase, construct, and maintain public roads,(135) bridges,(136) road and turnpikes,(137) and road districts.(138) Upon petition, the county must hold an election to determine if the county should assess and collect a special road tax.(139) In addition, counties have the power to acquire land to construct and operate a county airport.(140)

In the assignment of finance powers for the county system, the State has placed limitations on the ability of the counties to raise revenue. The state law makes counties observe statutory limits on bond issues including an overall limit of 5 percent of the total county budget.(141) Although the county must use any surplus from tax levies to retire bonds for the maintenance of roads and bridges,(142) the county is given the option of issuing turnpike bonds and assessing taxes to create a sinking fund for debt retirement and interest payment. The value of the bonds, however, may not exceed one-fourth of the assessed valuation of real property in the county.(143)

The role of the counties in providing for transportation in the State of Texas is significant. County roads comprise slightly over one-half of the total state roadway system. (In 1980, Texas counties were responsible for 136,059 miles of county roads, 947 miles of park and forest roads, and 11,499 bridges.) The property tax is the most important source of revenue to finance the county road and bridge system. In 1978, ad valorem taxes, with rates specified by the state constitution, accounted for 60.5 percent of county road revenues. Motor vehicle fees were the second largest source, accounting for 13.5 percent. The sale of bonds for the purpose of building road infrastructure increased from $25 million in 1974 to $69 million in 1978 to $112.4 million in 1982. Federal revenue-sharing funds allocated to Texas county road and bridge funds totaled $15.4 million in 1982. An additional $3.2 million for county road development in 1982 was granted under other federal programs that deal with community development and national forests. The need for additional funding for road and bridge construction and maintenance is critical. In 1978, for example, 31 percent of Texas bridges were found to be obsolete, and 51 percent were deficient.(144)

Another important responsibility of the county, assigned by the State, is in water supply and waste disposal. These powers are constrained, however, and can be exercised only upon petition by the county residents. For water supply, as an example, counties are permitted to issue revenue bonds if authorized by an election.(145) Upon such petition, the county commissioners' court may create water control and improvement districts for improvements and construction for irrigation, navigation, drainage, and the preservation and conservation of the natural resources within the county, including both underground and freshwater districts.(146) In addition, counties have the authority to create levee improvement districts to construct and maintain levees along creeks and streams, reclaim lands from overflows, and provide for proper drainage.(147) Multicounty cooperation is typical in this area of economic development. Water districts are usually more important for counties in West Texas and the Texas Panhandle.(148)

Counties are also allowed by state law to acquire, construct, operate, or maintain solid waste disposal systems; to contract for solid waste collection;(149) and to regulate within unincorporated areas of the county (not including city extraterritorial jurisdictions) the disposal, transportation, and collection of solid waste.(150) State legislation allows counties to issue bonds for solid waste facilities.(151) Texas counties may also acquire land on which to locate dumping and garbage disposal areas and have the right of eminent domain for this purpose.(152) In addition, they may establish licensing procedures for private sewage facilities.(153)

Texas counties have been granted few statutory powers for land-use control in unincorporated areas, although the state government has provided substantial authority to municipalities. The State itself exercises control in floodplain areas, highway development, and water development funding. For the most part, however, the State delegates little of its authority to the counties and there is no systematic government involvement in land-use regulation beyond the powers exercised by cities.(154) Texas counties do have powers to establish and enforce appropriate zoning regulations for airports within their jurisdictions.(155) The counties have also been given broad regulatory authority to comply with the provisions of the National Flood Insurance Act. Under state law, a commissioners' court may adopt building and development standards for floodplains in order to qualify residents in unincorporated areas.(156) Other state legislation dealing with land-use control has come in the way of "bracket bills" (bills that are limited to particular geographic areas or certain size population centers) that specify that designated areas of the state are eligible for county regulation. Most of these areas are in the Texas Gulf Coast counties, on Padre Island, or on land adjacent to reservoirs.(157)

State law does give counties authority to adopt minimal subdivision regulations applying to unincorporated areas. These standards apply to roads, the width of streets, and drainage systems.(158) This regulatory authority is insufficient. The counties have the power to require platting when the plats do not provide for sufficient rights-of-way, but they do not have other tools such as the sanction of fines, the denial of utility service for noncompliance, injunctions, and the denial of building permits. Furthermore, counties cannot require standards for the provision of utilities, minimum lot size, setbacks, building lines, or the reservation of space for parks and recreational facilities.(159)

The problem with land-use and subdivision controls in Texas counties is that land developers frequently plan and lay out new areas for urban residences long before settlement occurs and while these areas are still outside any city limits. Also, modern industries increasingly acquire land and build outside existing urban areas. These developments may escape city regulation, but they produce a need for services such as sewage and waste disposal, water supply, and transportation. As a consequence, urban growth beyond the limits of incorporated cities has led to a multiplication of special districts, whose creation has served to increase available services in Texas counties.(160)

The provision of utilities is one area in which a county can develop its potential economic resources. State law provides counties with the authority to cooperate with other public or private entities in the financing and construction of electric generating facilities.(161) Counties with a population greater than 5000, also have the power to acquire (not through eminent domain) a natural gas system and sell any natural gas not needed by the county.(162)

To generate operating revenues for the county, the commissioners' court has financial responsibility in setting the tax rate, authorizing expenditures, and issuing bonds, in addition to its duties as a fiscal agent of the State and county in collecting taxes for the State. The Texas Constitution limits the levy that counties can place on their citizens. The current limit on the county ad valorem levy is eighty cents for each one hundred dollars of property valuation.(163) The county may also levy fifteen cents for each one hundred dollars of property valuation for the added maintenance of the public roads if the property-tax-paying voters approve it by election.(164) Specific grants of tax authority, in addition to all other ad valorem taxes, are used for the construction and maintenance of farm-to-market and lateral roads, and flood control.(165) In counties whose tax valuation decreases as much as 7 percent a year, the county may issue certificates of indebtedness for operating expenses and assess taxes to repay those certificates.(166) Counties whose population is over one million inhabitants may also issue certificates of indebtedness, but only for certain purposes.(167) The state law also specifies the terms for indebtedness. For example, the counties may not fix the maturity for bonds to exceed thirty years, and the interest rate may not exceed 5.5 percent per annum.(168)

The property tax constitutes the greatest single source of Texas county revenues. From 1975-76 to 1980-81, total county property taxes increased from $470.9 million to $893.9 million, but still were only about half the total general revenue of all Texas counties. The second largest revenue source was charges and miscellaneous fees, which accounted for 33.3 percent in 1981, followed by federal government funds (6.8 percent), state funds (5.2 percent), and other taxes (3.9 percent). Using inflation-adjusted figures, the property tax increased in the same five-year period by 24 percent, charges and miscellaneous fees by 38 percent. State funds decreased by 5.7 percent, federal funds by 22.3 percent, and other taxes by 10.5 percent.(169) Direct expenditures by all Texas counties on interest and debt from 1975-76 to 1980-81 increased from $26 million to $49.6 million, registering a 24.7 percentage change based on inflation-adjusted figures. Nevertheless, county expenditures for debt and interest remained about 2.7 percent of total county direct expenditures. County debt alone increased from $603.8 million to $1,060.7 million from 1975-76 to 1980-81, an inflation-adjusted increase of 14.8 percent. Of that debt,

90.6 percent was long-term, full-faith and credit, general obligation debt.(170)

At present, Texas counties do not have ordinance-making authority.(171) The lack of this authority restricts the ability of counties to coordinate and develop their economic resources and control the pattern of development within their boundaries. Counties do have the opportunity to seek special legislative authority on a case-by-case basis, but that process could result in each of 254 counties possessing a separate and distinct set of laws. A degree of continuity and coordination is needed to avoid such a situation. Ordinance-making authority could be predicated on a local option election.(172)

In order to gain a perspective on the attitudes and priorities of economic development within Texas county governments, a questionnaire was designed to assess the role and attitudes of county judges, the executive officers of the Texas county commissioners' courts. The questionnaire was mailed to the sixty largest urban counties in the state, and responses were received from nineteen counties. Although the response rate was low and the representativeness of the sample uncertain, insight into the role and performance of county governments in the economic development process can nonetheless be acquired from the results of the survey. In this portion of the report, a summation of the results is provided.

Questions in the survey consisted of seven categories: finance, services, transportation, water use and supply, land-use controls, governmental cooperation and responsibility, and political attitudes toward economic development and growth.(173)

The results revealed a consensus on economic and political priorities. Sequentially, the top four priorities for attention were: (1) road development and maintenance, (2) the lack of county ordinance authority, (3) the financing of county facilities and services, and (4) a lack of industrial and business development in the county. The second group of county development priorities were concerned with water use and supply, and waste management. In order, they were (5) water supply, (6) solid waste management, (7) water pollution, and (8) drainage. The third and least urgent set of development concerns included (9) planning and zoning, (10) flooding, (11) water district regulation, (12) preserving open spaces, and (13) city annexation of county land.

In their responses to questions about governmental responsibility in transportation, one-half of the respondents felt that roads are exclusively a county responsibility, while one-quarter believed that this function should be shared by both the county and state governments.

In the area of finance, 76 percent of the respondents indicated opposition to increased property taxes for financing county facilities and services, while 94 percent perceived an increase in nonproperty taxes and other revenue sources as a partial solution to their financing problems. Eighty-three percent of the respondents felt that an increase in financial resources through federal revenue sharing was desirable, with 59 percent of the respondents indicating that direct federal aid would suffice.

Forty-one percent of the respondents rejected direct federal aid as a solution to their county's financing problems, although 82 percent noted a desire to obtain greater state commitments to fund county development and services. Responses were almost equally split when the counties were asked if they should provide more services as a means of encouraging county growth and development.

When asked about debt limits, 82 percent of the respondents said they did not favor the removal of state constitutional limits on the incurrence of county debt. On the other hand, 72 percent of the respondents indicated that they believed that counties should not hesitate to increase their debt to finance necessary projects if they cannot be financed by current revenues. Several respondents recognized the need for alternative financing methods and the need for more state funds to pay for facilities and services that traditionally have been provided by some Texas counties, such as the financing of indigent health care. In terms of governmental levels of responsibility, 73 percent of the respondents felt that the county should be the primary source of funds for county activities.

Despite difficulties in finding revenue sources to finance capital development projects, Texas counties are nonetheless continuing to finance and build facilities in their counties. Seventy-three percent of the respondents indicated that their county faced additional extraordinary infrastructure needs that competed for scarce capital funds. Almost one-quarter of the total infrastructure projects consisted of public buildings. Another 25 percent of total capital projects was used for the construction of county jails. Sixteen percent of the projects consisted of solid waste facilities, 12 percent were for airport construction, 12 percent were for road development, 8 percent were for parks, and 4 percent were for the construction of port facilities. The level of capital expenditures ranged from three to fifteen million dollars. The greatest financial constraints to the financing of these projects were voter resistance to bond issuances and an inadequate tax base.

The respondents' answers indicated a consensus about the role and effectiveness of county powers in shaping the course of economic development through land-use policy tools. The respondents identified the following priorities for effective land-use management tools in their counties: subdivision practices (94 percent), building code practices (82 percent), and zoning practices (76 percent). In general, two-thirds of the respondents believed that counties should utilize strong land policies (such as the ones listed above) to shape the quality and direction of their county's growth. As a land-use control tool, the respondents overwhelmingly favored planning on the county level. Ninety-four percent of the respondents agreed that counties should seek cooperation with adjoining counties in planning for county growth and development. Seventy-nine percent of the respondents discouraged statewide control of county development.

For water use and supply, the respondents first were asked to indicate whether a particular measure was effective in dealing with water use and supply problems. Second, the respondents were asked to rank each of the measures in terms of effectiveness. With the most effective measures ranked sequentially and the rate of affirmative responses, the results were: (1) regional planning (94 percent), (2) land-use controls and planning (86 percent), (3) floodplain zoning (81 percent), (4) river basin planning (75 percent), (5) regulation of water district development (83 percent), (6) higher water and sewer rates (23 percent), and (7) greater control of municipal utility districts (60 percent). No consensus emerged, however, on which level of government(s) should be responsible for water use and supply.

For solid waste management, the greatest frequency of intergovernmental interaction occurred between the county and city council members within the county (71 percent), between the county and city administrators (63 percent), and between the county and state administrators (60 percent). Forty-six percent of the respondents indicated that solid waste management should be a joint city-county governmental responsibility, while 30 percent of the respondents felt that this issue should be a state-county responsibility.

Regulation of municipal utility districts is another area of the survey that is linked with water supply and service finance provision. Sixty-one percent of the respondents urged promotion of MUD development. On the other hand, 58 percent of the respondents believed that MUD development could be restricted if their county had a greater taxing authority.

Finally, the respondents' perceptions on growth and development were measured. Eighty-eight percent of the respondents affirmed their county's role in the promotion of county growth and development, with only 38 percent preferring that current county growth be maintained. All respondents indicated that attracting industrial firms to their county was desirable, while 94 percent said that they favored attracting commercial activities. Seventy-seven percent of the respondents advocated setting aside county land for future large-scale industrial development sites, although 42 percent of the respondents felt that this type of promotion should be a joint city-county effort. In the effort to promote growth in their counties, the greatest frequency of intergovernmental interaction occurred between the county and city council members (88 percent), between the county and city administrators (85 percent), and between the county and state legislators from the county (73 percent).

In conclusion, the results of this survey indicate that Texas county policymakers wish to play an active role in developing the economic resources in their counties. Their ability to shape the direction of this development process is inhibited largely by the political and fiscal constraints on increasing revenue sources for financing facilities and services. The counties want the state and federal governments to provide a larger share of the funds that are needed by the counties, especially for activities that are mandated by the State. The future of Texas counties in financing economic development will still be dependent on the political will of county voters and the expansion of the counties' tax bases.

Although Texas counties do not have substantial regulatory authority in controlling growth or ordinance-making authority, they will continue to utilize the powers that they have been granted. Control of land-use practices, regional planning, and city-county cooperation are all areas in which the counties can gain influence in their economic development process.

IX. CONCLUSIONS

Some Texas local governments may be on the verge of losing their traditional autonomy with respect to financial matters. Sales tax revenues are quite sensitive to the poor economic fortunes of certain localities, and property taxes may not be able to grow rapidly enough to meet the financial needs of these cities. Although Texas cities do not adequately assess or plan for future revenue needs, the ratings of bond issues for most of them are remarkably stable, and thus the prospects for financing future infrastructure are favorable.

Texas cities rarely use either traditional powers, such as zoning and eminent domain, or more recently authorized tools, such as tax abatement and tax increment financing, for the purpose of stimulating economic development. The most commonly used tool for the development or redevelopment of targeted areas has been the industrial development corporation. Although some reservations still exist, this mechanism has, so far, proved the most acceptable to public and private concerns. On a broader scale of development, the use of foreign trade zones has brought about impressive accomplishments in international trade and notable effects in employment.

Finally, of the two nonmunicipal governments examined, water districts have a more significant impact on economic development than do counties. The limited regulatory authority of counties hinders their ability to influence development activities. Special districts provide the infrastructure services in unincorporated areas in the absence of county authority. This may result in fragmented development patterns.

ENDNOTES

1. Dennis W. Carlton, "The Location and Employment Choices of New Firms: An Econometric Model with Discrete and Continuous Endogenous Variables," *Review of Economics and Statistics* 65 (August 1983): 440-49.

2. Texas Comptroller of Public Accounts, *1983 Annual Financial Report* (Austin, Texas, 1983), pp. 9-15.

3. Texas, *Constitution*, art. 8.

4. Tex. Rev. Civ. Stat. Ann., art. 1066f (Supp., 1984).

5. Texas, *Constitution*, art. 8, sec. 9.

6. Ibid., art. 8, sec. 1.

7. Tex. Prop. Code Ann., sec. 26.07 (1984).

8. Interview with Gary Watkins, Assistant to Director, Texas Municipal League, Austin, Texas, July 21, 1982.

9. Glen Hahn Cope and W. Norton Grubb, "Restraint in a Land of Plenty: Revenue and Expenditure Limitations in Texas," *Public Budgeting and Finance* 2, no. 4 (Winter 1982): 143-57.

10. Tex. Rev. Civ. Stat. Ann., art. 1031 (Supp., 1984).

11. Cope and Grubb, "Restraint," p. 148.

12. Texas Comptroller, *1983 Report*, pp. 51-53.

13. Texas, *Constitution*, art. 8.

14. Cope and Grubb, "Restraint," p. 148.

15. Texas, *Constitution*, art. 8, sec. 9.

16. Ibid., art. 9, sec. 3. Cities of five thousand or less population can levy a maximum tax rate of $1.50 per $100 of assessed valuation, although cities granted home rule charters by the State, permitting them to enact their own ordinances, may set lower rates under the terms of their charters. Towns and villages operating under Chapter 11 of the General Laws of the State of Texas may levy a maximum of 25 cents per $100 assessed valuation (see chap. 11, Tex. Rev. Civ. Stat. Ann., 1984).

17. Texas, *Constitution*, art. 8, sec. 21.

18. Tex. Prop. Code Ann., sec. 26.07 (1984).

19. The provision requires 10 percent of those citizens who voted in the most recent local election to petition for the referendum. If the referendum issue carries by majority vote, the increase is then rolled back to the 8 percent level. This provision has been fully effective only

since 1982. Since that date, five rollback elections have been held. A 17.6 percent increase in Rosenberg and a 49 percent increase in Seabrook were rolled back to the 8 percent level in 1982. An attempt to roll back a 64.7 percent rate in Rowlett failed the same year. In 1983, a 14.9 percent increase in League City was rolled back, while an attempt to set a 5 percent limit in Odessa was invalidated (interview with Gary Watkins, July 21, 1982).

20. Ibid. Corpus Christi enacted a maximum rate of 48 cents per $100 valuation by referendum in 1980, setting the rate below the 80 cents per $100 valuation permitted by the Texas Constitution for all municipalities. A provision enacted at the same time limits future tax increases to 6 percent of all taxable property value in any one year. In 1979 Baytown established a 60 cents per $100 valuation maximum rate and limited future tax increases to 10 percent a year. That same year Galveston set a 40 cents maximum rate and a 5 percent limit on future increases.

21. Cope and Grubb, "Restraint," p. 148.

22. Tex. Rev. Civ. Stat. Ann., art. 1066f (Supp., 1984).

23. Tax Information Division, Texas Comptroller of Public Accounts.

24. Ibid.

25. Ibid. Tax collections rose 12.5 percent among the communities in the Dallas-Fort Worth area, while the communities along Interstate Highway 35 from Waco to San Antonio experienced a combined growth in sales tax revenue of 11.8 percent between 1982 and 1983.

26. Albert Preston, Jr., State and Local Taxes on Business (Princeton, N.J.: Tax Institute of America, 1964), pp. 5-11.

27. Tex. Rev. Civ. Stat. Ann., art. 1066f (Supp., 1984).

28. Tax Information Division, Texas Comptroller of Public Accounts.

29. Tex. Rev. Civ. Stat. Ann., art. 1269, sec. 3a (Supp., 1984).

30. Texas Tourist Development Agency, "1983 Tax Survey," Austin, Texas, 1983 (25 leaves).

31. Ibid. San Antonio, for example, received $4.4 million from the tax in 1982, a substantial 36 percent increase over 1981. This was used to fund a visitor's bureau, chamber of commerce convention promotions, local arts groups, and a civic center.

32. Tex. Alco. Bev. Code Ann., sec. 202.02 (1978).

33. Tex. Rev. Civ. Stat. Ann., art. 1031 (Supp., 1984).

34. Texas Municipal League, Texas Municipal Law Handbook and Index: A Reference Manual for Texas City Officials (Austin, Tex., May 1982), pp. A-8 - A-10.

35. Texas, Constitution, art. 6, sec. 5.

36. Texas Municipal League, Texas Municipal Law Handbook and Index. Laws relating to infrastructure are found in Tex. Rev. Civ. Stat. Ann., arts. 46, 118, 1175, 1187, 1269, 2368, 4477, 6081 (Supp., 1984); art. 8351 (1967); art. 835 (1964); arts. 1015, 1086, 1108, 1109, 1111, 1114, 1118, 1178, 1179, 1180 (1963).

37. Interview with David Spurgin, Administrative Assistant, Lt. Governor's Office, Austin, Texas, March 16, 1984.

38. William E. Claggett, Planning for Infrastructure Needs in Texas: The Scope of the Problem (Dallas: University of Texas at Dallas, 1983), p. I-2.

39. Claggett, Planning, p. IV-25.

40. Interview with William E. Claggett, March 16, 1984.

41. Claggett, Planning, p. I-5.

42. Ibid., p. I-7.

43. Peter E. Wilson, The Future of Dallas' Capital Plant (Washington, D.C.: Urban Institute, 1980).

44. Texas, Constitution, art. 6, sec. 2, art. 3, sec.52; Tex. Rev. Civ. Stat. Ann., art. 703a (1964), art. 703b (Supp., 1984), art. 717k-1 (Supp., 1984), art. 717k-6 (Supp., 1984), art. 717k-2 (Supp., 1984), art. 1021 (1963), art. 2368a.1 (Supp., 1984).

45. Advisory Commission on Intergovernmental Relations, Significant Features of Fiscal Federalism, 1976-1977, vol. 2 (Washington, D.C., 1977), pp. 83-90.

46. Interview with Steve Bickerstaff, Attorney, Bickerstaff, Heath and Smiley, Austin, Texas, March 16, 1984.

47. Texas Comptroller of Public Accounts, "Growth of Texas Public Debt Slows," Fiscal Notes 7, no. 81 (June 1981), p. 7.

48. Arthur Ziev, Recent Trends in Local Government Debt in Texas (Austin: Lyndon B. Johnson School of Public Affairs, University of Texas, 1982), p. 20.

49. Ziev's analysis of Texas municipalities with populations less than 50,000 is based on a random sample of 25 cities, a necessity considering there are 1,075 municipalities in this category. Random- sample cities were derived by dividing 1,075 by the desired sample size, 25, which equals 43. Next, every forty-third small city was selected from an alphabetical list; this process was repeated until a sample of 25 was obtained. The resulting sample cities all had populations between 25,000 and 50,000.

50. Roland Robinson and Dwane Wrightsman, *Financial Markets* (New York: McGraw-Hill, 1980), p. 11.

51. Interview with Elbert Morrow, Bond Attorney, Dumas, Huguenin, Boothman and Morrow, Dallas, Texas, March 16, 1984.

52. Ibid..

53. Seven of the nine cities in Texas whose population exceed 150,000 were surveyed: Austin, Corpus Christi, Dallas, El Paso, Fort Worth, Houston, and Lubbock. Only Arlington and San Antonio were not included in the survey. The two smaller cities are Amarillo and Irving. Their responses to the study did not appear to differ much from the bigger cities. Interviews were conducted by telephone with the planning director of each of the nine cities or the director's designated representative. Each director received a copy of the questionnaire in advance of the interview. Interviews lasted between thirty and forty-five minutes.

54. Tex. Rev. Civ. Stat. Ann., arts. 976a and 1011a-1011j (1963); Stuart A. MacCorkle, *The Texas City: Its Power to Zone* (Austin, Tex.: Institute of Public Affairs, University of Texas, 1955), p. 6; Charles M. Haar, *Land-use Planning: A Casebook on the Use, Misuse and Reuse of Urban Land*, 3d ed. (Boston: Little, Brown & Co., 1977), p. 444. Haar provides further details about the federal model and discusses its use by various states.

55. Lyndon B. Johnson School of Public Affairs, *A Matrix Analysis of Growth Policies in Austin*, Policy Research Project Report Series, no. 58 (Austin, Tex., 1983), pp. 4, 16, and 18; also see Isaac M. Singer, *Texas Practice: Municipal Law and Practice*, vol. 22 (St. Paul, Minn.: West Publishing Co., 1976), pp. 224-5.

56. Tex. Rev. Civ. Stat. Ann., art. 970a, sec. 4 (1963), and art. 1175 (Supp., 1984).

57. Ibid., sec. 10b (1963).

58. Ibid., sec. 5 (1963).

59. Ibid., arts. 969b and 1109b (1963).

60. Ibid., arts. 3264, 3266, and 3268 (Supp., 1984).

61. Texas Industrial Commission, *Directory of Industrial Development Corporations* (Austin, Tex., July 29, 1983), p. 53.

62. Texas Industrial Commission, *Financing Industrial Facilities in Texas* (Austin, Tex. [1980]), p. 25.

63. The national purpose of the bonds is "to promote industry and enhance the industrial capability of the nation" (Patricia Cuthbertson, "Small Issue Industrial Revenue Bonds: Public Policy Issues and the Texas Experience" (Professional Report, Lyndon B. Johnson School of Public Affairs, University of Texas, Austin, Tex., 1984), p. 8).

64. Ibid., p. 43.

65. National Association of State Development Agencies, National Council for Urban Economic Development, and Urban Institute, <u>Directory of Incentives for Business Investment and Development in the United States</u> (Washington: Urban Institute Press, 1983), p. 26.

66. Texas Economic Development Commission, <u>Industrial Revenue Bonds for Commercial Projects</u> (Austin, Tex., March, 1983), p. 19.

67. Ibid., Summary.

68. Ibid., p. 26.

69. National Association of State Development Agencies, et al., <u>Directory</u>, p. 27.

70. Texas Economic Development Commission, <u>Industrial Revenue Bonds for Non-Commercial Projects</u> (Austin, Tex., October, 1983), pp. 38-40.

71. To qualify as a reinvestment zone, the governing body, following a public hearing, "must determine that the area substantially impairs or arrests the sound growth of the city, retards the provision for housing accommodations, or constitutes an economic or social liability in its present condition and use by reason of the presence of a substantial number of substandard, slum, deteriorated, or deteriorating structures, the existence of conditions that endanger life or property by fire or other cause, or any combination of such factors or conditions" (Legal Subcommittee, Industrial Development Corporation Committee, Mayor's Task Force on Housing and Economic Development for Southern Dallas, Memorandum, August 19, 1983, pp. 7-8).

72. Texas House Study Group, <u>Tax Increment Financing: Texas Tries a New Urban Development Tool</u>, Texas House Study Group special legislative report, no. 82 (Austin, Tex., June 11, 1982), p. 12.

73. Daniel R. Mandleker, Gary Feder, and Margaret P. Collins, <u>Reviving Cities with Tax Abatement</u> (New Brunswick, N.J.: Center For Urban Policy Research, 1980), p. 47.

74. Texas House Study Group, <u>Tax Increment Financing</u>, p. 4.

75. James A. Maxwell and J. Richard Aronson, <u>Financing State and Local Governments</u> (Washington, D.C.: Brookings Institute, 1977), p. 32.

76. Texas House Study Group, <u>Tax Increment Financing</u>, p. 21.

77. Joshua Levin, "Creative Financing of Urban Growth and Redevelopment: An Analysis of the Rationale and Implementation of Tax Increment Financing in Texas" (Professional Report, Lyndon B. Johnson School of Public Affairs, University of Texas, Austin, 1982), p. 13.

78. Ibid., pp. 97-98.

79. Rose M. Rubin and Samuel Ogden, "Prospects for Tax Increment Financing in Texas," Texas Business Review, January 24, 1983, p. 32.

80. Levin, "Creative Financing," pp. 107-32.

81. Texas House Study Group, Tax Increment Financing, pp. 5-6.

82. Ibid., p. 17.

83. Texas House Study Group, Enterprise Zones, Texas House Study Group Daily Floor Report, Tex. H.B. 1125, 68th Leg. (May 4, 1983), p. 19.

84. An urban enterprise zone is located within a central city of a standard metropolitan statistical area (SMSA), and has a minimum population of four thousand. A rural enterprise zone is not located in a central city of an SMSA, and has a population of at least twenty-five hundred individuals (Texas Enterprise Zone Act, Tex. H.B. 1125, 68th Leg. (1983), pp. 5-6).

85. To be eligible for a Level I designation, a zone must meet the following population criteria: unemployment must be at least 1.5 times the state average, at least 70 percent of the residents must make below the median income, and the population must have decreased by at least 10 percent between 1970 and 1980. In approving local zones, the state Enterprise Zone Board gives preference to depressed areas in which local governments are willing to reduce tax rates or fees other than property taxes (Texas House Study Group, Enterprise Zones, pp. 19-20).

86. Ibid.

87. "Enterprise Zones," Urban Lawyer 15, no. 1 (Winter 1983): 283.

88. Lawrence Revzan, "Enterprise Zones: Present Status and Potential Impact," Governmental Finance 12, no. 4 (December 1983): 34.

89. Ibid., p. 32.

90. Rochelle L. Stanfield, "The Administration May Be Overselling Its Plans for Urban Enterprise Zones," National Journal, January 23, 1982, p. 153.

91. 19 U.S.C.A., sec. 81a (1978).

92. U.S. Congress, Senate, April 21, 1982, p. 104.

93. Manny Ellenis, "Six Major Trends Affecting Site Selection Decisions to the Year 2000," Dun's Business Month 122, no. 5 (November 1983): 116.

94. City of San Antonio pamphlet, 1983.

95. The sixteen public corporations authorized to apply for FTZ licenses are the following: (1) Laredo Trade Zone Corporation at the Laredo Port of Entry, (2) McAllen Trade Zone Corporation in Hidalgo County at

the McAllen Port of Entry (an amendment in 1979 provided for a subzone of this FTZ in Starr County), and (3) Harlingen Trade Zone Corporation in Cameron County, adjacent to the Port of Entry, in 1965; (4) San Angelo Trade Zone Corporation in Tom Green County, 1967; (5) Amarillo Trade Zone Corporation in Potter and Randall counties, 1975; (6) Galveston Port of Entry Trade Zone, (7) Houston Port of Entry Foreign Trade Zone, (8) El Paso Trade Zone Corporation, adjacent to the Port of Entry, (9) San Antonio Foreign Trade Zone Corporation, and (10) Brownsville Navigation District Foreign Trade Zone at the Port of Entry, in 1977; (11) Dallas-Fort Worth Regional Airport Foreign Trade Zone Corporation, 1979; (12) Eagle Pass Foreign Trade Zone Corporation, (13) Del Rio Foreign Trade Zone Corporation, (14) Starr County Foreign Trade Zone Corporation, (15) Southeast Texas Foreign Trade Zone Corporation, and (16) Midlothian Foreign Trade Zone at the port limits of the Dallas-Fort Worth Regional Airport Port of Entry at Midlothian, Ellis County, all in 1983. This last FTZ was created by preliminary state legislation that permitted joint airport boards to establish FTZs where the population in the two or more cities had a combined population of 100,000.

96. The Tower Report, February 1984.

97. Data collected from interviews with public officials and private individuals connected with Texas FTZs.

98. Interview with Frank Birkhead and Joyce Dean, McAllen Chamber of Commerce, McAllen, Texas, February 29, 1984 and February 22, 1984.

99. Interview with Robert Jacobs, El Paso International Airport, El Paso, Texas, February 23, 1984.

100. Interview with Betty Houghtaling, Brownsville Navigation District, Brownsville, Texas, February 23, 1984.

101. Interview with Jorge Veregada, Larado International Airport, Laredo, Texas, February 23, 1984 and March 2, 1984.

102. Interview with John Massey, Galveston Port of Entry Trade Zone, Galveston, Texas, February 22, 1984.

103. Interview with Bill Okerland, Houston Port of Entry Foreign Trade Zone, Houston, Texas, February 22, 1984.

104. Interview with Paul Seagan, Darrell Sedin Company, Dallas, Texas, February 22, 1984.

105. Interview with David Katz, San Antonio Foreign Trade Zone Corporation, San Antonio, Texas, February 22, 1984.

106. Interview with L. Howard, City Hall, Midlothian, Texas, February 28, 1984.

107. Interview with Birkhead, McAllen Chamber of Commerce, McAllen, Texas, February 29, 1984.

108. Tex. Rev. Civ. Stat. Ann., art. 7151 (Supp., 1984).

109. Interview with David Katz.

110. Interview with Paul Seagan.

111. Tex. Rev. Civ. Stat. Ann., art. 7173 (Supp., 1984).

112. Interview with David Katz.

113. Tex. Alco. Bev. Code Ann., chap. 66, secs. 66.03 and 66.04 (1978); and chap. 67, sec. 67.01.

114. Interview with Bill Okerland.

115. Matthew D. Breitemberg, ITC Investigation, 1983.

116. Interview with Morris Winn, Coordinator, Job Training and Employment, Governor's Planning Office, Austin, Texas, November 29, 1983.

117. Telephone survey of twenty-five Texas SMSA cities' finance and personnel divisions, March 14-21, 1984.

118. Carol E. Kasworm and Cora Hilliard, "Employee Development in the 1980's," in Economic and Business Issues of the 1980's, ed. Joseph E. Pluta (Austin: Bureau of Business Research, University of Texas at Austin, 1980), p. 124.

119. Interview with Kathleen Gamil, Manager, Training and Development, Houston Natural Gas, Houston, Texas, March 16, 1984.

120. Interview with Weldon Holliway, Director, Employment and Training, Brown and Root, Inc., Houston, Texas, March 16, 1984.

121. David Tees, A Fresh Look at Special Districts in Texas (Arlington: Institute of Urban Studies, University of Texas at Arlington, 1973), p. 70.

122. Bureau of Business Research, Area Economic Studies, Corpus Christi: Economic Impact of the Port (Austin: University of Texas at Austin, 1973), pp. 8-9.

123. Ibid., pp. 13-15.

124. These districts were created under secs. 60, 61, 62, and 63 of the Tex. Water Code Ann. of art. 16, sec. 59 of the Texas Constitution.

125. Coastal Management Program, The Coastal Economy: An Economic Report (Austin: General Land Office of Texas, 1975), p. 60.

126. Virginia Lacy Perrenod, "Urban Fringe Special Districts Along the Upper Texas Gulf Coast: Accountability and Impact Upon the Environment," Public Affairs Comment (Lyndon B. Johnson School of Public Affairs) 27, no. 4 (August 1981): 1.

127. Ibid., pp. 1-4; Tees, "Special Districts," p. 70; House Interim Committee on Water Supply and Waste Disposal in the Metropolitan Areas, Water Supply and Waste Disposal in Texas Urban Areas (Austin, Tex., January 1975), p. 19; Woodworth G. Thrombley, Special Districts and Authorities in Texas (Austin: Institute of Public Affairs, University of Texas at Austin, 1959), p. 12; and John Mitchell, "The Use of Special Districts in Financing and Facilitating Urban Growth," Urban Lawyer 185, no. 5 (1973): 186-99.

128. Thomas Muller and Grace Dawson, The Economic Effects of Annexation: A Second Case Study in Richmond, Virginia (Washington, D.C.: Urban Institute, 1976), pp. 3-5; and Southern Growth Policies Board, Suburbs in the City: Municipal Boundary Changes in the Southern States, Research Report (Triangle Park, N.C.: Commission on the Future of the South, 1980), pp. 3-5.

129. Southern Growth Policies Board, "Suburbs," pp. 45-49.

130. Perrenod, "Urban Fringe," p. 3.

131. Ibid.; Tees, "Special Districts," p. 70; Mitchell, "Use of Districts," pp. 186-99; Thrombley, Special Districts, p. 12; and House Interim Committee, Water Supply, p. 19.

132. Texas, Constitution, art. 11, sec. 1.

133. Texas Advisory Commission on Intergovernmental Relations, Handbook of Governments in Texas (Austin, Tex., December 1981), p. II-3.

134. Under authority of Tex. Rev. Civ. Stat. Ann., county commissioners are responsible for adopting a system for laying out, draining, and repairing public roads (art. 6763, 1960), and establishing roads connecting land to the road system (art. 6711, 1960). The state law also gives the court the power to condemn or acquire rights-of-way for the purpose of developing the counties' road systems (arts. 6673e-1 and 6674n, 1977), and counties may join together to form intercounty road districts (art. 778a et seq., 1964).

135. Ibid., art. 718 (1964).

136. Ibid., art. 785 (1964).

137. Ibid., art. 752a (1964).

138. Ibid., art. 778a et seq. (1964).

139. Ibid., arts. 6790-6792 (1960).

140. Ibid., art. 2351 (Supp., 1984).

141. Ibid., art. 722 (1964).

142. Ibid., art. 723 (1964).

143. Ibid., art. 752a (1964).

144. Texas Advisory Commission on Intergovernmental Relations, Current County Road Problems in Texas (Austin, Tex., January 1981), p. 5.

145. Tex. Rev. Civ. Stat. Ann., art. 2352e (1971).

146. Tex. Water Code Ann., secs. 51, 52, and 53 (Supp., 1984).

147. Ibid., sec. 55 (Supp., 1984).

148. Texas Department of Water Resources, Permits Division, Texas Register of Water Districts (Austin, Tex.,

149. Tex. Rev. Civ. Stat. Ann., art. 4477, sec. 8 (Supp., 1984).

150. Ibid., sec. 18 (1976).

151. Ibid., art. 4478 (Supp., 1984).

152. Ibid., art. 2351g-1 (Supp., 1984).

153. Tex. Water Code Ann., sec. 26.032 (Supp., 1984).

154. Texas Advisory Commission on Intergovernmental Relations, "Development Standards in Unincorporated Areas," Austin, Tex., 1978, p. 6.

155. Tex. Rev. Civ. Stat. Ann., art. 463 (1959).

156. Ibid., art. 8280 (1984).

157. Ibid., art. 2372 (Supp., 1984).

158. Ibid., art. 6720 (1960).

159. Texas Advisory Commission on Intergovernmental Relations, "Development Standards," p. 8.

160. Edwin Otto Stene, The Impact of the Texas Constitution on County Government (Houston: Institute for Urban Studies, University of Houston, 1973), p. 3.

161. Tex. Rev. Civ. Stat. Ann., art. 1435a (Supp., 1984).

162. Ibid., art. 2372 (Supp., 1984).

163. Texas, Constitution, art. 8, sec. 3.

164. Ibid.

165. Tex. Rev. Civ. Stat. Ann., art. 7048a, secs. 2 and 7 (Supp., 1984).

166. Ibid., art. 717 (Supp., 1984).

167. Ibid., art. 717b.1 (Supp., 1984).

168. Ibid., art. 752i (1964).

169. Texas Advisory Commission on Intergovernmental Relations, Handbook, pp. II-8 and 9.

170. Ibid.

171. Stene, Impact of Texas Constitution, p. 8.

172. Judge Horace Groff, Grayson County, Texas, Testimony before the Committee on County Affairs, State of Texas, December 9, 1983.

173. The survey's respondents were from the following Texas counties: Anderson, Angelina, Bell, Comal, Ellis, Galveston, Grayson, Hale, Jefferson, Jim Wells, Johnson, Kaufman, Lamar.

CHAPTER 5:
CONCLUSIONS

I. INTRODUCTION

Over the past twenty years, Texas has experienced remarkable growth and change within its economy. The relative importance of agriculture and energy production has decreased, while the manufacturing, construction, and private services producing sectors of the economy have increased. The very favorable business climate in Texas has brought about much of this growth, with incoming industries citing transportation facilities, access to raw materials, and a large available workforce as factors influencing their location decisions.

Although the Texas economy has experienced continual growth throughout the last two decades, 1983 saw a decline in the rate of growth that was caused by a number of factors. Severe weather conditions in West and South Texas resulted in disastrous losses in the agricultural sector. The drop in world oil prices depressed the petroleum industry and caused high unemployment in Houston and other areas dependent upon petroleum-related production. The devaluation of the Mexican peso produced a sharp decline in trade along the Texas-Mexico border.

Until recently, an explicit statewide economic development policy was not a priority for state elected officials. In spite of a strong pro-business attitude among state leaders, lack of interest in policy formulation and goal setting was attributable to a general complacency about the Texas economy, which was viewed as being strong and healthy. Unexpected fluctuations in the economy during the past few years, as well as a certain lag in less developed parts of the state, have caused growing concern among business, academic, and political leaders in Texas about the future structure and direction of the state's economy.

State and local governments have recently begun an active involvement in industrial recruiting and in policy planning for future economic growth. This was evident in the formation of the Texas 2000 Commission under former Governor Clements, and more recently with Governor Mark White's creation of the Governor's Office of Economic Development in an effort to facilitate greater state involvement in economic development and industrial recruiting. Government involvement is also apparent at the local level; for example, San Antonio's mayor has established an economic development staff dedicated to promoting the city as an ideal business location and to developing national and international markets for the city's products.

While this degree of direct involvement in economic development is a fairly recent innovation for state and local governments, concern for economic growth has been in evidence throughout the history of this state, as reflected in many state laws and programs. The State has affected economic development, either directly or indirectly, in three broad areas:

- Through state regulatory policies and practices;

- Through direct state actions and expenditures; and

- Through the powers granted to local governments.

II. GOVERNMENT REGULATION

The regulatory environment in Texas is generally cited as one of the most attractive features for new firms locating in the state. Despite rhetoric attempting to minimize the role of the State, state laws have a substantial impact on creating the business climate in the state. Labor laws, banking and insurance regulations, utility and transportation regulation, and taxation levels together comprise the State's business regulatory climate. An example of the State's positive and interventionist role can be seen in the Catastrophe Property Insurance Pool, a creation of state government, which provides insurance coverage against wind and water damage to the Texas coast. This Act has had a very positive influence on economic development on the Gulf Coast, particularly in tourism and residential development--development that, in the absence of the Act, probably would not have occurred to the same degree.

One area of possible concern is the State's prohibition of branch banking. Banking regulations influence economic development by either facilitating or obstructing the flow of capital to various sectors of the economy. While the law originated in populist attitudes against large financial institutions, the effect of the law may have placed businesses in small communities at a disadvantage, making it more difficult for them to obtain sizable loans necessary for expansion and other business purposes. The recent growth in bank-holding companies, however, will probably mitigate any negative effects of the branch prohibition in small communities.

In the area of taxation Texas is relatively conservative, levying neither a corporate nor a personal income tax. The State imposes a modest tax burden on firms located or operating within Texas. In the past, state and local governments have operated within a tax system that has provided for a level of public goods and services compatible with this modest tax burden. Increased demand for services and reductions in revenues collected from historically dependable sources will force both state and local governments to seek new sources of revenue. Statistical studies cited above suggest that state business tax rates do not have a significant effect on economic growth in a state, which implies that the State of Texas does have some flexibility in generating additional revenue to meet this increased demand for services, without affecting growth rates.

The State has been heavily dependent on oil and gas severance taxes for many years. These taxes currently make up a quarter of the State's total revenue collections. Collections from severance taxes have declined as the price of oil has declined during the past two years. It is apparent, therefore, that a substitute source of revenue will have to be found, as in-state oil and gas production is expected to decline through the end of the century.

State and local governments rely on retail sales taxes as major sources of revenue. At the state level, a constantly expanding economy provided a steadily growing source of revenue from this tax through 1983, when recession conditions in Houston and the Golden Triangle and in the border region caused a drop in collections. At the local level, communities in these areas tended to suffer a very rapid loss in sales tax revenue, while growing communities in other regions experienced a steady growth in revenue. Because of heavy reliance on sales tax revenue for local government fiscal needs, some communities will be better able to provide public goods needed to attract development than others.

Local governments are also very dependent on property taxes, which are subject to several legal and constitutional limitations. Exemptions for certain property and classes of taxpayers as well as ceilings on allowable rates and provisions for taxpayer rollbacks of annual rate increases serve to constrain localities' use of property taxes. While less sensitive to temporary economic conditions, property taxes also do not grow as quickly as sales taxes as a revenue source. Consequently, some communities in Texas may soon reach their taxing capacity and may have trouble meeting growing revenue needs. It is possible that local governments want to turn to the state government for relief just at the point the State is experiencing reductions in its severance tax revenues. New sources of income for both state and local governments may be necessary, as a result, by the year 2000. The State should be able to broaden its revenue base through new taxes or expansions of existing tax bases without significantly detracting from its desirability as a location for new firms. This is possible because Texas enjoys a very beneficial combination of other factors that make it attractive to business, and because taxes are a relatively unimportant factor in a firm's location decision.

One bright spot in the State's revenue picture is that most bonds marketed by the state government and its subdivisions receive high ratings, thus assuring that interest rates paid on this borrowing will be relatively low. Since bonds are the major source of financing for most infrastructure construction undertaken by both state and local government, the relatively low cost of capital will reduce the taxpayers' and ratepayers' costs for infrastructure.

III. DIRECT STATE ACTIVITIES

Texas state government sets a broad policy framework for development that relies on elected city and county officials to solve urban problems but provides assistance and cooperation in various ways, such as aiding in the provision of basic services and altering unduly restrictive constitutional and legal provisions that adversely affect fiscal priorities of local governments. The State's primary funding categories are education, welfare, and highway programs. In 1983, education comprised 51 percent of state spending, welfare 16 percent, and highways 11 percent.

State aid to cities and counties has both explicit and implicit effects on local economic development. Programs that aid general government services, especially programs supporting highways and public transportation, directly enhance the attractiveness of an area to business. State aid can indirectly affect development by freeing local dollars for other efforts. State aid improves intergovernmental equity among localities within the state as well as the distribution of services across regions. In fact, from 1977 through 1983, a generally increasing but erratic pattern of state aid developed, apparently in response to decreasing levels of federal aid. Intergovernmental assistance can be helpful in financing costly community and economic development efforts.

The two state agencies most directly involved in economic development are the Texas Department of Community Affairs (TDCA) and the Texas Economic Development Commission (TEDC). TDCA, using federal funds from the Community Development Block Grant program (CDBG) is the principal state agency assisting with economic development in small cities. The criteria TDCA has adopted in the administration of the CDBG program place a priority for funding on distressed small cities. Many efforts of both agencies are designed to assist local governments, community organizations, and small businesses in development efforts, such as TDCA's role in the Job Training Partnership Act and TEDC's role in industrial promotions. While the actual effectiveness of these two agencies is difficult to assess, it is clear that such efforts are low priorities of the State of Texas since these programs are supported at levels lower than most other states. This may be explained by the relative prosperity in the state or the reluctance to increase state taxes.

IV. EDUCATION

The training and development of human capital is essential to meet the needs of a diversified economy. Texas's transition from an economy based on agriculture and natural resources to one based on manufacturing and producer services in urban areas will require a well-educated workforce, an essential element for economic development. The State's educational policy must address the need to provide training programs, specifically in public schools, which will provide the basis for a trainable and retrainable workforce. The State's responsibility for supporting job training efforts is accomplished through public schools and postsecondary institutions. A cooperative working relationship between Texas state government, business and industry, and educational institutions is important. Adjustments in educational funding or programs should be made to address the needs of disadvantaged populations to prepare those persons to meet the expanding needs of a diversified economy. It can not be overemphasized that a well-educated and trained workforce represents the best investment for the future.

V. WATER

The distribution and limitation of water resources is the most significant environmental constraint on development in Texas. There is an uneven distribution of water in Texas, with some areas experiencing water shortages while other areas are prone to flooding. The Texas Department of Water Resources (TDWR) is mandated by law to prepare and maintain a comprehensive water plan for orderly development and management of water in the state. While TDWR appears to serve well in its role of granting permits and analyzing needs, it functions largely in a reactive capacity since other levels of government are responsible for constructing and funding water works. TDWR does provide capital to small municipalities in developing their water supplies. That aid only accommodates present needs and is not adequate to meet the needs of all small cities in Texas, much less provide for future growth. With revenue constraints in many of the larger cities, there is also a question of their ability to meet future needs through current fee mechanisms. Studies are needed of the effects of water availability on economic development and on financing methods for future water resource development. The capability of many municipalities to finance future water capacity needs is not certain. Additional financial resources may need to be provided by the State to assist local governments in meeting these needs.

VI. TRANSPORTATION

Transportation facilities play a distinct role in conditioning the pattern of growth by linking consumption and production centers within and outside a region. On the other hand, the absence of an adequate transportation system may adversely affect the development of a region. Growing regions with limited transportation infrastructure will almost certainly require additional facilities. Relative to other state programs, highway spending declined in Texas during the 1970s and early 1980s, although it still remained a significant share of the state budget. While heavily populated districts (i.e., Houston, Dallas, San Antonio, and Fort Worth) disbursed the most money in construction and maintenance projects, expenditure figures by size of population showed that the rural districts were receiving the greatest per capita investment in highways. Furthermore, it was found that high population and economic growth occurred in districts with relatively low per capita expenditures. It was not clear whether this occurred due to economies of scale in heavily populated, fast-growing districts which reduced their costs or due to inadequate planning of investment in other areas, increasing costs.

Poor highways and bridges slow movement of goods and may also discourage industry from locating in a particular region. For this reason, maintaining the quality of highways and bridges is vitally important to the economic growth of Texas; to do otherwise could impede state efforts to attract industry and to move people and goods efficiently within state borders. Maintenance will increase in importance as the existing highway system suffers wear. Because 11 percent of Texas highways are in poor condition, heightened maintenance activity must be undertaken in order to preserve the quality of the state's original highway system. While deteriorating infrastructure does not yet seem an impediment to development, except perhaps in Houston, this may become a serious problem in the future.

VII. TOURISM

Texas ranks third among the states in the nation in terms of dollars spent by tourists. This fact is primarily attributed to the state's strong convention market. While Texas has been successful in attracting tourism, state government itself allocates relatively little in terms of financial resources for the promotion of tourism. The primary agency responsible for tourism activity, the Texas Tourist Development Agency (TTDA), offers technical assistance and advisory services to chambers of commerce, convention bureaus, and individual city promotional activities. While these local efforts have contributed significantly to tourism, coordination among the tourism-related state agencies might improve their effectiveness.

VIII. LOCAL GOVERNMENTS

Local governments, utilizing powers designated by the State while relying on their own fiscal resources, have been able to maintain a level of public goods and services that have been attractive to economic development. They also have been given considerable latitude by the state government in terms of development tools using local means to encourage industrial relocation.

Local governments in Texas, except counties, have traditionally had authority to act to promote economic development. City governments can encourage and regulate growth through the use of zoning, eminent domain, and annexation powers. Eminent domain and annexation for economic development purposes have been little used in recent years. Texas municipalities have extraterritorial jurisdiction powers that permit them to exercise limited types of control over areas adjacent to their boundaries, though these appear insufficient to regulate growth completely. Special districts, ranging from port authorities to municipal utility districts, are formed for the express purpose of providing services to promote development. County governments lack ordinance-making power and other tools, particularly financing powers, that would be useful in promoting and controlling growth in unincorporated areas. Special districts attempt to fill the gap in authority between cities and counties, but they tend to promote erratic development and service delivery.

IX. ECONOMIC DEVELOPMENT TOOLS

Foreign trade zones have proven effective in creating employment and in encouraging international trade in several Texas communities. These zones are slightly restricted by state laws requiring that their property and inventory be noted for taxation purposes, which works against the purpose of having a duty-free zone for international trade. New zones have been approved but have not been activated because of current world economic conditions and the lack of customers.

Several types of economic development devices have been created by acts of the state legislature. Of these, industrial revenue bonds have proven most popular for financing construction projects and business ventures. These bonds are issued through industrial development corporations, 359 of which have been formed in Texas. There is some concern that the popularity of these tax-free bonds might crowd municipal bonds from the marketplace and might lead to federal restrictions because of the loss of federal tax revenue caused by this financing mechanism. Also, some critics of IRBs cite the use of these bonds by large, highly profitable firms that could obtain financing through conventional means. It is arguable whether or not this practice constitutes an actual abuse, but it has not become of particular concern in Texas as yet. In fact it might well serve as a mechanism for targeting development in particular parts of the state.

Tax abatement has been an available tool since the passage of the enabling legislation in 1981. Property tax abatement contracts have not yet been used in Texas, although Waco has designated a reinvestment zone in the city. There is some question as to the actual value of tax abatement as an incentive for development. Even though there is little proof that tax abatement actually induces investment, there are studies which suggest that such property tax differentials can give one location an advantage over another, other factors being equal. If this proves to be the case, tax abatement initiatives could place Texas cities in competition with each other and not make any net contribution to the state as a whole.

Tax increment financing has proven more popular in Texas than tax abatement. A number of cities have created tax increment districts, but have not begun projects because of pending litigation in El Paso involving the use of school taxes in tax increment financing. This litigation centers on a question of jurisdictional equity problems between cities and school districts. These problems result from the fact that only cities may establish tax increment districts, although school districts, which have higher tax rates, tend to contribute more heavily to tax increment financing funds. Once this case has been decided, the future of tax increment financing as a development tool will be more easily judged.

Enterprise zones, though authorized by law, have not yet been formed in Texas. They provide a more comprehensive approach to development than tax increment or tax abatement districts. Whether they are effective as a job creation mechanism remains to be seen, as proposed federal enterprise zones are geared toward large businesses, which create comparatively few jobs per dollar invested.

X. SUMMATION

The growth prospects of any state and its cities are related to many factors including its natural resource endowment, the composition and skill level of its labor force, the economic structure in the state, national business cycles, and national economic policy. In this study, it has been observed that state government also affects economic development in many ways. While the economic base of Texas was largely shaped by its natural resource endowment, the evolution of its two principal sectors--agriculture and petroleum--has to a significant extent been affected by state laws regarding water rights, state efforts in water resource development, and by state regulation in the form of the Railroad Commission.

The economic base of the state is now shifting, and the advantages offered by the state to agriculture and petroleum are less important to the location decisions of urban-based economic activity. Fortunately, the state has been able to attract a significant share of the country's growth industries, the so-called high-technology firms. Even so, this project has found that if state government is to assume a larger role in fostering growth, all aspects of state government need to be reviewed in developing a broad-based policy.

The state regulatory environment clearly contributes to the positive business climate in the state. It is also clear that one component of this business climate, low tax rates, has contributed to low revenues and, subsequently, to relatively low levels of services. While low levels of services were not inconsistent with a rural, natural-resource-dominated economy, they may be less well suited for an urban, industrial-service-based economy. Revenue constraints will certainly limit state efforts in export promotion, industrial development, training programs, tourism, promotion, and so forth, but an underfunded education system may seriously undermine future growth possibilities. The state's public and private universities seem to position the state very well in relation to the research activities of the growth industries, but it is not clear that the state's labor force offers any relative advantages to manufacturing activities and may in fact be relatively unattractive given current education and skills levels. The lack of relationship between state tax rates and rates of economic growth discussed in Chapter 2 can be explained by the fact that enhanced public services, made possible by increased revenue, actually make a state more attractive and more supportive of business development.

One of the most difficult problems to be faced by the state will be the uneven nature of economic development within its borders; specifically, rapid growth in some areas and near stagnation in others. The decisionmakers in Texas will be faced with a basic question of equity: should it be a matter of policy to attempt to distribute economic growth more evenly, or should the prevailing pattern of development winners and losers be allowed to continue? State government may need to consider specific measures to relieve the fiscal crises of depressed cities highly dependent upon the sales tax.

Local governments will be forced to deal with important gaps in their authority to manage growth, particularly because of differences in planning and zoning powers between city and county governments. The gaps in service delivery and regulatory authority in the territory lying between city corporation limits and county boundaries have been filled by a variety of special districts that have tended to promote patchwork development and erratic delivery of services to residential and industrial developments. While these activities may not adversely affect development in the short run, they may result in more costly service provision or infrastructure replacement activities in the future.

Changes in the national economy, specifically the emergence of new growth sectors, have benefitted the economy of Texas and, in particular, a number of cities in the state. This development is occurring during a period of substantial change in federal-state relations, which is forcing states to assume additional responsibilities. This economic and intergovernmental transition creates an opportunity and a challenge for state government. How well this challenge is met will partially determine whether the state's economy, and that of individual Texas cities, will continue to be attractive and prosperous. The state inherited a rich legacy that required little attention to prosper; future growth will depend upon the willingness of state government to nurture and develop its evolving, more diversified urban economy.

APPENDIX I: ECONOMIC DEVELOPMENT TOOLS IN OTHER STATES

Government in each of the fifty states is involved in some type of economic development activity aimed at encouraging the growth of private industry within its borders. Appendix I examines state economic development activities in the other fourty-nine states to provide a frame of reference for assessing economic development efforts by Texas. Section I looks at the major tools states use to encourage industrial growth. Section II examines in depth the economic development activities in eight states that are considered to offer progressive programs for economic development: Arizona, California, Florida, Illinois, Massachusetts, Minnesota, New York, and North Carolina.

I. STATE ECONOMIC DEVELOPMENT TOOLS

The information in this section is derived largely from the Directory of Incentives for Business Investment and Development in the United States by the National Association of State Development Agencies, the National Council for Urban Economic Development, and the Urban Institute. The 1983 publication provides a comprehensive inventory of economic development activities in the fifty states. This section defines the major economic development tools used within the U.S., and lists the states in which they are currently employed.

A. STATE AND LOCAL BONDS

States, local governments, and special districts/authorities may issue tax-exempt bonds to raise capital for public purposes. Four types of bonds are available.

Industrial Revenue Bonds: Municipal bonds payable solely from project revenues to finance private industrial development. The structure of IRB financing varies according to state law. The following states issue industrial revenue bonds:

California	Massachusetts	New Jersey
Connecticut	Michigan	New York
Delaware	Missouri	Ohio
Hawaii	Montana	Oregon
Illinois	Nebraska	Rhode Island
Maine	Nevada	Vermont
Maryland	New Hampshire	West Virginia

All states except Alaska, Rhode Island, New Jersey, Hawaii, and Connecticut permit localities within their borders to issue industrial revenue bonds.

General Obligation Bonds: Most are issued by state and local governments to finance public use facilities. Should default occur, the local or state government issuer must pay outstanding principal and interest from its general revenues. Missouri is the only state which issues general obligation bonds in conjunction with its economic development activities. Louisiana, Mississippi, Missouri, North Dakota, and Tennessee permit local governments to issue general obligation bonds as part of their economic development efforts.

<u>Umbrella Bonds</u>: A single issue of tax-exempt industrial bonds providing loan funds for several individual business projects. Most are directed toward small-business growth and expansion. Umbrella bonds are issued by:

Alaska	Michigan
Connecticut	Minnesota
Iowa	Missouri
Maine	Nebraska
Maryland	Nevada

<u>Industrial Revenue Bond Guarantees</u>: Guarantees commit the state authority administering the program to pay outstanding principal and interest on a bond issue in case of default by the issuing company. They are used to increase the marketability of the bonds. Industrial revenue bond guarantees are provided by:

Arkansas	New Jersey
Kentucky	New York
Maine	North Dakota
Maryland	Ohio
Massachusetts	Rhode Island
Missouri	

B. DIRECT STATE LOANS

Direct loans are used by the state to fill a gap in availability of financial capital from traditional private sector lenders. They are targeted toward specific industries, certain size companies, or minority/disadvantaged businesses. Direct state loans are offered by:

Alaska	Montana
California	New Jersey
Connecticut	New York
Florida	Ohio
Hawaii	Oklahoma
Illinois	Oregon
Indiana	Pennsylvania
Kentucky	Texas
Louisiana	Vermont
Minnesota	West Virginia

C. LOAN GUARANTEES

Loan guarantees are used to reduce the lenders' risk by leveraging private sector financing with guarantees of loans by private or governmental lenders. Usually, states guarantee only a portion of the loan. The following states provide loan guarantees:

California   Mississippi
Connecticut   Missouri
Indiana   New Hampshire
Louisiana   New Jersey
Maine   Ohio
Maryland   Vermont
Minnesota

D. STATE-FUNDED INTEREST SUBSIDIES

These subsidies are used to encourage private sector lenders to make loans to businesses at lower interest rates. Missouri is the only state which currently provides interest subsidies.

E. STATE-FUNDED OR CHARTERED EQUITY/VENTURE CAPITAL CORPORATIONS

This tool is used to develop small, innovative businesses by forming companies that provide venture capital for start-up financing. Small Business Investment Companies (SBICs) are the most frequently used structure. Equity/venture capital corporations are funded or chartered by the following states:

Alaska   Massachusetts
Connecticut   Michigan
Indiana   New York
Maine   Wisconsin

F. PRIVATELY SPONSORED DEVELOPMENT CREDIT CORPORATIONS

These credit corporations function as a publicly chartered, private development bank to provide medium-term working capital and loans for construction and expansion to new and existing businesses. They usually require that the firm has been turned down by one or more lenders. Loans rarely exceed $500,000 to $600,000. This development tool is used by:

Arkansas   Michigan
Florida   Missouri
Georgia   Montana
Iowa   Nebraska
Kansas   New Hampshire
Kentucky   New York
Maryland   North Dakota
Massachusetts   South Carolina

G. ENTERPRISE ZONES

Enterprise zones are designated economically distressed areas within which incentives are given to businesses which locate or expand there. Tax concessions are the major incentive used by states to encourage development of a stable economy and creation of jobs within the enterprise zone. Enterprise zones have been established in:

Connecticut	Maryland
Florida	Minnesota
Kansas	Missouri
Kentucky	Ohio
Louisiana	

H. CUSTOMIZED INDUSTRIAL TRAINING

Customized industrial training is used to reduce the initial costs of opening a new facility by providing a trained workforce. States can either design and administer the training, or they can provide a grant to companies to provide their own training. All states except Alaska, Arizona, Minnesota, Montana, New Hampshire, Maine, Oregon, Utah, Washington, Wisconsin, and Wyoming offer direct customized industrial training and/or grants to companies.

I. TAX INCENTIVES

Tax incentives are used to reduce a business's tax liability and to increase its chance of operating profitably. The state may refrain from levying a tax or may provide partial tax reductions. These reductions may include exemptions of activities or items from taxation, reductions of the base upon which the income tax is computed, subtraction of tax credits from the tax due to reduce actual tax payments, and abatement of property taxes for a specified period of time. The following is a list of the major areas in which tax exemptions, deductions, credits, or some other form of special treatment are given to businesses and the number of states offering such incentives.

1. <u>Business Inventory</u> - thirty-seven states, including Texas.

2. <u>Energy and Fuel Conservation Measures</u> - forty-two states, including Texas.

3. <u>Goods in Transit</u> - forty-three states, including Texas.

4. <u>Industrial Fuels and Raw Materials</u> - forty-three states. Texas does not offer this incentive.

5. <u>Industrial Machinery and Equipment</u> - forty-five states, including Texas.

6. <u>Investment Tax Credit</u> - twenty-three states. Texas does not offer this incentive.

7. <u>Job Creation Tax Credit</u> - nineteen states. Texas does not offer this incentive.

8. <u>Pollution Control Equipment</u> - forty-one states. Texas does not offer this incentive.

9. <u>Property Tax Abatement</u> - thirty-two states, including Texas.

10. <u>Research and Development</u> - The following states offer this incentive:

California	New York
Indiana	Rhode Island
Maine	Vermont
Maryland	Virginia
Massachusetts	Washington
Minnesota	West Virginia
New Jersey	Wisconsin

II. ECONOMIC DEVELOPMENT PROGRAMS OF SELECTED STATES

A. NORTHEAST

The two states chosen from the Northeast are Massachusetts and New York. High-technology industries in Massachusetts benefit from programs providing venture capital financing to early-stage, high-risk, technology-based companies. While 50 percent of the FY 1982 Massachusetts Commerce Department budget was designated for economic development, the state offers no assistance for small business and minority-owned business or research and development efforts. New York relies heavily on state-issued industrial revenue bonds for a variety of economic development needs. Unlike Massachusetts, New York provides extensive assistance to small business and minority-owned business and uses 100 percent of its state Commerce Department budget for economic development. Research and development aid is provided directly by state universities.

B. SOUTHEAST

Florida and North Carolina were chosen to represent economic development efforts in the Southeast. In Florida, privately sponsored development credit corporations in conjunction with direct state loans comprise the highest valued group of economic development tools. Enterprise zones have also been heavily promoted, with one hundred receiving certification as of December 1, 1982. Thirty-four percent of the FY 1982 Florida Commerce Department budget was used in economic development efforts. In North Carolina, only 7.79 percent of the FY 1982 state Commerce Department budget was designated for economic development, perhaps explaining the limited number of programs offered. The state basically provides locally issued industrial revenue bonds and customized industrial training with a focus on manufacturing firms. Research and development has been encouraged in recent years through state-provided research and the North Carolina Triangle Institute.

C. WEST

The two representative states from this region are Arizona and California. Similar to efforts made by Massachusetts, economic development programs in California emphasize the special needs of high-technology companies. These programs include worksite education and training for jobs in electronic and technical areas as well as a $2 million loan program for financing new product development. For FY 1983, the budget for economic development was $7.9 million, or 36 percent of the total state budget. Economic development efforts in Arizona are much more limited than those in California, consisting primarily of locally issued industrial revenue bonds. The state provides assistance for small business, but offers no programs to encourage minority-owned business or research and development. Arizona does have the Office of Economic Planning and Development, which is devoted exclusively to fostering economic growth within the state.

D. MIDWEST

Minnesota and Illinois were chosen as representatives of the Midwest. In Minnesota, a number of programs exist to aid expanding small businesses in the state, including locally issued industrial revenue mortgages, umbrella bonds, direct state loans, and a loan guarantee program known as the Minnesota Plan. In FY 1982, 50 percent of the state budget was used for economic development programs. Illinois relies on state-issued industrial revenue bonds for job creation, environmental control equipment, and medical care facilities. Localities may also issue industrial revenue bonds, while direct state loans are targeted for projects in areas of high unemployment. Ninety-nine percent of the FY 1982 budget for the Illinois Department of Commerce and Community Affairs was used for economic development programs in the state. Both Minnesota and Illinois are among the six states whose percentage of the budget used for economic development is extremely high.

E. COMPARISONS WITH TEXAS

Compared to efforts by Texas in economic development, these states provide a more diverse "menu" of programs to assist business. Texas relies solely on locally issued industrial revenue bonds, direct state loans targeted to communities in rural areas for industrial locations and expansion, and customized industrial training provided cooperatively between the Texas Economic Development Commission and local public education systems. Industrial revenue bonds are the most used program, with 242 issues totaling $950 million in 1982. No research and development assistance is provided by the state. Overall, the level of commitment to economic development by the State of Texas is relatively lower than the other states examined, despite Texas's consistently high standing in business climate surveys. The eight states will be examined below in greater detail.

Massachusetts

DIRECT FINANCIAL INCENTIVES

PROGRAM: Industrial Revenue Bonds - State Issued
PURPOSE: To provide lower-cost financing for private businesses to create jobs, revitalize the state's commercial centers, and strengthen the tax base of the state and local communities.
FOCUS: Must be used for the construction, acquisition, or improvement of plant and equipment located in the state; working capital and refinancing are not permitted.
VOLUME: 183 bonds approved in 1981 totaling $221,891,900.

PROGRAM: Industrial Revenue Bonds - Locally Issued
PURPOSE: To authorize municipalities to create industrial development financing authorities to issue industrial revenue bonds.
FOCUS: Same as above.
VOLUME: 243 projects were approved in 1981 totaling $297,321,500.

PROGRAM: Industrial Revenue Bond Guarantees
PURPOSE: To provide guarantees of all tax-exempt loans to younger or smaller companies unable to obtain long-term loans to finance plant and equipment purchases.
FOCUS: Must be secured by a first-mortgage lien on the new or improved plant or equipment to be financed. Projects must create or retain employment in the state that is substantially full-time and nonseasonal, paying 1.5 times the minimum wage.
VOLUME: Seven projects approved in 1981 totaling $6,504,331.

PROGRAM: State-funded or -chartered Equity/Venture Capital Corp.
PURPOSE: To provide venture capital financing to early-stage, high-risk, technology-based companies in the state through the Massachusetts Technology Development Corporation (MTDC). To create jobs and other benefits for residents of depressed areas of the state through the Massachusetts Community Development Finance Corporation (CDFC).
FOCUS: MTDC provides financing on a coventure basis with investors from the private sector up to $500,000. CDFC funds are invested in conjunction with locally based community development corporations (CDCs) which act in a partnership with companies seeking to expand or locate in the community represented by the CDC.
VOLUME: In 1982, MTDC approved loans totaling $625,000 and capital investments totaling $550,000. Since 1975, CDFC has committed $5,102,000 in investment funds.

PROGRAM: Privately Sponsored Development Credit Corporations

PURPOSE: The Massachusetts Business Development Corporation (MBDC) pools money from financial institutions to provide medium- and long-term loans to promising firms that do not qualify for loans from conventional lenders. The Massachusetts Capital Resource Company (MCRC) offers high-risk capital from Massachusetts-based life insurance companies to promote growth in Massachusetts' manufacturing and industrial operations.

FOCUS: MBDC makes loans for working capital, new equipment or energy conservation, leveraged buyouts when a significant job loss is at stake, second mortgages, and government-guaranteed loans. MCRC makes long-term unsecured loans to companies rejected by lending institutions, offers subordinated loans to rapidly growing companies, and provides growth capital to young firms needing capital infusions.

VOLUME: Since 1953, MBDC has approved $95,815,000 in loans. MCRC is capitalized at $100 million, with sixteen companies receiving $16.4 million in 1981.

PROGRAM: Customized Industrial Training
PURPOSE: Bay State Skills Corporation (BSSC) matches nonprofit and private sector training resources with high-demand occupations in the state. The state provides 50 percent of the training cost, and the company is expected to contribute 50 percent.

VOLUME: Established in 1981 with $8 million appropriation. Since then, 71 training programs approved for 5,562 trainees at cost of $5 million.

BASIC BUSINESS TAXES

CORPORATE INCOME TAX: Corporations are classified as tangible property corporations or intangible property corporations. Tangible corporation rates equal $7 per $1,000 of taxable tangible property value plus 8 1/3 percent of taxable net income. Intangible property corporations are taxed at rate of $7 per $1,000 taxable net worth plus 8 1/3 percent of taxable net income.

SALES AND USE TAXES: 5 percent sales tax plus 5 percent tax on transfer of possession by rental or lease.

PROPERTY TAX: Property taxes are based on four classifications: residential, open space, commercial, and industrial. Since 1980, total taxes levied on property cannot exceed 2.5 percent of property's full and fair cash value.

TAX EXEMPTIONS, DEDUCTIONS, CREDITS, AND SPECIAL TREATMENT

PROGRAM: Job Creation Tax Credits
PURPOSE: To target nine classifications of workers. To encourage corporations to locate in urban municipalities and to hire employees who live in an "eligible section of substantial poverty."

PROGRAM: Investment Tax Creation
PURPOSE: To allow manufacturing corporations, agricultural/fishing enterprises, and research and development corporations to benefit from 3 percent credit against state excise tax on the cost of depreciable property purchased during the year.

PROGRAM: Property Tax Abatement
PURPOSE: To exempt realty owned by economic development corporations that exist to expand jobs from property taxation for seven years.

PROGRAM: Business Inventory
PURPOSE: To exempt business inventories for manufacturing and non-manufacturing companies from property taxation.

PROGRAM: Goods in Transit
PURPOSE: To exempt export sales of tangible personal property shipped to purchasers in foreign countries from sales or use taxation.

PROGRAM: Research and Development
PURPOSE: To exempt from sales and use taxation all machinery and replacement parts used in corporations engaged in research and development.

PROGRAM: Pollution Control Equipment
PURPOSE: To exempt from corporate income tax the cost of pollution control facilities.

PROGRAM: Industrial Machinery and Equipment
PURPOSE: To exempt from sales, use, and property taxation certain categories of machinery.

PROGRAM: Industrial Fuels and Raw Materials
PURPOSE: To exempt from sales and use taxes certain categories of fuels and raw materials.

PROGRAM: Energy and Fuel Conservation Measures
PURPOSE: To exempt from income and property (ten years) taxation solar- or wind-powered systems.

New York

DIRECT FINANCIAL INCENTIVES

PROGRAM: Industrial Revenue Bonds - State Issued
PURPOSE: (a) To alleviate unemployment and promote economic and urban development in project areas through the issuance of tax-exempt industrial revenue bonds; (b) to provide lease financing to medium and large companies for large-scale industrial or commercial development projects that cannot be completely financed through IRB programs because of federal limits on project size; and (c) to assist municipalities and private industry in complying with state and federal environmental standards through the issuance of special purpose, tax-exempt pollution control revenue bonds against the credit of the borrowing company.
FOCUS: Bond proceeds may be used for (a) construction, expansion, or renovation of an industrial plant, including purchase and installation of equipment; (b) projects approaching or exceeding $10 million or smaller projects that are part of a larger, multiyear development program in a single geographic area; and (c) projects with no loan limit and a minimum bond amount of $500,000.

VOLUME: In 1982, (a) one bond issue totaling $5 million; (b) seven projects totaling $35 million; and (c) two bond issues totaling $35.1 million.

PROGRAM: Industrial Revenue Bonds - Locally Issued
PURPOSE: To finance business and industrial projects through bonds issued by local industrial development agencies (IDAs).
FOCUS: Counties, cities, towns, villages, and Indian reservations are eligible to establish IDAs.
VOLUME: In 1981, 295 bond issues totaling $528,412,000.

PROGRAM: Umbrella Bonds
PURPOSE: To stimulate the expansion of private sector employment through the authorization of loans for industrial development/expansion by the Job Development Authority (JDA).
FOCUS: Priority is given to projects that revitalize distressed localities, especially those that involve reuse, reconstruction, or new construction of plants and buildings.
VOLUME: In 1981, JDA participated in 128 loans totaling $92.5 million.

PROGRAM: Industrial Revenue Bond Guarantees
PURPOSE: To assist small- or medium-size industrial and commercial businesses and developers in obtaining lower-cost, tax-exempt financing by guaranteeing a portion of industrial revenue bond issues.
FOCUS: Companies that have experienced good earnings growth and are in good financial condition but whose credit is not strong enough to secure needed permanent financing.
VOLUME: In 1982, two bond issues totaling $5 million.

PROGRAM: Direct State Loans
PURPOSE: To provide direct loans to new businesses in distressed rural communities for environmentally sound development projects.
FOCUS: Communities in counties not within SMSAs or in counties with fewer than 150 persons per square mile.
VOLUME: Program established in 1982 with a capital base of $800,000. No projects funded to date.

PROGRAM: State-Funded or -Chartered Equity/Venture Capital Corporations
PURPOSE: To meet the capital financing needs of small businesses in distressed areas through equity investment.
FOCUS: Projects which (1) are start-ups or expansions for small business; (2) will provide neighborhood services near existing housing projects lacking services; (3) are necessary to ensure sufficient occupancy of a retail structure; or (4) require security for tax-exempt industrial revenue bonds.
VOLUME: In 1982, twenty-seven projects totaling $47.5 million.

PROGRAM: Privately Sponsored Development Credit Corporations
PURPOSE: To share the risk of loaning to firms seeking to expand in the state by pooling the money of New York financial institutions.
FOCUS: Companies whose capital requirements may be just beyond the limitations of conventional bond financing.
VOLUME: In 1982, fourteen loans totaling $4,108,000.

PROGRAM: Customized Industrial Training
PURPOSE: To provide reimbursement to private employers for costs associated with hiring and training economically disadvantaged workers in New York City.
FOCUS: Trainees and firms must reside in New York City.
VOLUME: In 1982, 32 companies participated, and 166 trainees were involved. Annual budget is $409,000.

BASIC BUSINESS TAXES

CORPORATE INCOME TAX: All domestic and foreign corporations are subject to an annual franchise tax for the privilege of employing capital, doing business, owning or leasing property, or maintaining an office in the state. Four different computation methods are used.
SALES AND USE TAXES: Four percent sales tax is levied on retail sales. Some cities impose additional taxes ranging from 1 to 4 percent.
PROPERTY TAX: All real property subject to taxation at local level. Tangible and intangible personal property are exempt from taxation.

TAX EXEMPTIONS, DEDUCTIONS, CREDITS, AND SPECIAL TREATMENT

PROGRAM: Job Creation Tax Credit
PURPOSE: To grant corporations a credit equal to 50 percent of the new capital investment amount against the corporate franchise tax payable in each of three years succeeding the year of the original investment.

PROGRAM: Investment Tax Credit
PURPOSE: To provide a credit against corporate franchise tax at a percentage of new capital investment in buildings and/or depreciable tangible property used for manufacturing, processing, assembling, and production.

PROGRAM: Property Tax Abatement
PURPOSE: To exempt from property taxation industrial/commercial facilities financed by a local industrial development agency, some industrial/commercial construction in New York City, and industrial/commercial facilities outside of New York City at a cost of more than $10,000.

PROGRAM: Research and Development
PURPOSE: To exempt from sales and use taxation property directly consumed or used in research and development.

PROGRAM: Pollution Control Equipment
PURPOSE: To exempt from sales and use taxes pollution control facilities, machinery, and agents.

PROGRAM: Industrial Machinery and Equipment
PURPOSE: To exempt from sales and use taxes certain categories of machinery.

PROGRAM: Industrial Fuel and Raw Materials

PURPOSE: To exempt from sales and use tax ingredients consumed in manufacturing, mining, agriculture, and research; building parts; packaging materials; fuel for aircraft; and supplies and fuel for commercial vessels.

PROGRAM: Energy and Fuel Conservation
PURPOSE: To exempt from property taxation solar- or wind-energy-producing equipment installed prior to July 1, 1988.

PROGRAM: Businesses in Low-Income Areas
PURPOSE: To provide a credit against the corporation franchise tax for businesses operating a facility in low-income areas.

Florida

DIRECT FINANCIAL INCENTIVES

PROGRAM: Industrial Revenue Bonds
PURPOSE: To provide industrial revenue bonds for eligible enterprises.
FOCUS: Cities, counties, industrial development authorities, and special districts may issue bonds for projects located within and outside the bonding authority's jurisdiction.
VOLUME: In 1982, 148 bond issues totaling $525,410,856.

PROGRAM: Direct State Loans
PURPOSE: To provide funds to local community development corporations, which in turn make loans to private businesses.
FOCUS: Monies can be used by CDCs to establish new businesses, to provide financial assistance to existing businesses, and to aid economic development in designated enterprise zones.
VOLUME: In 1982, five loans totaling $1.6 million.

PROGRAM: Privately Sponsored Development Credit Corporations
PURPOSE: To make loans for industrial purposes in Florida through the Florida Industrial Development Corporation.
FOCUS: Loans can be used for working capital or capital projects. Amounts can range from $75,000 to $500,000.
VOLUME: In 1981, nine loans totaling $1.8 million.

PROGRAM: Enterprise Zones
PURPOSE: To provide tax relief and other assistance to eligible businesses within designated enterprise zones.
FOCUS: Areas with high percentages of substandard housing units, low per capita income, high percentages of population with incomes below poverty level, and a high unemployment rate.
VOLUME: As of December 1, 1982, one hundred enterprise zones had been certified.

PROGRAM: Customized Industrial Training
PURPOSE: To provide on-the-job-training and shop instruction to ensure that new workers are ready when a new facility opens.
FOCUS: Training for skilled and semiskilled operations requiring learning time of one year or less.

VOLUME: In 1980 and 1981, eighty-five programs were conducted.

BASIC BUSINESS TAXES

CORPORATE INCOME TAX: Income tax on corporations and franchise tax on banks and savings associations. Rate is five percent of net income with a $5,000 exemption.
SALES AND USE TAXES: Five percent rate on retail sale. Use tax is 5 percent on price of each item brought into Florida.
PROPERTY TAX: Both real and tangible personal property are subject to taxation.

TAX EXEMPTIONS, DEDUCTIONS, CREDITS, AND SPECIAL TREATMENT

PROGRAM: Job Creation Tax Credit
PURPOSE: To provide a credit against corporate income taxes for businesses creating new jobs for residents of enterprise zones.

PROGRAM: Investment Tax Credit
PURPOSE: To provide income tax credit of up to $50,000 to businesses with facilities in enterprise zone. To provide credit against income taxes of 50 percent of the amount of contributions by businesses to community improvement projects.

PROGRAM: Property Tax Abatement
PURPOSE: To provide cities and counties with the option of granting a ten-year exemption from property taxes to new and expanding businesses.

PROGRAM: Business Inventory
PURPOSE: All business inventories are exempt from property taxation.

PROGRAM: Goods in Transit
PURPOSE: To exempt from property tax for 180 days goods in transit.

PROGRAM: Pollution Control Equipment
PURPOSE: To assess pollution control equipment at salvage value rather than fair market value.

PROGRAM: Industrial Machinery and Equipment
PURPOSE: To exempt from sales and use taxes new or expanding businesses, electrical or steam energy production, aircraft, vessels, and fuels.

PROGRAM: Other Exemptions
PURPOSE: No personal income tax; no corporate income tax on foreign source income.

North Carolina

DIRECT FINANCIAL INCENTIVES

PROGRAM: Industrial Revenue Bonds - Locally Issued
PURPOSE: To authorize counties to establish authorities to issue industrial revenue bonds for tax-exempt financing for private businesses.
FOCUS: Proposed new facilities must create new jobs at wages above the average manufacturing wage paid in that county or at least 10 percent above the average manufacturing wage in the state, and be environmentally sound.
VOLUME: In 1981, 128 bond issues totaling $399,656,000.

PROGRAM: Customized Industrial Training
PURPOSE: To provide training for new and expanding industries as well as upgrading or retraining existing employees.
FOCUS: Programs carried out by fifty-eight community colleges and technical institutes. Primary focus on manufacturing firms.
VOLUME: In 1982, 80 companies received training for 5,819 employees. Annual budget was $2,223,848.

BASIC BUSINESS TAXES

CORPORATE INCOME TAX: Six percent on portion of net income allocable to the state.
SALES AND USE TAXES: Retail sales taxed at 3 percent.
PROPERTY TAX: Levied by local authorities, not state.

TAX EXEMPTIONS, DEDUCTIONS, AND CREDITS

PROGRAM: Business Inventory
PURPOSE: To reduce the impact of property tax on manufacturers' inventories, the state allows a credit against the corporate income tax for such taxes paid on inventories of raw materials and goods in the process of manufacture that are excessive.

PROGRAM: Goods in Transit
PURPOSE: To exempt from sales and use taxes exported property, motor vehicles, property awaiting shipment, and imported property.

PROGRAM: Pollution Control Equipment
PURPOSE: To allow property used to reduce pollution to amortize the cost over sixty months for corporate income tax purposes.

PROGRAM: Industrial Machinery and Equipment
PURPOSE: To exempt from sales and use taxation boats and supplies purchased by commercial fishermen. To reduce sales and use taxes to 1 percent for manufacturing equipment (including that purchased by contractors), telephone and telegraph company equipment, laundry and dry cleaning equipment, freezer locker equipment, and radio and television station equipment.

PROGRAM: Industrial Fuels and Raw Materials
PURPOSE: To exempt from sales and use taxation property incorporated into a manufactured product; products from mines, forests, and farms; agricultural products for manufactures; fuel and property for ocean-going

vessels; and packing and shipping materials. To reduce to 1 percent the sales and use tax on coal, coke, fuel oil, laundry fuel, and packing supplies for freezer locker plants. To exempt from property tax nuclear materials, cargo containers, and motor vehicle chassis.

PROGRAM: Energy and Fuel Conservation Measures
PURPOSE: To provide a corporate income tax credit for a portion of costs for installation of solar heating, cooling, and hot water systems; wind energy devices; methane gas facilities; and solar cooling or heating systems.

California

DIRECT FINANCIAL INCENTIVES

PROGRAM: Industrial Revenue Bonds - State Issued
PURPOSE: To issue industrial revenue bonds for pollution control purposes.
FOCUS: Bond proceeds can be used to finance the entire cost of a pollution control project, including land and buildings, as well as equipment installation, engineering, and professional and financial expenses.
VOLUME: In 1982, $217,305,000 in bonds issued to twenty-eight firms.

PROGRAM: Industrial Revenue Bonds - Locally Issued
PURPOSE: To allow cities and counties to issue IRBs to finance land acquisition, building construction, equipment purchases, fees, and other project costs.
FOCUS: Industrial activities and projects for energy development.
VOLUME: In 1982, eighteen IRBs totaling $97,350,000.

PROGRAM: Direct State Loans
PURPOSE: To provide a revolving fund for loans to small businesses for working capital and fixed assets.
FOCUS: Businesses located in certain distressed areas.
VOLUME: In 1981, twelve loans totaling $3.4 million.

PROGRAM: Loan Guarantees
PURPOSE: To provide loan guarantees for small businesses.
FOCUS: Maximum loan guarantee of $350,000.
VOLUME: In 1982, forty-one guarantees totaling $5,534,500.

PROGRAM: Customized Industrial Training
PURPOSE: To design and operate training programs for specific skills in which there are shortages in California.
FOCUS: Targeted toward economically disadvantaged and handicapped workers with obsolete skills, minorities, displaced workers, and veterans.
VOLUME: In 1982, 95 active programs for 6,835 trainees and 344 employers.

BASIC BUSINESS TAXES

CORPORATE INCOME TAXES: 9.6 percent of taxable income.
SALES AND USE TAXES: 4.75 percent on retail goods.
PROPERTY TAX: No tax levied by state; rates vary by locality.

TAX EXEMPTIONS, DEDUCTIONS, CREDITS, AND SPECIAL TREATMENT

PROGRAM: Job Creation Tax Credit
PURPOSE: To allow a credit for banks and corporations equal to 10 percent of wages paid in first two years of employment of disadvantaged employee.

PROGRAM: Business Inventory
PURPOSE: To exempt business inventories from property tax.

PROGRAM: Goods in Transit
PURPOSE: To exempt from sales tax property shipped outside state by retailer or common carrier, property purchased for export, and cargo containers used outside state.

PROGRAM: Research and Development
PURPOSE: Research and development expenses are deductible in determining net taxable income.

PROGRAM: Pollution Control Equipment
PURPOSE: To allow a credit against corporate income tax liability of 20 percent of cost of installing pollution control equipment by metal finishers.

PROGRAM: Industrial Machinery and Equipment
PURPOSE: To exempt from sales and use taxes commercial watercraft and vessels, trucks, trailers, and aircraft used out of state, and tangible personal property purchased by foreign air carriers for use outside state.

PROGRAM: Industrial Fuels and Raw Materials
PURPOSE: To exempt from sales and use taxes water, gas, electricity, containers, raw material, and aircraft fuel.

PROGRAM: Energy and Fuel Conservation Measures
PURPOSE: To allow deductions for energy conservation and solar system expenses over a thirty-six-month period. To allow a corporate income tax credit for 20 percent of cost incurred for purchase/lease of commuting vehicles as part of a ride-share program.

Arizona

DIRECT FINANCIAL INCENTIVES

PROGRAM: Industrial Revenue Bonds - Locally Issued

PURPOSE: To allow cities and counties to establish Industrial Development Authorities or Pollution Control Authorities for the purpose of issuing IRBs.
FOCUS: Pollution control purposes, many other uses.
VOLUME: In 1982, sixty bonds totaling $679,824,219.

BASIC BUSINESS TAXES

CORPORATE INCOME TAX: Ranges from 2.5 percent to 10.5 percent on net taxable income.
SALES AND USE TAXES: 4 percent of gross income for most industries; 2.5 percent for mining industries. Sales tax rate of 4 percent.
PROPERTY TAX: Commercial/industrial property taxed at 25 percent of full market value, all others by classification system.

TAX EXEMPTIONS, DEDUCTIONS, CREDITS, AND SPECIAL TREATMENT

PROGRAM: Business Inventory
PURPOSE: To exempt manufacturers' and merchants' inventories from taxation.

PROGRAM: Goods in Transit
PURPOSE: To exempt property in transit from taxation.

PROGRAM: Pollution Control Equipment
PURPOSE: To amortize over a sixty-month period cost of pollution control devices.

PROGRAM: Industrial Machinery and Equipment
PURPOSE: To exempt these from sales tax.

PROGRAM: Energy and Fuel Conservation Measures
PURPOSE: To allow corporations to take either a deduction against gross income for cost of purchase and installation of solar energy devices or a credit against tax liability for corporate income tax purposes.

Minnesota

DIRECT FINANCIAL INCENTIVES

    PROGRAM: Industrial Revenue Bonds - Locally Issued
    PURPOSE: To allow counties, municipalities, redevelopment agencies, and port authorities to issue IRBs.
    FOCUS: Eligible projects include industrial, commercial, tourism, health care facilities, harbor development, electric power development, telephone systems, and pollution control facilities.
    VOLUME: In 1981, 413 bonds totaling $949,489,700. In 1982, 266 bonds totaling $669,716,150.

    PROGRAM: Industrial Revenue Mortgages - Locally Issued
    PURPOSE: To provide municipalities an alternative to IRBs in providing reduced interest financing to private companies.
    FOCUS: Same as above.
    VOLUME: Program authorized by legislature. No mortgages to date.

    PROGRAM: Umbrella Bonds
    PURPOSE: To provide low-interest loans to small businesses for fixed asset financing by issuing tax-exempt industrial revenue bonds.
    FOCUS: Only for-profit businesses are eligible. Excluded activities include banks and financial services, real estate brokerages, legal/medical/accounting/engineering and other professional consulting services, recreation facilities, and food and beverage service facilities.
    VOLUME: In 1981, five loans totaling $835,000.

    PROGRAM: Direct State Loans
    PURPOSE: (a) To provide low-interest financing to new or expanding small businesses in the state; (b) to provide Minnesota-based Indians resources to start or expand a business; and (c) to provide low-interest loans to small manufacturing firms located in distressed areas in the state.
    FOCUS: (a) Projects which increase number of jobs created and ensure high likelihood of repayment; (b) long-term, fixed asset financing (not available for working capital or to repay/consolidate existing debt); and (c) industrial manufacturing firms that qualify as small under the U.S. SBA.
    VOLUME: (a) In 1982, four loans totaling $500,000; (b) in 1980-81, four loans totaling $67,500; (c) in 1981, one loan for $75,000.

    PROGRAM: Loan Guarantees
    PURPOSE: Also known as "The Minnesota Plan." Allows long-term, fixed-rate financing to small businesses as alternative to umbrella bond program.
    FOCUS: Ability to lock in fixed-rate financing over a fifteen- to twenty-year period.
    VOLUME: Became effective in 1982 with $30 million bond issues. No figures available.

    PROGRAM: Enterprise Zones

PURPOSE: To encourage business growth in areas characterized by high levels of poverty and unemployment, population erosion, and decaying infrastructure.
FOCUS: Businesses which manufacture or process goods by physical change or provide office, research and development, warehousing, ports, or other facilities within the zone.
VOLUME: Zones operable in July 1983. No figures available.

BASIC BUSINESS TAXES
CORPORATE INCOME TAX: 9 percent on first $15,000 of taxable income, 12 percent on remaining income. Two methods of allocating allowed for corporations whose income is between in-state and out-of-state sources.
SALES AND USE TAXES: 5 percent sales tax.
PROPERTY TAXES: Most assessed value of commercial and industrial property is 43 percent of market value, to which mill rate is applied to obtain property tax. Mill rates are established by local cities, counties, school districts, and special tax districts.

TAX EXEMPTIONS, DEDUCTIONS, CREDITS, AND SPECIAL TREATMENT

PROGRAM: Property Tax Abatement
PURPOSE: To allow a deferral of property tax in initial stages of development in development districts, industrial development districts, and redevelopment projects.

PROGRAM: Business Inventory
PURPOSE: To exempt all inventories from property tax.

PROGRAM: Goods in Transit
PURPOSE: To exempt from sales tax all sales of property delivered outside the state or sold to a common carrier.

PROGRAM: Research and Development
PURPOSE: To grant a deduction from gross income for research and experimental expenses.

PROGRAM: Pollution Control Equipment
PURPOSE: To exempt all property used for pollution control (except waste disposal land) from property tax. To grant a corporate income tax credit of 5 percent of cost of pollution control equipment in year of purchase.

PROGRAM: Industrial Machinery and Equipment
PURPOSE: To allow exemption from sales and use taxation of common carriers' rolling stock, commercial aircraft, flight equipment, and telephone equipment.

PROGRAM: Industrial Fuels and Raw Materials
PURPOSE: To exempt from sales and use tax all materials consumed in production of personal property for retail sale, petroleum products, raw materials, and containers.

PROGRAM: Energy and Fuel Conservation

PURPOSE: To reduce property tax for owners installing solar, wind, or methane gas systems before 1984.

Illinois

DIRECT FINANCIAL INCENTIVES

PROGRAM: Industrial Revenue Bonds - State Issued
PURPOSE: (a) To create jobs in areas of substantial and persistent labor supplies through tax-exempt IRBs; (b) to provide financing for acquisition or construction of environmental control facilities; and (c) to provide high-quality medical care at low cost to for-profit nursing homes.
FOCUS: (a) Location in areas of high unemployment; (b) any firm intending to obtain air, water, or solid waste facilities for pollution control; and (c) for-profit nursing homes and not-for-profit health care institutions.
VOLUME: (a) In 1981, sixteen projects creating 2,053 jobs totaling $70,325,000; (b) in 1981, thirteen companies received $138,202,000; and (c) in 1982, fourteen bonds totaled $292,697,083.

PROGRAM: Industrial Revenue Bonds - Locally Issued
PURPOSE: To allow home rule municipalities, non-home rule special municipalities and counties, airport authorities, and special districts to issue economic development revenue bonds.
FOCUS: Projects which stimulate private investment in projects promoting local economic development.
VOLUME: In 1981, no bond issues.

PROGRAM: Direct State Loans
PURPOSE: To encourage economic development by assisting manufacturing or other industrial projects that create or retain jobs in eligible designated areas.
FOCUS: Manufacturing or industrial projects located in areas of high unemployment.
VOLUME: In 1981, fourteen projects totaling $968,698.

PROGRAM: Customized Industrial Training
PURPOSE: (a) To provide grants to firms to cover a portion of salaries of workers being trained; and (b) to provide funds to public school districts and community colleges to conduct initial high-impact training program.
FOCUS: (a) New and existing firms; and (b) to meet the training needs of business establishments locating in communities within the state and local firms expanding in current location.
VOLUME: (a) In 1982, 27 firms with 2,326 trainees and annual budgets of $1.4 million; and (b) in 1981, 30 firms received training assistance on first-come, first-served basis. Budget for 1981 was $750,000.

BASIC BUSINESS TAXES

CORPORATE INCOME TAX: 4 percent on corporate net income.
SALES AND USE TAX: 4 percent for both taxes.
PROPERTY TAX: Property is assessed and equalized at one-third of actual value.

TAX EXEMPTION, DEDUCTIONS, CREDITS, AND SPECIAL TREATMENT

PROGRAM: Investment Tax Credit
PURPOSE: To provide a credit against corporate income tax to increase investment in capital equipment.

PROGRAM: Property Tax Abatement
PURPOSE: To provide local tax districts with the capability to abate any portion of the district's taxes applying to industrial firms newly located within Illinois or expanding an existing facility.

PROGRAM: Goods in Transit
PURPOSE: To exempt from use tax goods stored in transit and building materials for use outside state.

PROGRAM: Pollution Control Equipment
PURPOSE: To exempt from sales and use tax the sale, use, or transfer of pollution control facilities. To exempt from property taxation water- and air-pollution control equipment.

PROGRAM: Industrial Machinery and Equipment
PURPOSE: To exempt from sales and use tax manufacturers' and graphic arts machinery and equipment, carriers' interstate rolling stock, and motor vehicles used for rental.

PROGRAM: Industrial Fuels and Raw Materials
PURPOSE: To exempt from sales tax watercraft fuel, newsprint and ink, and raw materials and component parts incorporated into tangible personal property.

PROGRAM: Energy and Fuel Conservation Measures
PURPOSE: To exempt from use taxes devices fueled by low sulphur dioxide emission coal. To allow a special valuation property tax on newly installed solar energy heating and cooling systems.

APPENDIX II: THE ROLE OF TEXAS STATE GOVERNMENT IN THE ADMINISTRATION OF FEDERAL PROGRAMS IN URBAN ECONOMIC DEVELOPMENT

In addition to the various state and local efforts in local economic development discussed in this report, there are several federal programs that offer various types of assistance to Texas state and local governments. The purpose of this appendix is to delineate the eight most important programs which make federal aid available to cities for economic development purposes: General Revenue Sharing, Urban Development Action Grants, Community Development Block Grant Entitlements, the Job Training Partnership Act, Public Housing, Urban Mass Transit, Wastewater Construction, and Economic Development Administration programs.

A. GENERAL REVENUE SHARING

The objective of General Revenue Sharing is to provide financial assistance to general purpose local governments. Based on a formula including population, per capita income, the federal individual income tax liability, taxes, transfers, and other variables, funds are automatically allocated to eligible governments. The money is provided directly to the locality; no state agency is responsible for the pass-through of any funds.

The recipient government may use the funds for any purpose which is a legal use of its own-source revenues. Any person, group, or agency may seek such funds from the recipient local government.(1) The federal agency administering this program is the Department of the Treasury, which has supplied approximately $247 million to Texas cities and counties in FY 1982.(2)

B. URBAN DEVELOPMENT ACTION GRANTS (UDAGs)

The objective of UDAGs is to assist severely distressed cities and/or pockets of poverty in alleviating economic deterioration through public and private investment in specific projects. These investments are intended to strengthen the economic, employment, and tax bases of these cities. UDAG awards are made on a project-by-project basis. Proposals for projects to alleviate pockets of poverty which originate from local governments in collaboration with private investors are considered separately from those submitted by distressed cities and urban counties. The primary criterion for each category is the comparative degree of physical and economic distress among applicants.

Projects which include financial assistance from the state or other public entities receive more favorable consideration than those which do not. No activity will be funded unless there is a firm commitment of private resources to the proposed project. Federal assistance is provided to discrete projects which can be completed in approximately four years.

No assistance may be provided for projects intended to facilitate the relocation of industrial or commercial plants or facilities unless the Secretary of Housing and Urban Development finds that such relocation does not significantly and adversely affect the unemployment level or economic base of the area from which the plant or facility is to be moved. UDAGs provide funds directly from the federal Department of Housing and Urban Development to the recipients, rather than passing the money through a state agency.(3)

Eight projects in Texas received UDAG funding in 1983. The federal contribution to these projects varied from $110,000 in Pottsboro to $3.5 million in Ft. Worth.(4) The average small-city grant for FY 1982 was $981,000, and the average large-city grant for the same year was $2 million.(5) Texas received $8.475 million in UDAG grants in 1983, which was 1.5 percent of the total UDAG awards made in that year.(6)

C. COMMUNITY DEVELOPMENT BLOCK GRANTS (CDBGs)

The primary objective of CDBGs is to develop viable urban communities by providing decent housing and a suitable living environment and by expanding economic opportunities, principally for persons of low and moderate income. The entitlement component of the program distributes funds by formula among urban jurisdictions. These grants are based upon the greater of two formula amounts. One formula uses data on poverty, population, and overcrowded housing, while the other uses data on housing built before 1940, poverty, and growth lag in population.

Eligible economic development activities under the program fall into three basic categories: site development, business development, and planning and administrative services. Site development includes the acquisition of real property and the acquisition, construction, or rehabilitation of specified public, commercial, and industrial facilities. The business development category allows cities to fund nonprofit organizations which provide direct assistance to business in the area, and to finance private, for-profit entities if such assistance furthers local economic development. The planning and administrative services category may only receive 20 percent of a city's block grant for activities such as comprehensive economic development planning and individual project planning, and reasonable costs for the development of a management planning capacity.(7)

The federal administrative agency for the CDBG program is the Department of Housing and Urban Development. The Community Development Division of the Texas Department of Community Affairs (TDCA) is the state agency responsible for the pass-through of the funds. Texas received approximately $216 million from this entitlement in FY 1982.(8) TDCA also administers the nonentitlement portion--the small-cities program discussed in Chapter 3.

D. JOB TRAINING PARTNERSHIP ACT

This program, which is a important form of federal aid to cities, is fully described in Chapter 3 of the text of this report.

E. MASS TRANSIT

Federal urban mass transit system funding and assistance comes primarily from the U.S. Department of Transportation's Urban Mass Transportation Administration. This federal agency assists in the development of mass transportation facilities, equipment, techniques, and methods. In addition, the agency is involved in the planning and establishment of areawide urban mass transportation systems and provides assistance to state and local governments in financing such systems.(9) In FY 1981, the State of Texas received approximately $34 million in operating assistance funds and $32.6 million for capital development expenditures. These funds were then passed on to localities in the state. The federal funds for capital expenditures accounted for about 95 percent of the state's total capital funds. The federal operating funds accounted for about 19 percent of total state operating revenues. During that same year, federal commitments to the state totaled approximately $70.7 million, of which $34 million was for operating expenses, $33 million for capital expenses, and $3.7 million for planning.(10)

F. ECONOMIC DEVELOPMENT ADMINISTRATION (EDA)

This federal agency has the responsibility of promoting long-range economic development of areas with severe poverty and unemployment problems. The agency also assists in the development of public facilities and private enterprises to help create new, permanent jobs.(11) In 1983, Texas was the recipient of fifty-one EDA projects which totaled $12.4 million in federal funds. The largest programs were public works projects and business loans. This agency also provides project grants for state and local economic development planning organizations.(12)

G. WASTEWATER CONSTRUCTION GRANTS

Administered through the Texas Department of Water Resources, this federal program is part of the activity of the Environmental Protection Agency (EPA). The EPA develops national water programs, technical policies, and regulations for water-pollution control and water supply. It also is involved in the management and operation of wastewater activities.(13) For FY 1983, the federal government provided the State of Texas $92.9 million for wastewater construction out of its $2.4 billion budget for this purpose.(14)

H. PUBLIC HOUSING

The U.S. Department of Housing and Urban Development administers federal public housing programs through its Texas regional offices. The HUD division associated with the programs is the Community Planning and Development Office. It is responsible for the development of viable urban communities, principally for moderate- and low-income communities. The specific purposes include elimination of slums and urban blight, funding and management of increased low- and moderate-income housing, improvement of health conditions, conservation of existing housing, and improvement of public services. The funding mechanisms used are entitlement grants, formula grants, and project grants to localities.(15) Total expenditures for public housing in the state of Texas for FY 1982 were approximately $197 million.(16)

ENDNOTES

1. *1983 Catalogue of Federal Domestic Assistance,* (Washington, D.C.: Government Printing Office, 1983), pp. 529-30.

2. Interview with Frank Sturzel, Executive Director, Texas Municipal League, Austin, March 1, 1984.

3. *1983 Catalogue,* pp. 363-65.

4. Interview with Jim Legrotte, Sr., Economic Development Specialist, Region 6 HUD Office, Austin, March 5, 1984.

5. *1983 Catalogue,* pp. 363-65.

6. Interview with Jim Legrotte, March 5, 1984.

7. *1983 Catalogue,* pp. 360-61.

8. Interview with Frank Sturzel, March 1, 1984.

9. *1983 Catalogue,* pp. 502-10.

10. State of Texas, State Department of Highways and Public Transportation, *1981 Texas Transit Statistics* (Austin, Tex., 1983), pp. 9-15.

11. *1983 Catalogue,* pp. 95-101.

12. Interview with Clara Seay, Assistant to Regional Representative of the Economic Development Administration, Austin, Texas, April 24, 1984.

13. *1983 Catalogue,* pp. 701-8.

14. Interview with Bob Klinker, Permits Division, Wastewater Division, Texas Department of Water Resources, Austin, Texas, April 24, 1984.

15. *1983 Catalogue,* pp. 365-67.

16. Interview with Frank Sturzel, March 1, 1984.

BIBLIOGRAPHY

Advisory Commission on Intergovernmental Relations. The Intergovernmental Grant System as Seen by Local, State, and Federal Officials. Vol. A-54. Washington, D.C., March 1977.

_____. Significant Features of Fiscal Federalism, 1976-1977. Vol. 2. Washington, D.C., 1977.

_____. State Aid to Local Government. Washington, D.C., April 1969.

_____. The States and Intergovernmental Aids--The Intergovernmental Grant System: An Assessment and Proposed Policies. Vol. A-59. Washington, D.C., February 1977.

Advisory Council for Technical-Vocational Education in Texas. Vocational Education in Texas-Unified Report to the State Board for Vocational Education: Governor of Texas, State Legislature. Austin, December 1982.

Advisory Council on Intergovernmental Relations. Block Grants: A Comparative Analysis. Washington, D.C., October 1977.

Ady, Robert M. "Shifting Factors in Plant Location." Industrial Development 150, no. 6 (June 1981): 15.

Alexandrides, C. G. The Case For Export Development of States: A Comparative Analysis with Recommendations. Atlanta: Southern Consortium for International Education, 1982.

American Gas Association Inc. Gas Facts. Arlington, Va., 1982.

Anderson, James, Richard Murray, and Edward Farley. Texas Politics: An Introduction. New York: Harper & Row, 1971.

Anderson, Terry L. "Institutional Underpinnings of the Water Crisis." CATO Journal 2, no. 3 (Winter 1982): 759-92.

Arondahl, William. Director of Tax Records, State Board of Insurance, Austin, Texas. Interview, February 23, 1984.

Austin American-Statesman, April 11, 1984, p. B-2.

_____, February 24, 1984, p. A-1.

Barnes, Alan, ed. Benchmarks for 1983-84 School District Budgets in Texas. Austin: Texas Research League, July 1983.

Bee, Ed. Harlingen Chamber of Commerce, Harlingen, Texas. Interview, February 28, 1984.

Benton, Wilbourn. Texas: Its Government and Politics. New Jersey: Prentice-Hall, 1977.

Bergsman, Joel. *Research on Urban Economic Development and Growth Policy*. Washington, D.C.: Urban Institute, 1972.

Birkhead, Frank. McAllen Chamber of Commerce, McAllen, Texas. Interview, February 29, 1984.

Breitemberg, Matthew D. *Assessing Costs and Benefits of Foreign Trade Zones: Testimonies before the U.S. International Trade Commission*. ITC Investigation 332-165, November 16, 1983.

Brown, Dick. Executive Director, Texas Municipal League, Austin, Texas. Interview, December 5, 1983, and March 16, 1984.

_____. "Why Firms Locate in Texas - And What That Means for City Officials." *Texas Town and City* 69 (July 1982): 13-14.

Buchanan, G. Sidney. "Texas Navigation Districts and Regional Planning in the Texas Gulf Coast Area." *Houston Law Review* 10, no. 3 (March 1973): 533-97.

Bynum, Raymon L. Cover letter, "To the Participants of the 1983 School Administrators Advisory Conference on Education." Austin: Texas Education Agency, January 25, 1983.

Charles River Associates. *The Role of Transportation in Regional Economic Development*. Lexington, Mass.: Lexington Books, 1971.

Choate, Pat, and Susan Walter. *America in Ruins: Beyond the Public Works Pork Barrel*. Washington, D.C.: Council of State Planning Agencies, 1981.

City of Austin. *Austin Tommorrow Comprehensive Plan*. Austin, Texas: City of Austin, Planning Department, 1980.

City of Dallas. *Memorandum by Mayor's Task Force on Housing and Economic Development for Southern Dallas*. Dallas: Industrial Development Corporation Legal Subcommittee, August 19, 1983.

City of San Antonio. *Foreign Trade Zones*. San Antonio, Tex.: Office of International Relations, 1983. (Pamphlet.)

Claggett, William E. *Planning for Infrastructure Needs in Texas: The Scope of the Problem*. Dallas: University of Texas at Dallas, 1983. (Draft.)

_____. Professor, University of Texas at Dallas, Dallas, Tex. Interview, March 6, 1984.

Claitor, Diana. "Special Report: Texas." *Hollywood Reporter*, August 9, 1983, pp. T-6, T-10, and T-11.

Clark, Don. Assistant Director of Travel Services, Travel Information Division, Texas Department of Highways and Public Transportation, Austin, Texas. Interview, April 11, 1984.

Claunch, John M. *The Government of Dallas County, Texas*. Vol. 5. Dallas: SMU Press, 1954.

Commerce Clearing House. *State Tax Handbook*. Chicago, 1982.

Commission on Interstate Cooperation. *Comparisons of Wisconsin's Total State and Local Taxes with the National Averages*. Madison, 1978.

Committee for Economic Development. *Public-Private Partnership: An Opportunity for Urban Communities*. New York, 1982.

Computer Printout on Number and Location of Water Districts in Texas. Provided by Tom Buckingham, Permits Department, Texas Department of Water Resources. Austin, September 15, 1983.

Conklin, Neal. City of Dallas, Dallas, Texas. Interview, March 16, 1984.

Coordinating Board of Texas College and University System, Enrollment Projects Press Release. Austin, March 1984.

──────. *Postsecondary Educational Supply and Occupational Demand*. Austin, Spring 1983.

Cope, Glen, and Norton Grubb. "Restraint in a Land of Plenty: Revenue and Expenditure Limitation in Texas." *Public Budgeting and Finance* 2, no. 4 (Winter 1982): 143-56.

Copeland, Tim. Texas Film Commission, Austin, Texas. Interview, April 11, 1984.

Cornia, Gary C., William A. Testa, and Frederich Stacker. *State-Local Fiscal Incentives and Economic Development*. Columbus, Ohio: Academy for Contemporary Problems, 1978.

Council of State Community Affairs Agencies. *Economic Development--The State's Perspectives*. Washington, D.C.: U.S. Department of Commerce, Economic Development Administration, 1981.

Cuthbertson, Patricia. "Small Issue Industrial Revenue Bonds: Public Policy Issues and the Texas Experience." M.P.A. Report, University of Texas at Austin, 1984.

Davidson, W.N. III, and P.R. Chandy, Jr. "Regulatory Environment for Public Utilities: Indication of the Importance of the Political Process." *Financial Analysts Journal* 39, no. 6 (November-December 1983): 50-53.

Davis, Phil. Texas Tourist Development Agency, Austin, Texas. Telephone Interview, March 30, 1984.

Dean, Joyce. McAllen Chamber of Commerce, McAllen, Texas. Interview, February 22, 1984.

Dennis, N. DeTray. *The Incidence of State and Local Taxes under Fiscal Changes: Methodology*. Santa Monica, Calif.: RAND Corporation, 1980.

DePodwin, Horace J. Discharging Business Tax Liabilities. New Brunswick, N.J.: Rutgers University Press, 1956.

Donovan, Dennis J. "Twelve Key Questions for Site Selection Decision-Makers." Industrial Development 151, no. 4 (July/August 1982): 12-15.

Douglas, Jim. Director, Texas Catastrophe Property Insurance Association, Austin, Texas. Interview, February 24, 1984.

Downing, Diane E. "Thinking for the Future: The Promise of MCC." Austin 25, no. 8 (August 1983): 105-10.

Dubin, Jeffery A., and Peter Navarro. "Regulatory Climate and the Cost of Capital." In Regulatory Reform and Public Utilities. Edited by Michael A. Crew. Lexington, Mass.: Lexington Books, 1982.

Due, John F. "Studies of State-Local Tax Influences on Location of Industry." National Tax Journal 14 (June 1961): 165.

Due, John F., and John F. Mikesell. Sales Taxation. Baltimore: Johns Hopkins University Press, 1983.

Duerksen, Christopher J. Environmental Regulation of Industrial Plant Siting. Washington, D.C.: Conservation Foundation, 1983.

Dworak, Robert J. Taxpayers, Taxes and Government Spending: Perspectives on the Taxpayer Revolt. New York: Praeger, 1980.

East Texas Council of Governments. Guide to Federal and State Environmental Legislation. Kilgore, Tex., 1977 revisions, August 1977.

Education Commission of the States. A Summary of Major Reports on Education. Denver, Colo.: Education Commission of the States, November 1983.

Ellenis, Manny, Development Counsellors International. "Six Major Trends Affecting Site Selection Decisions to the Year 2000." Dun's Business Month 122, no. 5. (November 1983): 116-30.

Eubank, J. Amarillo Chamber of Commerce, Amarillo, Texas. Interview, February 26, 1984.

Facts and Figures. Report to the Texas 2000 Commission, Office of the Governor. Austin, Tex., 1982.

Fehrenbach, T. R. Seven Keys to Texas. El Paso: Texas Western Press, 1983.

Feistritzer, C. Emily. The Condition of Teaching. Princeton: Carnegie Foundation for the Advancement of Teaching, 1983.

"The Fifty Legislative Climates." Industrial Development 151, no. 1 (January/February 1982): 4-19.

Financing Local Government. New York: New York Conference Board, 1967.

Fisher, James, and Dean Hanink. "Business Climate: Behind the Geographic Shift of American Manufacturing." *Economic Review* (Federal Reserve Bank of Atlanta) 67, no.6 (June 1982): 20-30.

Florida Advisory Council on Intergovernmental Relations. *The Federal Block Grants: A Guide for State and Local Officials*. Tallahassee: Secretary of State, August 1981.

Foster, Robert. "Economic and Quality of Life Factors in Industrial Location Decisions." *Social Indicators Research* 4 (July 1977): 247-65.

Fraser, D., and P. Rose. "Bank Entry and Bank Performance." *Journal of Finance* 27 (March 1972): 65-78.

Friedlaender, Ann F., and Richard H. Spady. *Freight Transportation Regulation*. Cambridge: MIT Press, 1981.

Fuller, Steve, Larry D. Makus, and Jack T. Lamkin, Jr. "Effect of Intrastate Motor Carrier Regulation on Rates and Service: The Texas Experience." *Transportation Journal* 23, no. 1 (Fall 1983): 16-29.

Galambos, Eva C. *Issues in Vocational Education*. Atlanta: Southern Regional Education Board, 1984.

Gamil, Kathleen. Director, Employment and Training Division, Houston Natural Gas, Houston, Texas. Telephone Interview by Billie Gonzales, March 16, 1984.

Gantt, Fred. *Governing Texas : Documents and Readings*. New York: Thomas Crowell Co., 1974.

Gardner, S. Roma City Hall, Starr County, Texas. Interview, February 27, 1984.

Gentry, Rick. Researcher, Institute for Insurance Information, Austin, Texas. Interview, February 26, 1984.

Gilmer, Robert W. "Regional Energy Costs and the Aluminum Industry." *Texas Business Review* 56, no. 6 (November-December 1982): 201-6.

Goodman, Susan, and Victor L. Arnold. "The State of Small Business in Texas." *Texas Business Review* 57, no. 5 (September-October 1983): 201-6.

Governor Mark White Press Release, January 24, 1984.

Grant, Alexander, and Co. *General Manufacturing Business Climates*. Chicago: Grant Thornton Co., 1983.

Groff, Horace. County Judge, Grayson County, Texas. Testimony before the Committee on County Affairs, Tyler, Texas, December 9, 1983.

Gronouski, John, and Gerard A. Rohlich. "Preliminary Report on Financing of Texas Water Resources." Unpublished. Austin: Lyndon B. Johnson School of Public Affairs, January 1983.

Haar, Charles M. Land-use Planning: A Casebook on the Use, Misuse, and Re-use of Urban Land. 3d ed. Boston: Little, Brown & Co., 1977.

Handbook for Tax Commissioners. Edited by J. Deveraux Weeks and Morgan B. Gilreath, Jr. Athens: University of Georgia, Institute of Government, 1976.

Hansen, Derek. "Banking and Small Business." Financing State and Local Economic Development. Edited by Michael Barker. Durham, N.C.: Duke University Press, 1983.

Hansen, Niles M. Intermediate Size Cities as Growth Centers. New York: Praeger Publishers, 1971.

Harris, Curtis C. Regional Economic Effects of Alternative Highway Systems. Cambridge: Ballinger, 1974.

Hatry, Harry P. Maintaining the Existing Infrastructure: Overview of Current Issues and Practices in Local Government Planning. Washington, D.C.: U.S. Department of Housing and Urban Development, 1982.

Haveman, Robert H. The Economics of the Public Sector. 2d ed. New York: John Wiley and Sons, 1976.

Hazlett, Thomas. "City Plan Pearl," New York Times, August 2, 1982.

Heath, Jim. San Angelo Chamber of Commerce, San Angelo, Texas. Interview, February 27, 1984.

Heilbrun, James. Urban Economics and Public Policy. New York: St. Martin's Press, 1981.

Hekman, John S. "What are Businesses Looking For? Survey of Location Decisions." Federal Reserve Atlanta 67 (June 1982): 6-19.

Hekman, John, and Alan Smith. "Behind the Sunbelt's Growth: Industrial Decentralization." Economic Review 65 (March 1982): 4-13.

"Helping the Schools Get Back to Work." Nation's Business 71, no. 9 (September 1983): 30.

Higgins, Dr. Jerry. Texas Department of Water Resources, Planning Division, Austin, Texas. Interview, November 10, 1983.

Higher Education Conference on New Federalism. Proceedings. Arlington, Tex.: Institute of Urban Studies, August 1982.

Hogsett, Tim. Program Section Leader, Grants-in-Aid Branch, Texas Department of Parks and Wildlife, Austin, Texas. Interview, October 11, 1983.

Holliway, Weldon. Director, Employment and Training Division, Brown and Root, Inc., Houston, Texas. Telephone Interview by Billie Gonzales, March 16, 1984.

Hopkins, R. Eagle Pass Chamber of Commerce, Eagle Pass, Texas. Interview, February 29, 1984.

Horvitz, P., and B. Shull. "The Impact of Branching on Performance." National Banking Review 2 (December 1964).

Houghtaling, Betty. Brownsville Navigation District Foreign Trade Zone, Brownsville, Texas. Interview, February 23, 1984.

House Interim Committee on Water Supply and Waste Disposal in the Metropolitan Areas. Water Supply and Waste Disposal in Texas Urban Areas. Austin, Tex., January 1975.

House Study Group, Enterprise Zones. House Study Group Daily Floor Report. Tex. H.B. 1125, 68th Leg. (May 4, 1983).

Howard, L. City Hall, Midlothian, Texas. Interview, February 28, 1984.

Humberger, Edward. Business Location Decisions and Cities. Washington, D.C.: Public Technology Inc. (Urban Consortium), 1983.

Humlum-Arhus, Johannes. Water Development and Water Planning in the Southwestern United States (Munksgaard: Kulturgeografisk Institut, 1969).

Ilhandfelt, Keith R., and Thomas P. Boehm. "Property Taxation and Demand for Home Ownership." Public Finance Quarterly 2, no. 1 (January 1983).

International Trade Administration. Texas Exports Mean Jobs. (Staff Research Paper.) Dallas: U.S. Department of Commerce, 1983.

Ireland, Evelyn. Director, Division of Research and Information Services, State Board of Insurance, Austin, Texas. Interview, December 5, 1983.

Isard, Walter. Introduction to Regional Science. Englewood Cliffs, N.J.: Prentice Hall, 1975.

Jacobs, Robert. Manager, El Paso Foreign Trade Zone Corporation, El Paso International Airport, El Paso, Texas. Interview, February 23, 1984.

Jenkins, Michael D., and Donald L. Sexton. Starting and Operating a Business in Texas. Sunnyvale, Calif.: Oasis Press, 1983.

Johnson, Harry L. State and Local Tax Problems. Knoxville: University of Tennessee Press, 1969.

Jones, Eugene W., Joe E. Ericson, Lyle C. Brown, and Robert S. Trotter, Jr. Practicing Texas Politics. 5th ed. Boston: Houghton Mifflin Co., 1977.

Kasworm, Carol, and Cora Hilliard. "Employee Development in the 1980's." In Economic and Business Issues of the 1980's, pp. 122-24. Austin: Bureau of Business Research, University of Texas, 1980.

Katz, David. Operator of San Antonio Foreign Trade Zone Corporation, San Antonio, Texas. Interview, February 22, 1984.

Kayne, Joseph. Director of Community Development Programs, Texas Department of Community Affairs, Austin, Texas. Interview, February 22, 1984.

Kerridge, Isaac Curtis. "The Advisability of Permitting Branch Banking in Texas." Thesis, University of Texas at Austin, 1970.

Kline, John M. State Government Influence in U.S. International Economic Policy. Lexington, Mass.: D. C. Heath & Co., 1983.

Korenich, Michael, and Benson Soffer. "Right-to-Work Laws as a Location Factor: The Industrialization Experience of Agricultural States." Journal of Regional Science 2 (1961): 41-56.

Kosta, Larry. Director of the Labor Division, Department of Labor and Standards, Austin, Texas. Interview, November 18, 1983.

Kraemer, Richard, and Philip Barnes. Texas: Readings in Politics, Government and Public Policy. San Francisco: Chandler Publishing Company, 1971.

Lake, Robert W. Real Estate Tax Delinquency: Private Disinvestment and Public Response. New Brunswick, N.J.: Center for Urban Policy Research, Rutgers University, 1979.

Lamb, Robert, and Stephen P. Rappaport. Municipal Bonds: The Comprehensive Review of Tax-Exempt Securities and Public Finance. New York: McGraw-Hill Book Co., 1980.

Lebowitz, J. Leon. "Recent Developments in Texas Corporation Law - Part II." Southwestern Law Journal 28, no. 5 (Winter 1974): 324-34.

Levin, Joshua. "Creative Financing of Urban Growth and Redevelopment: An Analysis of the Rationale and Implementation of Tax Increment Financing in Texas." University of Texas at Austin Professional Report, 1982.

Levin, Sharon G. "Suburban-Central City Property Tax Differentials and the Location of Industry: Some Evidence." Land Economics 50 (November 1974): 380-86.

Limiting State Taxes and Expenditures. Lexington, Mass.: Council of State Governments, 1978.

Liner, Donald C. "The Effect of Taxes on Industrial Location." Popular Government 39 (Supplement, 1973): 33-39.

Little, Mildred J. Camper's Guide to Texas Parks, Lakes, and Forests. Houston: Gulf Publishing Co., 1978.

Litvak, Lawrence, and Belden Daniels. Innovations in Development Finance. Washington, D.C.: Council of State Planning Agencies, 1979.

_____. "Innovations in Development Finance." In *Financing State and Local Economic Development*. Edited by Michael Barker. Durham, N.C.: Duke University Press, 1983.

Loflin, Leslie. "User Charges as a Municipal Revenue Option: A Survey of Selected Texas Cities." MPA Report, University of Texas at Austin, 1981.

Losch, August. *The Economics of Location*. New York: John Wiley and Sons, 1967.

Lumsden, Keith, and Craig Peterson. "The Effect of Right-to-Work Laws on Unionization in the United States." *Journal of Political Economy* 83, no. 6 (December 1975): 1237-48.

Lyndon B. Johnson School of Public Affairs. *Guide to Texas State Agencies*. 5th ed. Austin, Tex., 1978.

_____. *A Matrix Analysis of Growth Policies in Austin*. Policy Research Project Report Series no. 58. Austin, Tex., 1983.

_____. *The Promotion of Exports from Texas*. Policy Research Project Report Series no. 46. Austin, Tex., 1981.

MacCorkle, Stuart A. *The Texas City: Its Power to Zone*. Austin, Tex.: Institute of Public Affairs, University of Texas, 1955.

MacCorkle, Stuart A., and Dick Smith. *Texas Government*. 5th ed. New York: McGraw-Hill, 1964.

MacCorkle, Stuart A., Dick Smith, and Janice C. May. *Texas Government*. New York: McGraw-Hill, 1974.

Makay, Rik. Associate Director, Employment and Training Division, Texas Department of Community Affairs, Austin, Texas. Interview, February 22, 1984.

Malone, Frank. "Rail Renaissance in Mexico." *Railway Age*, April 13, 1981.

Mandleker, David R., Gary Feder, and Margaret P. Collins. *Reviving Cities with Tax Abatement,* New Brunswick, N.J.: Center For Urban Policy Research, 1980.

Mansfield, Edwin. *Microeconomics: Theory and Applications*. 2d ed. New York: W. W. Norton & Co., 1980.

_____. *Microeconomics: Theory and Applications*. 4th ed. New York: W. W. Norton & Co., 1982.

Marshall, Ray. Lecture Notes from International Economics Class, Lyndon B. Johnson School of Public Affairs, Austin, Texas, January 16, 1984.

_____. Professor of Labor Economics, Lyndon B. Johnson School of Public Affairs, Austin, Texas. Interview, November 22, 1983.

Massey, John. Operator of the Galveston Port of Entry Trade Zone, Galveston, Texas. Interview, February 22, 1984.

Maxwell, James A. Financing State and Local Governments. Washington, D.C.: Brookings Institution, 1969.

Maxwell, James A., and J. Richard Aronson. Financing State and Local Governments. 3d ed. Washington, D.C.: Brookings Institution, 1977.

McAllen Chamber of Commerce. Economic Research Department. McAllen: 1982-83 Economic Facts and Figures. McAllen, Tex., 1983.

McCall, A., and M. Peterson. "Impact of De Novo Commercial Bank Entry." Journal of Finance 32 (December 1977): 1587-604.

McCleskey, Clifton. Innovations in Development Finance. Washington, D.C.: Council of State Planning Agencies, 1979.

McCleskey, Clifton, Allan Butcher, Daniel E. Farlow, and J. Pat Stephens. The Government and Politics of Texas. 6th ed. Boston: Little, Brown & Co., 1978.

McCrea, Joan. Texas Labor Laws. 3d ed. Houston: Gulf Publishing Co., 1978.

Mellow, Wesley. "Unionism and Wages." Review of Economics and Statistics 63 (February 1981): 43-52.

Meyers, Edward M. Urban Incentive Tax Credits: A Self-Correcting Strategy to Rebuild Central Cities. New York: Praeger, 1974.

Meyers, Frederick. Right-to-Work in Practice. New York: Fund for the Republic, 1959.

Mignano, Gregory. "California: Gateway for Trade." Business America 7, no. 3 (February 6, 1984): 10-14.

Mikesell, John L. Fiscal Administration: Analysis and Applications for the Public Sector. Homewood, Ill.: Dorsey Press, 1982.

Miller, E. Williard. Manufacturing: A Study of Industrial Location. University Park: Pennsylvania State University Press, 1977.

Misiolek, Walter, and Thomas C. Noser. "Coal Surface Mine Land Reclamation and Costs." Land Economics 58, no. 1 (February 1982): 67-85.

Moak, Lennox L. Municipal Bonds: Planning, Sale and Administration. Chicago: Municipal Finance Officers Association, 1982.

Morrow, Elbert. "Financing of Capital Improvements by Texas Counties and Cities." Southwestern Law Journal 25, no. 3 (August 1971): 373-427.

_____. Municipal Bond Attorney, Dumas, Huguenin, Boothman and Morrow, Dallas, Texas. Interviews, November 11, 1983, and March 16, 1984.

Muller, Thomas, and Grace Dawson. The Economic Effects of Annexation: A Second Case Study in Richmond, Virginia. Washington, D.C.: Urban Institute, 1976.

Musgrave, Peggy B. and Richard A. Public Finance in Theory and Practice. New York: McGraw-Hill, 1973.

Musgrave, Richard A. and Peggy B. Public Finance in Theory and Practice. New York: McGraw-Hill, 1980.

National Association of Regulatory Utility Commissioners. Annual Report on Utility and Carrier Regulation, 1981. Washington, D.C., 1981.

National Association of State Development Agencies. "1981-1982 Expenditure and Salary Survey for State Development Agencies." Washington, D.C., September 1982.

National Association of State Development Agencies, National Council for Urban Economic Development, and Urban Institute. Directory of Incentives for Business Investment and Development in the United States. Washington, D.C.: Urban Institute Press, 1983.

National Council for Urban Economic Development. CUED's Guide to Federal Economic Development Programs. Washington, D.C., 1981.

National Economic Research Institute. Economic Progress in Texas - The Critical Issues. Washington, D.C., November 1979.

Natural Resources Defense Council, Inc. Land-Use Controls in the United States. New York: Dial Press, 1977.

Navarro, Peter. "Public Utility Commission Regulation: Performance, Determinants, and Energy Policy Impacts." Energy Journal 3, no. 2 (April 1982): 121-42.

Neff, Pauline. "The Ambush of the Urban Cowboy." Texas Business 8, no. 8 (February 1984): 32-36.

Northcutt, Kaye. "Texas and Mexico: Two Nations, Indivisible." Texas Business 8, no. 5 (November 1983): 32-47.

North Texas-Oklahoma District Export Council. Export Information Manual for Arkansas, Louisiana, New Mexico, and Texas. Waco: Baylor University Press, 1980.

Norwood, Robert E. "Texas County Government: Let the People Choose." Austin: Texas Research League, 1983.

Office of the Governor. "Governor White's Economic Development Program." Austin, Tex., January 30, 1984.

_____. Texas Past and Future: A Survey. Austin, Tex., June 1981.

_____. Texas 2000 Commission Report and Recommendations. Austin, Tex., March 1982.

Okerland, Bill. Operator of the Houston Port of Entry Foreign Trade Zone, Houston, Texas. Interview, February 22, 1984.

Pascal, Anthony H. *Fiscal Containment of Local and State Government*. Santa Monica, Calif.: Rand Corporation, 1974.

Passmore, Leonard. Formerly General Counsel, Texas Bankers Association, Austin, Texas. Interview, February 21, 1984.

Patterson, Charles V. "An Analysis of Texas Law Controlling Multiple Office Banking." M.A. thesis, University of Texas at Austin, 1975.

Pechman, Joseph. *Federal Tax Policy*. 2d ed. Washington, D.C.: Brookings Institution, 1977.

Phares, Donald. *Who Pays State and Local Taxes?* Cambridge: Gunn and Hahn, 1980.

Phillips, Charles F. *The Economics of Regulation*. Homewood, Ill.: Richard D. Irvin, 1972.

Plaut, Thomas R. "Energy and the Texas Economy." *Texas Business Review* 57, no. 2 (March-April 1983): 69-73.

Plaut, Thomas R., and Joseph E. Pluta. "Business Climate, Taxes and Expenditures and State Industrial Growth in the U.S." *Southern Economic Journal* 50, no. 1 (July 1983): 99-118.

Pluta, Joseph E. *Economic and Business Issues of the 1980s*. Austin: Bureau of Business Research, University of Texas, 1980.

Pollard, Robert F. "Industrial Location Decisions in Texas." *Texas Business Review* 52 (July 1978): 125-27.

Port of Houston Magazine. September 1983.

Posner, Alan R. "Export Promotion Policies in Sunbelt States." *Texas Business Review* 55, no. 4 (July/August 1981): 152-56.

Posner, Bruce G. "A Report on the States." *INC.* 4, no. 10 (August 1982): 95-102.

Preston, Albert, Jr. *State and Local Taxes on Business*. Princeton: Tax Institute of America, 1964.

Prindle, David F. *Petroleum Politics and the Texas Railroad Commission*. Austin: University of Texas Press, 1981.

Property Tax Preferences for Agricultural Land. Edited by Neal A. Roberts and H. James Brown, Lincoln Institute of Land Policy. Montclair, N.J.: Allanheld Osmun, 1980.

Public Utility Commission of Texas. "New Rate Procedures Adopted." In *Annual Report 1982*. Austin, 1982.

Railroad Commission of Texas. Gas Utilities Division. _Municipal Assistance Packet._ Austin, 1983. (Pamphlet.)

_____. Oil and Gas Division. "A Chronological Listing of Important Historical Events, Legislative Acts, Judicial Decisions, Orders, and Other Related Data Regarding the Railroad Commission of Texas." Austin, Oct. 1, 1980. (Mimeographed appendix.)

_____. Transportation Division. "How to Obtain Trucking Authority." Austin, 1983. (Pamphlet.)

Rasnic, Carol D. "Federally Required Restoration of Surface-Mined Property: Impasse Between the Coal Industry and the Environmentally Concerned." _Natural Resources Journal_ 23, no. 2 (April 1983): 335.

Reagan, Michael D. _The New Federalism._ New York: Oxford University Press, 1972.

Reinshuttle, Robert J. _Economic Development: A Survey of State Activities._ Lexington, Ky.: Council of State Governments, 1983.

Research Triangle Institute. _Final Technical Report - A Study to Make Recommendations Regarding a Comprehensive State Occupational Education Program._ Submitted to the Texas Education Agency. Research Triangle, N.C., October 31, 1982.

_____. _Resume of Texas State Agencies Having Statutory Responsibility for Provisions of Vocational-Occupational Education._ Submitted to the Texas Education Agency. Research Triangle, N.C., 1984.

Revzan, L. H. "Enterprise Zones: Present Status and Potential Impact." _Governmental Finance_ 12, no. 4 (December 1983): 31-38.

_____. "State and Local Tax Policies and Industrial Location Decisions." _Popular Government_ 41 (Winter 1976): 14.

Richardson, Harry W. _Regional Economics._ Urbana: University of Illinois Press, 1979.

Robinson, Roland, and Dwayne Wrightsman. _Financial Markets._ New York: McGraw-Hill, 1980.

Rubin, Rose M., and Samuel W. Ogden. "Prospects for Tax Increment Financing in Texas." _Texas Business Review_ 57 (January 1983): 29-33.

Sackrey, Charles Melvin. "The Laws Regulating the Investment Policies of Life Insurance Companies Operating in Texas: An Interpretation and Analysis." M.A. thesis, University of Texas at Austin, 1963.

Schmenner, Roger W. "Location Decisions of Large Firms: Implications for Public Policy." _Commentary_ 5, no. 1 (January 1981): 3-7.

Schonert, Charles Gregory. "The Determinants of Texas Municipal Expenditures and the Effects of a Tax Reduction." M.P.A. Report, University of Texas at Austin, 1980.

Schroeder, Larry D. The Property Tax and Alternative Local Taxes: An Economic Analysis. New York: Praeger, 1975.

Seagan, Paul. Darrell Sedin Company, Dallas, Texas. Interview, February 22, 1984.

Shannon, John. Business Taxes in State and Local Governments. Lexington, Ky.: Lexington Books, 1972.

Singer, Isaac M. Texas Practise: Municipal Law and Practise. Vol. 22. St. Paul, Minn.: West Publishing Co., 1976.

Skorpa, Lidvard, Richard Dodge, C. Michael Walton, and John Huddleston. Transportation Impact Studies: A Review with Emphasis on Rural Areas. Austin: University of Texas at Austin, October 1974.

Smith, David M. Industrial Location: An Economic Geographical Analysis. New York: John Wiley and Sons, 1971.

Somerfeld, Raynard M. Tax Research Techniques. New York: American Institute of Certified Public Accountants, 1976.

Southern Growth Policies Board. Suburbs in the City: Municipal Boundary Changes in the Southern States. Research Triangle Park, N.C.: Commission on the Future of the South, 1980.

Spurgin, David. Administrative Assistant, Lt. Governor's Office, Austin, Texas. Interview, March 16, 1984.

Stanfield, Rochelle. "The Administration May Be Overselling Its Plans for Urban Enterprise Zones." National Journal 23 (January 1982): 153-57.

Stanford, Jay. Local Government Fiscal Structure in Texas: A Report Prepared for the Texas Urban Development Commission. Arlington: Texas Urban Development Commission, 1972.

State Job Training Coordinating Council. "Minutes of Council Meetings." Austin, 1983.

State of Texas. Comptroller of Public Accounts. Annual Financial Reports. Austin, 1977, 1978, 1979, 1980, 1981, 1982, and 1983.

_____. Education Workpaper. Vol. 1. Austin, June 1984.

_____. "Growth of Texas Public Debt Slows." Fiscal Notes 81, no. 7 (June 1981): 6-11.

_____. Texas Means Business: A Study of Fiscal Responsibility in Texas as Compared to Other States. Austin, 1977.

_____. Your New Corporation and the Texas Franchise Tax. Publication #96-198. Austin, October 1982.

_____. Comptroller of Public Accounts and Texas Economic Development Commission. A Brief Guide to Business Regulations and Services in Texas. Austin, August 1983.

_____. Governor's Office. Governor's Column #16. "Governor Mark White Reports." Austin, Texas, January 12, 1984.

_____. Legislative Budget Board. Fiscal Size-Up, 1982-1983 Biennium. Austin, 1983.

_____. Legislative Tax Handbook, Texas State Revenues, Comparative Data for the 1984-85 Biennium. Austin, January 1983.

_____. Report to the Joint Select Committee on Fiscal Policy. Austin, March 16, 1984.

_____. Trends in Texas State Government Expenditures. Austin, October 1983. (Booklet.)

_____. Lieutenant Governor's Office. "Financing Texas State Government--An Overview." Austin, September 1983.

_____. Department of Community Affairs. Community Development Program: Final Statement. Austin, May 1983.

_____. Employment and Training Programs in Texas. Austin, January 1983.

_____. 1983 Texas Community Development Program: Applications and Procedures Manual. Austin, July 1983.

_____. Planning Guidelines for Title II A, Job Training Partnership Act, July 1, 1984 - June 30, 1986. Austin, 1984.

_____. "Texas Community Development Program: 1984 Proposed Procedural Changes." Austin, 1984.

_____. "Texas Community Development Program Questionnaire." Austin, 1983.

_____. Local Government Services Division. How to Successfully Compete for Grant Dollars. Austin, April 1981.

_____. A Resource Guide for Local Governments. Austin, July 1982.

_____. Department of Highways and Public Transportation. History and Present Status. Austin, September 1982.

_____. Operational Planning Document Study. Austin, July 1982.

_____. Supplement to the Annual Financial Report for the Fiscal Year Ended August 31, 1981. Austin, 1981.

_____. Supplement to the Annual Financial Report for the Fiscal Year Ended August 31, 1982. Austin, 1982.

_____. Texas Transportation Finance Facts. Austin, 1982.

_____. A Statewide Delivery System. Austin, May 1983.

_____. State Purchasing and General Services Commission. Commodity Book. 7th ed. Austin, September 1978.

Stene, Edwin Otto. The Impact of the Texas Constitution on County Government. Houston: University of Houston, Institute for Urban Studies, 1973.

Strauss, Robert P., and Ronald S. Warren. "A Mixed Logit Model of the Relationship Between Unionization and Right-to-Work Legislation." Journal of Political Economy 87, no. 3 (June 1979): 648-55.

Swardson, Anne. "House Vote Removes Threat to Industrial Bonds." Dallas Morning News, November 18, 1983.

Talrico, Jean. Texas Economic Development Commission, Austin, Texas. Interview, November 29, 1984.

Tax Foundation Inc. Facts and Figures on Government Finance. New York, 1981.

Tees, David W. "A Fresh Look at Special Districts in Texas." (Paper prepared for Texas Urban Development Committee, Austin, Tex., 1971.)

Texas Advisory Council on Intergovernmental Relations. "Background on the HUD CDBG Non-entitlement Program." Austin, 1983. (Draft.)

_____. "Debt Position and Financial Condition of Local Governments in Texas." Austin, October 1983. (Draft.)

_____. A Handbook for Board Members of Utility Districts in Texas. Austin, 1983.

_____. Ordinance-Making Authority for Texas Counties: A Local Options Approach. Austin, 1976.

_____. Texas County Government Finance: Revenue and Spending Issues. Austin, 1977.

Texas AFL-CIO. "Labor Law Manual." Austin, 1967.

The Texas Almanac and State Industrial Guide. Dallas: A. H. Belo Corp., 1983.

Texas Commission for the Blind. 1980-82 Biennial Report. Austin, 1982.

_____. Part II of the Self-Evaluation Report to the Sunset Advisory Commission. Austin, 1983.

Texas Commission for the Deaf. Part II of the Self-Evaluation Report to the Sunset Advisory Commission. Austin, 1983.

Texas Committee on State and Local Tax Policy. *The Impact of the Texas Sales Tax on Industry: An Examination of the Provisions of the Texas Sales Tax.* Austin, 1968.

Texas Department of Human Resources. *1982 Annual Report.* Austin, 1982.

Texas Department of Water Resources. *Basic Information Regarding Permits and Other Authorizations Issued by the Texas Department of Water Resources.* Publication C-11, revised. Austin, November 1982.

_____. *Hazardous Waste Management in Texas.* Publication C-10, revised. Austin, July 1982.

_____. *Texas Department of Water Resources.* Publication C-8. Austin, 1983.

_____. *Texas Environment.* Publication C-15. Austin, October 1981.

_____. *Water for Texas - Planning for the Future.* Austin, February 1983.

_____. *Water Planning Information - Geographical Regions.* Austin, June 1983.

Texas Department on Aging. *1980 Biennial Report.* Austin, 1980.

_____. *Part II of the Self-Evaluation Report to the Sunset Advisory Commission.* Austin, 1983.

_____. *Training and Employment Opportunities for the Older Worker.* Austin, 1983.

Texas Economic Development Commission. *Industrial Revenue Bonds for Commercial Projects.* Austin, March 1983.

_____. *Industrial Revenue Bonds for Non-Commercial Projects.* Austin, October 1983.

Texas Education Agency. *Texas Public School Statistics.* Austin, 1982.

_____. *Texas School Law Bulletin.* Austin, 1982.

Texas Employment Commission. *Annual Report 1982.* Austin, 1982.

_____. *A Labor Market Information System.* Austin, May 1983.

_____. *A Local Delivery System.* Austin, May 1983.

_____. *A Statewide Delivery System.* Austin, May 1983.

The Texas Enterprise Zone Act. Tex. H.B. 1125, 68th Leg. (1983).

Texas General Land Office. "Activities of the Texas General Land Office." Austin, June 1983. (Mimeographed.)

Texas Good Roads/Transportation Association. *Texas Mobility Crisis Deteriorating Highways and Lagging Revenues*. Austin, March 24, 1982.

Texas Industrial Commission. *Directory of Industrial Development Corporations*. Austin, n.d.

Tex. Ins. Code Ann. (1956, as amended to 1981).

Texas Legislature. "Official Comprehensive Policy on Development of Urban Communities." Tex H.R. Con. Res. 61, 62d Leg., reg. sess., 1971 Tex. Gen. Laws 1.

_____. House. Intergovernmental Affairs Committee. "Development Standards in Unincorporated Areas." *TACIR*. Austin, 1974.

_____. Senate. *Text of Conference Committee Report. Senate Bill No. 179, Sixty-Eighth Legislature, Regular Session, 1983. Senate Journal*.

Texas Municipal League and Texas Department of Community Affairs. *Texas Municipal Law Handbook and Index*. Austin, 1982.

Texas Parks and Wildlife Department. *Sunset Commission Report, Administrator's General Statement*. Austin, 1983.

_____. *Sunset Commission Report, Self-Evaluation Report*. Vol. 2. Austin, 1983.

Texas Past and Future: A Survey. Prepared for the Texas 2000 Commission, Office of the Governor. Austin, June 1981.

Texas Rehabilitation Commission. *Part I of the Self-Evaluation Report to the Sunset Advisory Commission*. Austin, 1983.

Texas Research League. *Analysis*. Austin, May and June 1983.

_____. *Revenue and Tax Administration*. Austin, February 1975.

_____. *The Tax Relief Amendment: What Next?* Austin, 1979.

Tex. S.B. 50, 66th Leg., reg. sess. (1979).

Texas State Commission for the Blind. *1980-82 Biennial Report*. Austin, 1982.

Texas State Technical Institute. *Facts and Figures*. Waco, September 1981.

Texas Sunset Advisory Commission. *Final Report on Business and Professional Agencies to the Governor of Texas and Members of the Sixty-Eighth Texas Legislature*. Vol. 1. Austin, January 1983.

_____. *Final Report on Cultural and Advisory Agencies*. Vol. 2. Austin, January 1983.

Texas Tax Reporter, State and Local, All Taxes, All Taxables. Chicago: Commerce Clearing House, 1960. (Loose-Leaf.)

Texas Tech University. Southwest School of Municipal Finance. "Glossary of Words and Phrases of the Municipal Bond Industry." (Background document, Municipal Bond Session.) Lubbock, May 20, 1981.

Texas Water Quality Board. A Ready-Reference on Major Texas Water Pollution Control Legislation. Publication #71-01. Austin, 1971.

Thomas, Bob. Manager of the Jefferson County Airport, Beaumont, Texas. Interview, February 27, 1984.

Thrombley, Woodworth G. Special Districts and Authorities in Texas. Austin: Institute of Public Affairs, University of Texas at Austin, 1959.

Tompkins, Jack E. Report to the 68th Session of the Legislature. Waco: Texas State Technical Institute, March 1983.

Umphrey, Don. "The Economic Impact of the 1980 Film/Tape Industry in Texas." Austin: Texas Film Commission, January 1982.

Urs, Denise. "Large Cities in Texas Remain Fiscally Sound." Fiscal Notes 83, no. 12 (November 1983): 1-8.

U.S. Advisory Commission on Intergovernmental Relations. State Limitations on Local Taxes and Expenditures. Washington, D.C., 1977.

U.S. Congress. Housing and Community Development Act. 93d Cong., 2d sess., Title I, PL 93-383, 1974.

_____. Omnibus Budget Reconciliation Act. 97th Cong., 1st sess., Title III, PL 97-35, 1981.

_____. House. Job Training Partnership Act. 97th Cong., 2d sess., 1982, H.R. 97-889.

_____. Joint Economic Committee. Subcommittee on Monetary and Fiscal Policy. Location of High Technology Firms and Regional Development. Washington, D.C.: Government Printing Office, 1982.

_____. Senate. Office of Senator John G. Tower, Texas. The Tower Report. Washington, D.C., February 1984.

U.S. Department of Commerce. Bureau of the Census. Annual Summary of Manufacturers. Washington, D.C., 1983.

_____. City Government Finances, 1980. Washington, D.C., 1980.

_____. General Social and Economic Characteristics, Texas. 1980 Census of Population. Vol. 1, pt. 55. Washington, D.C., August 1983.

_____. Governmental Organization. Vol. 1. Washington, D.C., August 1982.

_____. International Trade Administration. A Basic Guide To Exporting. Washington, D.C.: Government Printing Office, 1981.

U.S. Department of Education. The Condition of Education. Washington, D.C.: National Center for Education Statistics, 1983.

_____. State Education Statistics. Washington, D.C.: Government Printing Office, 1984.

U.S. Department of Housing and Urban Development. Community Development Block Grant Program: Directory of Allocations for Fiscal Years 1978-1983. Washington, D.C.: Government Printing Office, 1983.

_____. Effects of the 1980 Census on Community Development Funding. Washington, D.C.: Government Printing Office, 1983.

_____. Implementing Community Development. Washington, D.C.: Government Printing Office, 1983.

U.S. Department of Transportation. Social and Economic Effects of Highways. Washington, D.C., 1976.

U.S. Executive Office of the President. America's New Beginning: A Program for Economic Recovery. Washington, D.C.: Government Printing Office, February 1981.

_____. Office of Management and Budget. Catalog of Federal Domestic Assistance. Washington, D.C.: Government Printing Office, 1983.

Vaughan, Roger J. The Urban Impacts of Federal Policies. Economic Development, Vol. 2. R-20280-KF/RC. Santa Monica: Rand Corporation, 1977.

Veregada, Jorge. Laredo International Airport, Laredo, Texas. Interviews, February 23, 1984 and March 2, 1984.

Weinstein, Bernard L. "Future of Texas High Tech." Dallas Morning News, January 20, 1984.

Weiss, L. "Concentration and Labor Earnings." American Economic Review 56 (March 1966): 96.

Welch, Terrence Scott. "An Analysis of Several Contemporary Intercity Family Tax Burden Studies." M.P.A. Report, University of Texas at Austin, 1981.

Wheat, Leonard F. Regional Growth and Industrial Location. Lexington, Mass.: D.C. Heath and Co., 1973.

Wheaton, William C. "Interstate Differences in the Level of Business Taxation." National Tax Journal 36 (March 1983): 83-94.

Wilder, Ronald P. "Foreign Trade and the Increasing Importance of Southern Ports." Texas Business Review 57 (May/June 1981): 96-99.

Williamson, Jodie. Executive Vice President, Del Rio Chamber of Commerce. Interview, February 27, 1984.

Wilson George W., Barbara R. Bergman, Leon V. Hirsch, and Martin S. Klien. _The Impact of Highway Investment on Development_. Washington, D.C.: Brookings Institution, 1966.

Wilson, Meg. Governor's Office of Economic Development, Austin, Texas. Interviews, January 20, 1984, and February 14, 1984. Telephone interviews, February 24, 1984, and April 11, 1984.

Wilson, Peter. _The Future of Dallas' Capital Plant_. Washington, D.C.: Urban Institute, 1980.

Wilson, Wesley M. _Labor Law Handbook_. New York: Bobbs-Merrill Co., 1963.

Winn, Morris. Coordinator, Job Training and Employment, Governor's Planning Office, Austin, Texas. Telephone interview by Billie Gonzales, November 29, 1983.

Ziev, Arthur. "Recent Trends in Local Government Debt in Texas." M.P.A. Report, University of Texas at Austin, 1982.

Zlatkovich, Charles P. _Texas Transportation Handbook_. Bureau of Business Research, University of Texas at Austin, 1976.

HC
107
.T4
E36
1985